Praise for *The Last*

"A brilliant and riveting book, a story that starts in pre-war Somalia and tells the whispers of war. *The Last Nomad* introduces the reader to the real lives in Somalia and the resilience of its people not only inside the nation but beyond."

—Abdi Nor Iftin, author of *Call Me American*

"In this agile personal history of trauma, civil strife, and asylum, debut author Salh vividly describes a youth divided between opposing worlds . . . Salh's prose radiates with deep empathy and sensitivity, a reflection of the gift for storytelling she inherited from her poet grandmother. This stuns with its raw beauty."

—*Publishers Weekly*

"Shugri Said Salh has had a life few of us could ever imagine . . . Salh's intense focus on her connection to her family and her culture packs an inspiring emotional wallop. As a nurse, she's crystal clear about why female genital mutilation is harmful to women. Yet her eye-opening description of undergoing it as a girl is filled with a surprisingly deep connection to her heritage. If you don't know much about the lives of Somali women before starting *The Last Nomad*, knowing Salh's story will make you want to learn more."

—Apple Books

"This stunning memoir is an exploration of identity, survival, and finding yourself wherever you are." —*A Mighty Girl*

"A onetime nomad reflects on the beauty and harshness of life in the Somali desert." —NPR

"A fascinating look at a disappearing culture. Told from the perspective of a girl growing into womanhood in a place where women's value and virtue hinges on the actions of men, Salh's stories of bravery and resilience intersplice with those of everyday joy and struggle. They show her forever navigating, with grace and skill, the place where two worlds collide as perhaps only a nomad can."

—Tracey Baptiste, author of
The Jumbies and *African Icons:
Ten People Who Shaped History*

"[A] beautifully written memoir . . . A tale of both physical danger and family warmth and traditions, both nomadic and urban. She brilliantly takes the reader along with her, whether that is in the desert tending her herd or in the city, protecting her family . . . A memoir that demonstrates the power of a young woman to adapt to many difficult changes in life, by an author who was truly inspired by the strength and power of women in her own family."

—*Library Journal* (starred review)

"A clear-eyed and moving chronicle of her coming-of-age during a tumultuous time in the history of her native Somalia . . . A thoughtful look at life in an often-misunderstood culture and region." —*Kirkus Reviews*

"Stunning . . . A clear-eyed, richly remembered memoir that takes its readers on the journey of a lifetime." —KQED

"An illuminating and engaging read . . . [Salh] offers an important perspective, carefully documenting her experiences and how they reflect geopolitical issues . . . A thoughtful and resonant celebration of the human spirit." —*Booklist*

"The prose is simple and open, and captivating. [Salh's] voice calmly teaches us about a stunning world most Americans are unfamiliar with, and the struggles of immigrating." —*Napa Valley Register*

"An intense, compassionate, and moving story of tradition and resilience." —*Book Riot*

"An absorbing attempt to explain, through vivid recollection and compassion for her own personal traumas and triumphs, how it feels to have experienced two such dramatically divergent lives." —*San Francisco Chronicle*

"A natural storyteller, Shugri Said Salh was born in the Somali desert and has endured war, refugee camps, loss and oppressive traditions on her way to finding her home."   —*Ms.* magazine

"A triumph of storytelling that illuminates the nomadic culture . . . As a testimony to human resilience as well as a love letter to Somalia and its people, *The Last Nomad* delivers accessible insights. Salh's hard-won wisdom endures in her sometimes painful, yet always riveting and entertaining book."

—*BookBrowse*

"Heartbreaking and soaringly inspirational . . . A devastating and gorgeous memoir."   —*Argus-Courier* (Petaluma, CA)

"The riveting and lyrical tale she tells is complex and reflects many angles of a patriarchal nomadic culture that is by turns oppressive and supportive, frightening and beautiful . . . Her storyteller's voice infuses her memoir with a playful, poetic spirit."

—*North Bay Bohemian*

"Salh writes lyrically and with reverence about her upbringing . . . She recalls with clear-eyed honesty the casual cruelties she witnessed in a homeland riven by clan warfare and a native culture that, for all its rich traditions, is rooted in misogyny."

—*The Press Democrat* (Santa Rosa, CA)

"A fascinating account of the life of a young girl growing up in a nomadic family in Somalia. Reading like a novel, the author provides an account of her life beginning when she was six years old and sent to live with her nomadic grandmother in the desert. Filled with fascinating details of her culture, I was totally immersed in this amazing memoir."   —Bookreporter.com

"This effortlessly told story documents both a personal and national history of strife. Salh's unforgettable memoir is about hardship, the 'rhythm and rituals of nomadic life,' and a victorious song at the end of personal and national trauma."

—*Isele Magazine*

THE LAST NOMAD

THE
LAST
NOMAD

Coming of Age in the Somali Desert

A MEMOIR

Shugri Said Salh

ALGONQUIN BOOKS OF CHAPEL HILL 2022

Published by
Algonquin Books of Chapel Hill
Post Office Box 2225
Chapel Hill, North Carolina 27515-2225

a division of
Workman Publishing
225 Varick Street
New York, New York 10014

First paperback edition, Algonquin Books of Chapel Hill, July 2022. Originally
published in hardcover by Algonquin Books of Chapel Hill in August 2021.
Printed in the United States of America.
Design by Steve Godwin.

A Note from the Author: I have changed the names of some of my friends and relatives to
protect their privacy. In addition, I have changed the spelling of a few names and words
to make them easier to read in English. For instance, my grandmother's name is correctly
spelled Xalima Xirsi Bille, but since the X in Somali sounds like an H in English, I spelled
it Halima Hirsi Bille to aid in pronunciation. Another change is that the letter C in Somali
makes a sound that doesn't exist in English. The closest approximation is a short A sound
when it's at the beginning of a word and an apostrophe when it's in the middle of a word, so
I made those spelling changes as well. For further information on how to pronounce Somali
words, please visit my website at www.shugrisalh.com.

Library of Congress Cataloging-in-Publication Data
Names: Salh, Shugri Said, [date]– author.
Title: The last nomad : coming of age in the Somali Desert, a memoir / Shugri Said Salh.
Other titles: Coming of age in the Somali Desert, a memoir
Description: First edition. | Chapel Hill, North Carolina : Algonquin Books of
    Chapel Hill, 2021. | Summary: "A fresh, captivating memoir about an indomitable
    woman's journey from her idyllic childhood with her nomadic grandmother in
    the deserts of Somalia to her escape from her country's brutal civil war and
    eventually to America"— Provided by publisher.
Identifiers: LCCN 2021000501 | ISBN 9781643750675 (hardcover) |
    ISBN 9781643751740 (ebook)
Subjects: LCSH: Salh, Shugri Said, [date]– —Childhood and youth. | Nomads—
    Somalia—Biography. | Mogadishu (Somalia)—Biography. | Somalia—Emigration
    and immigration. | Refugees—Somalia—Mogadishu—Biography.
Classification: LCC DT407.3.S25 A3 2021 | DDC 967.7305/3092 [B]—dc23
LC record available at https://lccn.loc.gov/2021000501

ISBN 978-1-64375-256-3 (PB)

10 9 8 7 6 5 4 3 2 1
First Paperback Edition

For my brother Guleed Said Haji-Mohamed,
also known by his poet name Gh Wiilwaal.
March 1976–April 2021
May the demons that haunted you throughout
your life finally let you rest in peace.
I will love you for eternity.

And for my mother, Ruqiyo Warsame Gurey,
my ageless desert flower,
and my nomadic grandmother Halima Hirsi Bille,
the strongest woman I have ever known.

CONTENTS

PROLOGUE

I AM THE last nomad.

How can I be the last one? Nomads still exist in that faraway desert where I grew up, so how can I make such a bold statement? What I am really trying to say is, I am the last person in my direct line to have once lived like that, and now I feel like the sole keeper of my family's stories. As I sit here in my home in California, weaving my tale for you, the weight of that responsibility urges me on. All of my ancestors on both sides of my family were nomads; they traveled the East African desert in search of grazing land for their livestock, and the most precious resource of all—water. When they exhausted the land and the clouds disappeared from the horizon, their accumulated ancestral knowledge told them where to move next to find greener pastures. They loaded their huts and belongings onto their most obedient camels and herded their livestock to a new home.

My nomadic family was at the mercy of the weather. At the end of *jilal*, the long dry season, when the clouds finally rumbled with rain, we looked up at the sky with renewed hope. As the desert quenched its thirst, the red earth crackled back to life. Responsibility eased, adults welcomed the rain with drums, singing, and dancing. Children got fat and healthy. Sitting around the fire at night, they soaked in the folktales and poems passed down from generation to generation. But despite the renewed abundance of food, we knew we had to preserve some of it for the dry season to follow. Sometimes, the drought hit harder than usual, killing both livestock and people. Bones and twigs soon littered the terrain where goats and sheep once happily grazed. In those times, my ancestors ceased singing under the moon, their drums hardened, and they longed for good news. Children no longer heard stories by the fire, and an old poet would bellow to the desert, voicing his agony. He would speak of a dying land taking his precious camels. His mournful poem would then travel through time and across borders, to remedy the pain of his people for years to come.

My three children, raised in California, know nothing of nomadic life except from the stories I have shared. As I sit here now in my comfortable suburban home listening to my teenage son excitedly tell me about his favorite YouTuber, I am reminded acutely of the void between my past and my present. I speak of a world of which he has little understanding. An old African proverb says, *When an elder dies, a library is burned.* I am not yet an elder, but I do feel like a portal between two worlds. I am the last person in my immediate family who holds this particular library of knowledge. As the years pass, the sense of urgency I feel about sharing my experience with my children and the world grows.

In my imagination, I have shared my story with each of you many times as we gathered under a clear black sky, its shiny stars guiding my ancestral wisdom. I have imagined you leaning in to me, as if I had brought news of water after a drought. I have poured us more tea, for I knew it was going to be a long night under the luminous moon; I wanted to get this tale of mine right. The fire between us has crackled with excitement, as if to nudge my story along. But now it is no longer enough for me to just *imagine* telling you my stories; I feel the need to bring you all to the fire and into my world.

Stories have always created understanding and connection between humans. In this era of great misunderstanding, I wish to help rein us back in to our shared humanity. The beauty of my culture was imprinted on me when I was very young, and I cherish it so deeply that my desire to share it only grows. Like an archeologist desperately excavating a forgotten world, I want to bring the details of my nomadic upbringing to life before it is lost forever. I don't want the library of my past to die with me. The resilience I learned from surviving life in the desert carried me through the unexpected death of my young mother, being chased from my country by civil war, and defying my clan's expectations after I dared to fall in love with a man from the "wrong" country. Though I was torn from nomadic life too early, it gave me a strong foundation and anchored me to that world despite the tumultuous twists and turns that followed.

I sometimes experience visions of my nomadic life here in California, despite the twenty-plus years and thousands of miles of distance between me and my homeland. Am I trying to assuage a longing left unfulfilled, or do these visions exist to keep me grounded and remind me of my roots? Just the other day, as I was sitting in the sun in front of Whole Foods eating sushi, a woman passed me carrying an African-style basket and an empty plastic water jug. Instantly, I was standing in front of my desert hut, eyes fixed on the scorching terrain, waiting for a glimpse of my uncle to appear, leading our camel back from collecting water. Water was often a day away, sometimes more, and the wait was trying on my young body. I actually laughed out loud at how odd it was for someone to be fetching water in a place where it is just a faucet away.

Certain stretches of highway that meander through the hills and valleys near my Northern California home always remind me of the lands where I once lived. My innate compass guides me as easily through this maze of roads and highways as it did through the endless, unmarked terrain of the desert. Driving one day, my eyes scan the horizon as I've always done, in an instinctive search for danger. No lions or hyenas, but I spot a car ahead of me swerving erratically. As traffic slows around me, my eyes settle on the golden, dry grass and the scattered green trees, mimicking the landscape of my past. Suddenly, I see myself sitting under an acacia tree with my herd of goats, vigilant in my mission to protect my precious animals from hungry predators as I wait for the heat of the midday sun to abate.

As the traffic resumes its pace and I drive on, my thoughts deepen and I ponder the journey my life took to bring me to this very road. I begin to shake with laughter. The man driving the car next to me stares at me like I'm crazy. *You have no idea who I am or where I come from*, I think as he speeds away. Dear Strange

Man, I am laughing in the comfort of my minivan, not because I am crazy, but because my journey to this highway began so very far away. It is ironic that I, of all my mother's nine children, am living this life. My mother's plan was for me to live permanently as a nomad, to be my grandmother's helper. Right now, I should be married to an old nomadic man, leading a nasty-tempered camel through the desert in search of water. If I failed to birth him sons or showed any signs of aging, he would not hesitate to take a younger wife. Despite my love for the culture and traditions of my youth, the guiding force of my grandmother, and my occasional longing for that simpler way of life, I am thankful for the life I have today.

My mother and father came from a world governed by a complex, conflict-filled clan system and the importance of your line of forefathers. A world where warring clans gave each other their young, virginal daughters to create allegiances and hoped-for peace. Could my parents ever have imagined a world where their desert daughter laughed with joy while skiing down a snowy mountain or drove endless hours to take her children to soccer practice, dance class, gymnastics, or simply to play with their friends?

As a teenager, my father left his family in the deserts of western Somalia, despite his mother's objection. He traveled a thousand kilometers, to Dire Diwe, Ethiopia, to get an education, and he never looked back. While visiting his nomadic sister decades later, my father spotted my fifteen-year-old mother herding her goats, her brown skin shimmering with the tone of the very desert she sprung from. He was instantly smitten by her beauty, but when he asked to take her hand in marriage, her mother refused. The men of her clan intervened, my grandmother relented, and my mother moved to the city with him.

My young mother found it more painful to disentangle herself from nomadic life than my father had. She was close to her mother and still wanted to be near her. She visited her mother often and sent each of us to stay with her mother—our *ayeeyo*—from time to time, usually during the rainy season so we could get fat and healthy. When I was a baby, my grandmother carried me on her back as she herded her goats and sheep, singing me old lullabies as she walked. As I got a little older, I sat by the fire while she told me stories and recited poems. My ayeeyo was a tall, regal woman who kept me close at night while the calls of lions and hyenas echoed in the distance. From my earliest childhood, my ayeeyo taught me how to be brave and resilient.

Because my mother had moved away, she felt it was her duty to provide a helper for her aging mother. In a society that saw daughters as a burden, I was my mother's fourth girl. Early on, she realized she would have to sacrifice one of her daughters to help our ayeeyo. I was that daughter, the chosen one. I would not grow up in the city with the rest of my family. I would not get an education, despite my father's wishes. *I am the last nomad.*

1 Nomads

Hooyaday aniga iyo calool adayg bay na dhashay.
Alongside with me, mother gave birth to an
indomitable will.
—Somali proverb, translated by Gh Wiilwaal

I RAN AS fast as my skinny little six-year-old legs could carry me. My heart pounded in my ears, and twigs snapped underneath as my feet skimmed the scorching desert floor. Before me, I saw nothing but vast, open land littered with rain-starved trees. The hot East African sun played tricks on my eyes, shimmering and dancing on the horizon. A glimmer of hope erupted as I glimpsed my ayeeyo's hut through this mirage. *Would I make it to my grandmother's before I was torn to pieces?* I was afraid my body was already too tired.

My ayeeyo's warning echoed in my ears even more loudly than my beating heart: *Leave those warthogs alone if you want to live.*

An hour before, I had been the one in power. When I spotted the herd grazing nearby, I had an urge to chase them. They broke into a trot, fleeing with their tails up in the air and their young trailing behind. Encouraged, I followed, throwing stones and twigs at them. Warthogs were ugly, useless creatures anyway. We never ate their meat, even if we were starving. My ayeeyo told me warthogs would run from me until they reached their home, but then would fight back viciously. I wanted to obey her, but I was also determined to test this theory myself. *Would they really turn vicious?* I felt elated to see them scared of little me. I continued my assault, targeting the small ones falling behind. Mother warthog warned me against bothering her young, sometimes circling back to intimidate me. But the whole herd was running, two by two, away from me. *I did it! I won!*

Then, suddenly, as if they heard my thoughts, all the adults turned, with their young tucked safely behind them, and charged me. I was now the prey.

I scanned the landscape as I fled, looking for a way to escape. Trees and bushes were few and far between in this arid desert; I was better off looking for a hole to hide in than a tall tree to climb. I desperately glanced over my shoulder and saw nothing but savage eyes, hooves pounding in the dust, and very long tusks, closing in fast. My lungs burned, my legs shook, and my red tunic clung to my body, drenched in sweat. Just when I thought all was lost, I felt a final surge of adrenaline; I practically flew into the hut, leapt up, and threw myself against its inner wall, clinging to it like a frightened monkey. For a moment I hung suspended, gasping for air and trembling, my eyes glued on the entrance, expecting the warthogs to stampede in. But I didn't need that last desperate acrobatic move: the warthogs had given up chasing me.

Now that I was safe, I examined my damaged feet. A long, thick thorn was deeply and painfully embedded in one sole. All I could do was wait for my family to return from animal herding so my uncle could pull it out with his well-used *toorey*, the short hunting knives all of the men in my tribe carried. I closed my eyes and pictured how brave I would be as he placed one toorey on each side of the thorn and pulled it straight out. The sun was directly above me so I knew it was midday; they wouldn't return until nightfall. It would be a long wait. I sat outside the hut, watching birds flit around me, keeping an eye out for the warthogs, and doodling in the sand. My misadventure hadn't deterred me from wanting to explore, but every time I tried to walk, the pain in my foot intensified, so I distracted myself with one of my favorite imaginary games. I built little huts made of twigs in the sand, pretending I had my own goats and sheep, and practiced calling them the way my ayeeyo did.

When the sun headed to its hole and the sky turned orange behind the acacia trees, I heard the sound of bleating goats approaching. I had managed to fence the young ones, knowing my ayeeyo would not be happy to see the *waharo* empty their mother's udders before the goats were milked. Now, I glimpsed her walking behind her goats, a herding stick in her hand. I couldn't miss her; she was a tall woman who always moved with great efficiency. Turning, I saw our camels approaching from the left and heard the wooden clacking of the *koor* bells worn around their necks. My *abti* Qoodaar, my mother's oldest brother, followed, singing to his herd, casually holding a long stick behind his neck with both hands. The melody of bleating goats, their crying babies, and bellowing camels, punctuated by the *koor*'s rhythm, thickened the air with music. I knew my family had come home.

JUST ONE YEAR earlier, I had been a city girl proudly wearing my schoolgirl uniform of white shirt and blue skirt, waiting with great anticipation to discover if I would be permitted to enter the first grade. I knew nothing except what I was told by the tall girl standing in front of me.

"I will make it into first grade because I can do this," she declared as she reached her right arm over her head and touched her left ear.

I was small for a five-year-old, so this caused me great distress. In reality, I shouldn't have been nervous. My father, a well-respected English and Arabic teacher and religious scholar, had already taught me more than I needed to know. If he said I should be in first grade, no one would go against him.

The teacher scrutinized us as we stood in line. Under his critical gaze, I straightened my back and stood stiffly, focusing on the tall girl's braids so I wouldn't draw attention to myself. Out of the corner of my eye, I saw endless lines of children in crisp blue and white uniforms standing in the middle of a dirt courtyard, surrounded by white stucco classrooms set against an encircling wall. I had never seen so many children gathered in one place, and they all towered above me. *Who will be my friend?* I thought as my eyes darted around.

Ten years earlier, one would not have seen so many girls or nomadic children going to school in a city. When Siad Barre took over Somalia in a military coup in 1969, he installed a program called "scientific socialism," which included building roads, hospitals, and farms and improving education. Even nomadic families sent their children to relatives in the city so they could get an education. In 1972, Barre hired a Somali linguist to write out our language using the Latin alphabet. Until that point, it had been mostly oral and, if written, was phonetically transcribed into another language, most commonly Arabic. (The Arab influence brought Islam to Somalia in the seventh century AD, and it remains an Islamic country today.) Despite his many faults, Siad Barre believed in education for all children, so there we were, all in uniform, a mixture of city boys and girls, and bewildered-looking nomads. I gazed up at the Somali flag waving in the wind as voices rose around me into the air, teachers and students singing songs praising the country and President Barre. The flag looked like the clear blue sky, and I imagined that the star in the middle was made from fluffy, white clouds. Whether due to nostalgia, pride, or a longing to see my home country again, to this day I have yet to see a flag as beautiful as the Somali flag.

I had spent the first five years of my life traveling back and forth between my ayeeyo's lands and my parents' house in the city of Galkayo, but during that first-grade year I lived the whole time in the city with my parents and siblings, in a huge stucco house my father built. When school was out, my siblings and I were sent back to the desert. This alternation between nomadic life and the city, not typical in our culture, represented a compromise between my nomadic mother and my well-educated father.

Even as a nomadic child, my father was restless and dissatisfied with the life he had been born into. He had a deep yearning for knowledge. But nomads depend on each other, and young boys were especially needed to help herd the camels far from home. His mother was unlucky and burdened because she had given birth to seven girls and only two boys. She truly needed her sons to take their place in the family.

This longing for education was so strong that in his teens he did the unthinkable: he attempted to steal money from his mother so he could run away. He got the money, but on his way out of their hut, he dropped it. Even though it was tied up in a red cloth and would be hard to miss on the dusty ground, my father kept turning frantically in circles, trying to find it. His movements caught his mother's attention and it became clear to her what was going on. His mother picked up the bundle and asked, "Is this what you are looking for?" It was like he was cursed not to see the money that day. Somalis truly believe that parents can bestow both blessings and curses on their children, so when my father couldn't see this red bundle of money lying in plain sight, he was convinced more than ever that his mother possessed godlike power.

"Forever you will move in circles if you ever try to deceive me another time," she warned. My father knew he would be cursed if he ever betrayed his mother again.

But something changed in her that day. She realized that this son of hers was so desperate for a world different from the one she had in mind for him that he would go to great lengths to escape. She finally released him with a blessing, saying, "May the stones of Galkayo turn gold for you." It was a clever chess move on her part that my grandmother forecast his success in a city that lay within her clan's lands. Like any mother, she wanted her son close by. Apparently, although he traveled around, he never felt settled until he finally dug up the stones of Galkayo to build his house there.

I don't know my father's exact age, only that he was born in the early 1920s. Even today, most Somalis don't know the exact date they were born. We might say, "He was born in *jilal*," and mark the birth by an important event, such as a bad famine or an unusually rainy season. My father, however, recorded the exact birthdate of each of his children, which was quite a feat since he fathered twenty-three. However, because Somalis don't generally celebrate birthdays, our actual birth dates were not something he shared with us. For the first eighteen years of my life, I didn't even have the concept of a birthday. I now celebrate mine on February 15, only because that's the random date I chose when Canadian officials created my documents granting me entry to North America. At least I didn't choose January 1 like most African immigrants.

When my father was a young man, the British held most of the land from Zeilah in northern Somalia to Garissa, Kenya. The whole region was known as Somaliland, not to be confused with Somaliland of the north, which later gained its independence from the British, or Italian Somaliland in the south. Somalia did not become a unified country until 1960. The British were employing young Somali men as domestic help, so my father decided to get a job at one of their military camps. The problem was that the British man in charge, Commander Smith, only spoke English and Swahili, so my father had no way of communicating with him. Since my father spoke Arabic, and a significant portion of Swahili vocabulary was derived from the Arabic language, he decided it would be faster to learn to speak Swahili than to learn English. He locked himself in a room for three days and taught himself five hundred Swahili sentences. When he was done, he marched over to the British encampment and, in Swahili, asked Commander Smith for a job.

Smith had a reputation for hiring young, poor Somali men, making them work for a month, and then refusing to pay them. Instead, he would falsely accuse them of a crime and dismiss them. My father had heard about this trick and wasn't going to let someone cheat him out of his hard-earned money. Toward the end of the month, my father was working in the kitchen when Smith entered and tried to pull his scheme on my father. He chose the wrong man at the wrong time.

My father had been chopping meat, and with a firm grip on his butcher's knife, yelled his innocence and accused the Englishman of repeatedly cheating his Somali employees. My father, knife in hand, chased that haughty man across a field. By the time someone intervened to stop the chase, their roles had reversed. Smith apologized to my father and even offered to help him with his education. My father learned English quickly. Smith was so impressed, he sent him to Mogadishu to get an English certificate, saying,

"The two-year program started six months ago, but you are already ahead of the game." Making good on that prediction, my father came back within a year and half with a certificate. He then worked for Smith, traveling and bringing goods from Kenya to Somalia.

Years later at our home in Galkayo, my siblings and I always sat together and shared family stories as the evening darkness gathered. This particular story was repeated often and with pride by my older siblings. When I first heard it, I thought, *My father is a hero!* I was impressed by his fortitude and angry at the man who had tried to humiliate him. I was proud he was my father at that moment, but that feeling did not live long enough to cushion the blow of the corporal punishment he often inflicted on my siblings and me. The reality was that my father was portrayed more admirably in the stories I heard about him than I found him to be in real life. At home he was serious and distant. I didn't spend nearly as much time with him as I did with my ayeeyo, and I couldn't bond with him in the same way. A palpable tension hung in the air around my father, warning me that engaging him in conversation would only lead to long lectures, more unpleasant homework, or undeserved punishment.

By the time he was in his midtwenties and had moved to Galkayo, a midsized town in Central Somalia, my father was fluent in both English and Arabic. People came to him and asked for his assistance when they had difficulty interpreting or understanding the Quran, and important government officials consulted him for help with English. Throughout his life, he educated many top-level government officials and ran his own private school from our large house. This earned my father the titles *Ma'alin*, teacher, and *Waadad*, man of God. My father had his faults, but he was adamant about one thing: all his sons *and daughters* must get an education. This was an unusual and bold view at that time, because girls' education was not highly valued. If a mother had money to educate only one child, she picked a son. But my father used to say, "If you educate a son, you educate one person, but if you educate a daughter, you educate the whole community."

My mother came from a different world. After she married my father as a teenager and went to live in the city, she felt it was her responsibility to provide her aging mother with a child to help her with the demands of nomadic life. My mother considered it an honor for one of us to be Ayeeyo's helper. She wanted to choose a child her mother was compatible with, and one suited to the harshness of the desert. My sister Arafo, though one year older than me, was fearful by nature. Even in the city, dark rooms frightened her. I, on the other hand, was a temperamental, strong-willed child who had learned early on that bravery was a virtue worth striving for. And my mother would never have given away a boy to be Ayeeyo's helper; domestic help was for girls. The reality was, my mother was giving birth to too many girls in a society that valued males over females. I was her fifth child and her fourth girl, so it was no great sacrifice for her to spare me as a gift to her own mother. I understand now that my mother was a woman of her time and circumstances, but sometimes, even today, I also can't help but wonder, *Was I dispensable?* In my low moments, the thought actually brings tears to my eyes. But when I am able to step back and take in the whole picture of the past, I am more understanding. I recall specific moments when she admired me for my bravery and resilience and I like to think she was honoring me with her choice.

My mother's biggest obstacle was convincing my father to allow me to live full time as a nomad. My parents' acrimony over my destiny hit a boiling point when I reached school age. My mother was so determined to provide my ayeeyo with help that she avowed that she would go herself if he didn't give in. Moving my ayeeyo to the city was never an option. My father had moved his own mother to the city and regretted it deeply; they had both watched as she slowly lost her independence and mobility. So after I finished first grade in the city, my father reluctantly agreed to let me go. My mother took me by the hand and headed to the desert.

All I recall from this particular trip was suffering terrible motion sickness on the long bus ride, a sensation that was mixed with the excitement of seeing my grandmother again. I did not grasp the full picture of what this trip meant. No one explained that I would grow up without my siblings and only occasionally see my mother. It was not until I was older that I learned the fight over my destiny had almost caused my parents to divorce.

WHEN I WAS living full time with my ayeeyo, my mother visited us from time to time. Looking back, I am amazed by my mother's ability to find us wherever we were in the vast, unforgiving red desert. By necessity, nomads are never stationary for long. They are constantly moving in search of water and fresh grazing land.

My mother traveled from the city to the edge of the nomadic lands by bus and then walked for many days at a time until she found us. She survived her journeys not only because she knew the harsh desert intimately but because of our built-in "nomadic network," which provided communication, food, and navigation. When she came to a hut, regardless of whether she knew its occupants, the nomads living there would give her shelter for the night and share their meal. Sometimes, in the rainy season, the season of plenty, they would slaughter a goat to share and give her meat to take along. This hospitality was commonplace among the nomads and was key to their survival. People shared because they knew they, too, might need that kind of hospitality in the future.

As they moved about the terrain, herding camels and other livestock long distances to find water, the nomads came into contact with each other, so they not only knew the land but knew where other tribes were currently located. To access this information, my mother had to give the "nomadic password," which was her full name and the name of her subclans. The Somali clan system, with its myriad clan wars, is remarkably complex and difficult to describe. The four core clans are Darod, Hawiye, Dir, and Isaaq. Each main clan branches into four or five main subclans, and they, in turn, split into many more sub-subclans, and so forth. Think of a big family tree, but with warring squirrels on the branches. Somali society uses a patrilineal system, so children always belong to their father's clan, not their mother's.

Somali children are taught to memorize the full name of each of their father's ancestors as far as ten to twenty generations back or more. You might see a little girl, only four or five years old, proudly reciting the names of her forefathers all the way back to the original member of the four clans. Although my father was serious about our education, he didn't feel it was necessary for us to memorize our clan lines. This created some awkward situations for me when I could not recite my forefathers' lineage to other kids my age. My ayeeyo and my mother belonged to the same sub-subclan, but only because my grandmother and grandfather happened to share a lower subclan. That was unusual: for the most part, nomads married their daughters off to other clans to create alliances so they could appeal to them in times of trouble or bad drought. Alliance was insurance, nomadic style.

When my mother went looking for us and came upon people from other subclans, she scrutinized their body language and reactions to make sure there was no recent animosity between the subclans. She had to be ready to flee, in case she had walked into enemy territory. Luckily, unlike men, women were not seen as much of a threat, but she did have to watch for other dangers, such as rape or forced marriage. The way nomads gave navigational information was not in coordinates but in environmental landmarks. They might tell my mother, "Oh, we heard they were headed to the *lafo Ayr*," which meant "the bones of the Ayr family," and signified an area where the Ayr clan had lost a lot of men in a war. Many areas were named for the warriors who died there. Other areas were named for the type of trees that grew there, the type of animals that lived there, or the harshness of that particular environment. She could be directed to *libaax yaale* ("the land where the lions lay") or *bali Higle* ("the reservoir Higle") or *bili badan* ("many reservoirs"), and she would understand exactly where to go.

I was always glad to see my mother, whom I called *hooyo*, but wasn't sad when she left, because I loved living with my grandmother. I loved the rhythm and rituals of nomadic life, from the sound of the baby goats demanding milk from their mothers every morning to the mysterious lullaby of the insects and birds that soothed me to sleep at night. I loved sitting around the fire, listening to the stories and poems my family members shared every evening. I could visualize myself in those heroic stories, whether they were legends about my ancestors or traditional Somali folktales. In the desert, I was treated like a big girl, as if I was part of something important. I was expected to be brave, and I was. My days were not structured or filled with schoolwork. When I stood in front of my ayeeyo's hut, all I could see was a vast, limitless land all around me, and I had the freedom to choose which direction to go. I could sit under a tree, just watching nature and being alone with my thoughts, or I could walk endlessly, exploring the myriad sights and sounds. I spent a lot of time climbing trees so I could see farther into the distance. When something caught my attention, I investigated it, often following an animal to its home. Around me, birds built nests, warthogs ran in groups, and foxes played hide and seek with me.

Although I enjoyed the freedom, nomadic life was not entirely carefree. I had work to do, and dangers abounded. Under my ayeeyo's watchful eye, I learned how to do the simple but important tasks of starting a fire, making flatbread using the hot sand under the fire, and looking after *waharo* (baby goats). Looking after waharo was my first job with the animals, given to me as a four- or five-year-old. I herded them close to our huts, and it served as a learning experience for both me and the waharo. At age five or six, I graduated to looking after a herd of older goats, which I would take farther from the huts in search of grass to eat. To get a bird's eye view of my herd, I climbed a tree or termite mound. From my perch, I watched all my goats below, scattered across the land, heads down, grazing contentedly.

Dudumo—termite mounds—rise like castle spires above the red desert, sometimes reaching the height of seventeen feet at their pointy peaks. They are shaped like a cone or stalagmite rising up from the ground, tricky to climb, yet are often the tallest things around for miles, so they are useful as both a landmark and to get the lay of the land. I quickly learned to climb with care, never leaving my foot or hand in a hole too long, for many other creatures also took advantage of the termites' building skill. Many times I placed my hand on a lizard, snake, or other scary crawler, who would be none too pleased with me for using their home as my play structure or watchtower. Like other nomadic children, I learned how to read landmarks. A tree that was twisted a certain way, unique rock formations, and clusters of dudumo all helped me navigate. Standing on top of a dudumo, I was convinced that the sky and desert met at a far-off point. I would walk toward it, thinking I would get to the meeting point, only to find it getting farther away as I neared. It was this kind of curiosity that often led me into danger, but I was rarely scared, for my ayeeyo taught me well.

As the sun dropped and evening neared, I would return to our cluster of huts with my herd of goats. We would tend to our animals, eat our dinner of camel's milk and dried meat, and then gather around the fire for stories and poems. At times, I mixed up the stories I heard with reality. Coupled with my curious nature and strong sense of duty, this created some interesting perceptions that sometimes came back to bite me. For example, I had often heard the adults talk about *guduudane*, or "the red one," who caused great destruction of the nomads' goats and sheep and seemed to magically appear and disappear. My mother's family often talked of demons that could possess people and then demand food offerings to leave them alone, so this idea swirled around in my head as I heard stories about "the red one" sucking the blood of animals. Then I grew confused. Was a guduudane a possessed person or a bloodthirsty beast?

One sunny, hot day, I was herding my baby goats not far from our huts when I spotted something red under a tree. Elated and proud to have discovered the despised guduudane, I yelled with urgency to anybody within hearing distance. My family knew I would not yell for help unless it was a life-threatening situation, so they came running. When they reached me, they saw nothing but a woman with a red head scarf sitting under a tree at the edge of our little village of huts. I stood, proudly waiting for someone to capture the "red one." I was convinced my discovery would end tales of the guduudane once and for all. But my mother, who was visiting at the time, calmly told me, "That is not what a red one looks like. Guduudane is not a human."

The "red one" I had spotted turned out to be a young woman eloping with her lover. It was a familiar Somali romance: a young camel herder wandering the desert spies a beautiful teenage girl herding goats and they run off together. The red-scarfed woman had stayed behind under the tree while her soon-to-be husband replenished their food and supplies from our encampment, partaking of the same hospitality my mother used when she traveled. The couple had left their subclans secretly and didn't want to be discovered until they reached the young man's nomadic lands—a common practice among clan youngsters who wanted to marry outside their family's expectations or didn't want to pay the bride dowry. Some men took the young woman's virginity on the way, making it that much more difficult for the other clan to take their daughter back. In nomadic culture, a young woman's virginity signified her value, and once that was lost, there was no point in fighting for her. After the women realized no danger existed and the couple quickly ran off, I heard my mother laughing with the other women over my mistake. I was confused as to why no one was running after the red one; I knew from the stories I heard around the fire that some humans could shape-shift so I wasn't convinced that the danger was over. But something about the way my mother dismissed my concern with ease told me that my quest to find the guduudane was not over. Much later, I found out that *guduudane* is the Somali word for a caracal, a feline the size of a bobcat. Funny to think that a young couple's elopement was put in peril because I mistook a red-scarfed woman for the ever-elusive cat!

Stories by the fire were not the only things that captured my imagination. One day, while herding my goats, I saw a straight, thin line in the sky above me. I stopped what I was doing and watched it. *Who is up there making that line in the sky?* It was so straight and so long it completely captured my attention. I knew about clouds, because studying rain patterns was important to nomads' survival. However, this line was completely different, and I instantly knew something had to be responsible for making it. This line made me wonder about the world that lay beyond mine, the same way the shining stars in the black night sky did as I slept in the open space in front of my ayeeyo's hut.

One of my nomadic relatives had told me about a people who lived in a faraway land who were the complete opposite of us. She said they walked on their heads instead of their feet, using their hands to aid them as they moved about. I tried to picture how they got around, ate, or took care of their children, and wondered how I could have a conversation with one of them, because I would just be looking at their feet. Nomads had no newspapers or books and hadn't seen photos of other people or places, so when they heard about people who were the opposite of themselves, they assumed these people must be opposite in every way, and must walk on their heads. When later I heard mention of "white people," I immediately put these two images together and believed that "white people" and "upside-down people" were one and the same. With this idea in my head, watching that perfect line in the clear, blue sky over Somalia, I wondered if the upside-down white people made it. I waved frantically at the line, trying to gain their attention. I was curious and not really afraid of them but was ready to run in case things went badly. The white line continued moving farther away, fading from view. Disappointed, I went back to herding my goats. But that fading white cloud left me wanting to know just who was living above us.

WHEN RAIN AND grass grew scarce, the animals had to be herded farther from our huts in search of grazing land, so it was no longer safe for me to herd them alone. My ayeeyo and other family members took over the herding, and I accompanied them to keep learning. As my ayeeyo moved the livestock around, I studied her every move. She dressed for working the land, with her long, flowing, vibrant *guntiino* (a single piece of cloth, similar to an Indian sari) tied over one shoulder. She wore it cinched up to midshin and tied it around her waist, ready to run after any predator that came after her goats. In contrast, city women wore their colorful and elaborate guntiino more stylishly, letting them flow to their ankles as they walked the city streets. With their matching head scarves and perfumed bodies, they dressed for beauty, not function.

My practical ayeeyo kept her herd together and moving, not with the help of sheep dogs but by throwing sticks along the edges of the group, accompanied by sharp shouts of *"Hooy hooy!"* Each animal in our herd had a name, and she called individually to any animal who was moving in the wrong direction. I copied her and

called after the animals, too. She constantly watched for predators, not an easy task when tending to more than a hundred sheep
and goats.

Herding animals was an all-day affair. When the sun hit midday and we could see the heat shimmering up from the ground in
the distance, my ayeeyo and I guided the animals to the closest
shade. Our goats stood under the trees, regurgitating and rechew-
ing the grass they ate earlier. I watched their stomachs, necks, and
mouths with intense curiosity to see if I could figure out how they
brought it up again. *Could I do this if I tried?* I worked on the skill
as I played around under the trees. When I felt hungry, I cupped
my hand under a goat's full udder and squeezed the warm, foamy
milk right into my hand. Other times I drank milk from a *dhiil*,
the waterproof vessel women wove tightly from grass. Because
it was wide in the middle and narrow on both ends, my ayeeyo
could carry the dhiil comfortably on her back as we walked.

I loved watching the whole ritual of *ulay*, the process of curing
the dhiil. After rinsing the dhiil with water, Ayeeyo lit a bundle
of small aromatic twigs from the *nagaar* shrub and inserted the
smoldering branches into the dhiil. She swirled them around vigorously and removed them, leaving the smoke inside. Then Ayeeyo
put the branches back into the fire to set them alight again, repeating the process until she felt the dhiil was sanitized. Performing
ulay regularly kept the milk from spoiling quickly. The dhiil's cap
served as a cup, and milk from a freshly sanitized dhiil had small
black particles in it that carried a distinctive, fresh herbal taste

that was very pleasing to my young palate. I liked it better than milk straight from the goat.

As we rested in the shade, my ayeeyo told me stories about tricky foxes who stalked goats, looking for children who were not being vigilant. I listened attentively to her tales as I doodled in the sand, soaking up our ancestral knowledge. Every once in a while, she would make sounds to scare away predators, such as foxes or the mysterious guduudane, who were stalking the herd.

One day, while we waited for the heat of the day to abate, she suddenly stopped in the middle of her story and looked intently at the herd. I followed her gaze to the resting goats. Then she hitched up her guntiino and leapt to her feet in one motion and ran, yelling, throwing rocks and branches. A guduudane had snuck in, crouching close to the red earth that camouflaged him, and silently attacked one of our goats. The large feline slunk away under my ayeeyo's assault, and the goat tried to stagger to its feet, a fatal wound on its neck.

Following the Muslim rules of *halal*, my ayeeyo quickly uttered *"Bismillah"* before the goat breathed its last breath, pulled out her knife, and slaughtered and skinned it. That evening, when we came back home, we cooked the meat over an open fire under the black sky, feasting while my ayeeyo reiterated the lesson learned: never let your guard down, because those sneaky predators are always looking for an opportunity to steal a meal.

Early on, I became so in tune with my ayeeyo that I could sense when trouble was brewing on the horizon. When I observed

Ayeeyo standing in front of our hut one day, her gaze fixed on the distance, her forehead wrinkled with worry, I knew something was wrong. Jilal, the drought season, was upon us. Since the dawn of time, nomadic poets have told tales about the devastation of jilal, the most dreaded season for nomads. Nothing shows the power of the red desert quite like jilal, with its relentless, merciless heat. As we came under its grip, our whole world dried up. Everywhere we saw scenes of death and destruction, fractured twigs and dry bones littering the ground, and rain-starved trees standing like skeletons. When our livestock no longer got enough water or grass, their milk dried up, and they succumbed to sickness and died. Even the massive, resilient, beloved camel yielded to jilal. The dry season could wipe out entire families and their animals in a matter of weeks.

When it was time to move to the next known food and water sources, I often heard adults talking about which areas would get rain and when. I had no idea they were following the accumulated knowledge of our ancestors, which informed them if we were experiencing a much harsher jilal than usual and would have to move farther away. In that case, we sent a scout ahead to find a waterhole or reservoir that hadn't dried up, grasslands that hadn't been ravaged, or an area with the prospect of rain— anywhere we could survive. The scout needed to have unusually good navigational and survival skills and the ability to foresee the weather. It could take anywhere from two to seven nights for a scout to return, provided he did not meet a predator more desperate than himself. The return of the scout meant the next day was moving day.

Moving days were always exciting for me but stressful for the adults. My ayeeyo moved with great efficiency as she dismantled our portable huts. We started packing at dawn's first light so we could start on our way before the sun got too high and hot. Several *hayin rati* (obedient male camel) were tied close by, ready to carry our houses and other belongings. I drank my breakfast, provided by the few goats whose udders hadn't gone dry yet, and headed toward my ayeeyo with a milk mustache, eager to help. She put a bridle on one of the camels, untied him, and gave a single tug. He followed her without complaint. When she reached the pile of sticks that had been our hut, I heard her say *"Ju!"* as she pulled the reins downward and ordered the camel to its knees.

Once the camel was sitting, Ayeeyo laid a tightly woven cloth on his back to prevent pressure points or chafing. She knew that even minor abrasions in the desert can turn deadly very quickly. Once the saddle was added, she attached the long, U-shaped branches that gave our hut its domed shape. She arranged them with the curved part along the sides of the camel, below the hump, and the straight parts pointing skyward, so they would not interfere with the camel as he walked. Several of these U-shaped branches were tied to each flank of the camel. Next, she secured four large woven water baskets within the curve of each U, creating side-walls for what would become a little house for my sister, young cousins, and me to rest in when we got tired. She put more soft, woven cloths on top of the saddle and covered it all with more mats. Along the front and back, she crossed two smooth sticks to create more support. The end result was that we had a totally enclosed, cozy little moving hut.

Our encampment usually consisted of my ayeeyo and myself, and my Uncle Qoodaar and his family. Other relatives and my siblings came and went. Our camps were set up in family groups, although they were always located within walking distance of other subclan members, for safety and protection. During the rainy season, we could have as many as eight huts in our encampment, but during the dry season, when people traveled at different times in search of water, it could be as few as two.

This was a big journey, regardless of the size of the group. In addition to the camels that carried our belongings, we had another fifty or more camels, which one of the men would herd ahead of us, and over one hundred goats and sheep. My ayeeyo tied the two rati that carried our belongings together and took the lead. Young camels in particular have a nasty temper and are known to sometimes bite the camel in front or create some kind of disturbance. Because my ayeeyo trained her camels herself, she knew exactly where to place them so they would not misbehave. She knew better than to trust young male camels, or *layli*, with any important job until they were out of adolescence and fully trained. The nomads had a saying: *Reerkii layli dhaansada, haamuhuu kalaayaa.* "The family who lets a layli fetch their water gets their water vessels destroyed."

My ayeeyo had one layli that was so out of control that he

used to destroy everything that stood in his way. Most of his victims were the baby goats that pranced happily around him after emptying their mother's udders. Time and time again, our family begged her to slaughter that layli, but my ayeeyo said he came from a long line of obedient rati. "Give him time," she assured them. As always, my ayeeyo knew what she was talking about, because this layli eventually grew up to become the most obedient camel she owned. He was so calm that kids played on him as he sat passively chewing his cud.

I started the journey on foot, watching one of my teenage cousins, who was herding our flock up ahead. She wore a rich, carthy terracotta-colored tunic and moved a big stick with great urgency from side to side as she pressured the sheep and goats to keep moving forward. Watching her rhythmic movements helped me keep pace with the others. Much farther ahead, I could see my young uncle Duran, my family's *geel jire*, herding the camels, but I didn't know how long I would be able to keep him in my sights. Geel jire were always young, resilient men, who herded the camels independently from the rest of the family. Even when we were camped, the geel jire were often alone with their herd for weeks at a time and wandered farther than the rest of the clan, since camels ate different plants than the sheep and goats and could go longer without water. Often, as the sun set, right before the night swallowed up the evening, I'd hear the wooden sound of the camels' koor, accompanied by the geel jire's singing, and watch the dark images of the trees and camels against the background of the dusky orange sky, and know all was right in my world.

Geel jire had to be brave and strong, as they were often in conflict with lions, hyenas, leopards, other clans, and any other danger the desert threw at them. We often saw geel jire from other clans pass by on our journey and could identify their subclan by the brand they used to mark their camels. I was excited to see and hear them approaching, but it was a different story for the older girls. Although most of these men were honorable, with deep pride in their families, we were taught to be wary of them because some took advantage of young women. Somali women were solely responsible for keeping their virginity. If they were raped, they were blamed, and rape brought dishonor to the whole family. We learned to guard our virginity with our lives.

When I eventually got tired of walking, my Uncle Qoodaar put me on his shoulders, where I could see the unfolding terrain better. When he could carry me no more, my ayeeyo brought the lead camel to his knees with one downward tug, and I clambered up. Initially, I was afraid I was going to fall off when the camel lumbered to his feet, but I quickly figured out how to counterbalance so I didn't fall in the dirt in front of the cranky camel's mouth or get hung up on his long neck when he dipped forward and backward. I sat inside that mini-hut feeling cozy and safe.

Riding a camel was soothing. The camel's flat feet moved steadily on the sandy desert floor, giving us a smooth ride. My sister and I sang songs, made up games, and kept ourselves entertained. We knew the adults had an important job to do, and we were never disobedient or demanding. Nomadic children only let their needs be known if there is a true emergency, such as threatening wild animals or a deadly snakebite—or in my case, when I imagined I saw a guduudane. We simply lived with the certainty that if there was water or food, we would be cared for. Life was predictable that way.

We stopped each nightfall, when most predators hunted and a moving herd became harder to defend. We unloaded all our camels so they could rest and established a safe area for the goats and sheep. We built a fire and ate thumbnail-sized bits of dried goat meat. In addition to this *oodkah*, children were given fresh, warm milk straight from the goat, and the adults drank tea with milk. We slept under the moon and hoped the fire would keep the lions and hyenas at bay. Even though I could hear predators out in the dark, I felt safe sleeping beside my ayeeyo. She would protect me. My ayeeyo was never afraid of the night hunters. She was not afraid of anything. I knew from her tales that the laughing hyenas were cowardly, opportunistic hunters, and courage belonged to the king of the desert, the lion. I once heard that she yanked one of her goats right out of a lion's mouth and sent the big cat back into the night with its tail between its legs. I remember being startled out of sleep one night as my whole family ran around yelling and waving torches, trying to scare away a lion determined to jump into the goat enclosure. Fear gripped me as I watched my ayeeyo disappear into the darkness toward the lion. She returned unharmed, her body language looking fiercer than ever. Watching her, I became a fearless child.

After several days of travel, we reached our destination. The women in the family instantly set about the tricky and labor-intensive task of putting together our portable hut. If a woman could not build her own *aqal*, she was shamed and deemed an incompetent wife. Somali society values a woman only if she is a "subservient girl" or an "obedient wife." If you couldn't even build your own *aqal*, rumors about you spread through the nomads like wildfire. Your daughter might not find a suitable husband and your sons would be looked down upon. In nomadic society, women carried the burden of keeping the family and clan honor. The division of labor between men and women was crystal clear and unchanging: men hunted, herded camels, and went to war, while women performed all the essential domestic chores. Women made all the materials needed to build their family's *aqal*. They wove grass for the hut's covering, then harvested flexible sticks for the frame, wrapping them with strips of animal skin that they had processed. Women used grass to weave sleeping mats and all of the necessary items for daily living, such as tightly woven milk bowls and storage vessels for milk and water. They also wove cloth strips into pads that cushioned both sleeping mats and the saddles of camels on moving day. Furthermore, they were responsible for herding goats, building enclosures for the live-stock with brush they harvested, and cleaning those enclosures, all while bearing and taking care of the children. No wonder that even as a child I noticed that beautiful, young, newly married ladies looked much older and haggard after only a few dry seasons, even if I didn't understand why. Reflecting on this today, I can't even imagine how these women survived. At the time, it seemed completely normal to me and I thought this would be my destiny. While I'm glad I've been spared that life, I still feel guilty if I pay someone to clean my house. I have three kids and a hectic work schedule, but an inner voice still shames and judges me because I should be able to handle all that myself like the women who came before me.

After the women finished building the huts, they moved on to building fences for the goats and sheep from bushes and branches they collected. Just as they finished, my uncle would return with our herd of camels. Camels were the nomads' lifeblood, and it was imperative that they be cared for extremely well. They provided milk, meat, and transportation. Given their high value, camels were also used as currency. Many camels might be used to pay for a good wife from a good family. Most important, they were used to perform *dhaan*, the act of fetching water from far-off sources, whether from rain, which filled natural reservoirs, or wells, which were dug in key spots across the land.

Our encampment had to be close to water, but far enough from it that we weren't in direct contact with predators or enemy subclans. This was more difficult when water was scarce. We were all just clinging to life; even my goats were weakened by the lack of water. When I used a small amount of water to wash my face and hands, my goats came running, eager to catch any drops that fell to the ground, only to be disappointed as any such drops were instantly swallowed by the dry desert. When a few licked my hands, I felt sorry for them and cupped my hands to give them a little drink, but then all the other goats swarmed around me and I had to grab my stick to scare them away.

When our water was nearly gone, someone took our rati to fill our water containers. During the drought, dhaan seemed to take an extra-long time, even though it was only a half-day's journey to the well. My lips would be cracked, my internal organs would feel as if they were drying out, and I desperately searched the wide horizon for our camel to appear. I had seen animals die from lack of water, their emaciated bodies succumbing to infection or bug bites. I had gone without water for a day or so before, but that day, as time elapsed and the sun beat down on me relentlessly, I started praying that no harm came to my uncle who was leading the dhaan. I grew excited when I was certain I could see our camel in the distance, only to be crushed by the realization that a mirage had hooked me with its false stories, a cruel joke nature plays when you are clinging to hope and life. When our camel finally appeared, laden with warm water, I drank gratefully, although I was so dehydrated that it took a long time for my mouth to become moist and lubricated again.

A few days later, after this water revived us enough to keep moving, we were able to herd our goats and sheep to the well my uncle had visited. Men and women, young and old, children of every age, goats, sheep, cows, and even warthogs all gathered around the life-giving source. Providing water for so many animals required teamwork, and the nomads helped each other so the line moved efficiently. Men sang as they fetched the water, and a symphony of other noises filled my ears as the animals drank from big wooden bowls. The first ones waddled away from the well, staggering under the weight of their distended bellies, and a new thirsty group came in. The camels took so long to fill their big stomachs that I got tired of watching them. I was curious to see, however, if the other nomads fed their camels salt after they drank, the way my ayeeyo did—a trick, I'd only later learn, that helped her camels retain their fluids as long as possible.

The rest of the dry season was spent just trying to survive. This was not a time for sitting around the fire at night sharing jokes and stories; we were tired and went straight to bed. We worked harder during jilal than any other time. Every bit of our energy was spent obtaining food and water and keeping our animals safe. In fact, all my best early childhood memories are from the rainy season. Jilal was only about survival. Despite our daily struggles, we knew this was part of a cycle. The rains would come again.

THE FIRST SIGN that the rainy season, *gu*, was approaching was the mating call of the *orgi*, or male goat. (The word *orgi* should not be confused with the English word *orgy*, which involves a mind-blowing group activity that neither Somali nomads nor orgi would ever consider doing.) Whether it was the scent of green grass, the promise of water, or just an ancient instinct, the female goats were always the first to go into heat. The orgi's reaction was immediate and intense. An orgi in rut truly seems possessed by demons.

One morning I watched as two orgi—one large and fierce-looking, the other small and weak—stationed themselves in the shade of a tree and yelled at all the female goats around them. Their tongues dangled from their mouths, shaking with the vibrations of their nonstop desperate bleating. Nearby, the female goats grazed and chewed their cud, holding their ground, unmoved by the pleading of the orgis. The two males had dirty clumps of some unknown substance that hung from their goat beards and radiated an odor that revolted my stomach.

I became increasingly curious about what was going on. Once in a while, the big orgi lost control, and I would see him on top of a female, moving his lower half fast before she slipped away. Then he was standing alone again, screaming, his upper lip pulled back as he pointed his mouth into the air, covered in his own urine. (The act of getting urine onto one's face is a trick an orgi in heat performs.) I kept one eye on the amorous goats and one eye out for my ayeeyo. While my grandmother was patient and kind, I assure you she would not have been happy to see a girl curious about mating. The minute any married Somali women, who were the self-appointed watchdogs of younger women's sexuality, saw a girl intensely or purposefully observing mating animals, they cursed and threw twigs at her. But that day my ayeeyo didn't seem to notice my stares. She was busy near the hut, skinning a young male goat as it hung from a tree. She could skin a large orgi in a matter of minutes, let alone a small one. Like a surgeon with years of experience, she could remove the most delicate tissue almost effortlessly.

My ayeeyo suddenly left her work by the hut and to my surprise captured the smaller of the two orgi. When she carried him by his legs roughly around to the side of the hut, I thought she was going to slaughter him. Were we expecting visitors? Or was she starting to store excess meat for the next jilal already? My eyes followed her as she picked up two large, thick slabs of wood by the side of the hut. With a quick, determined motion she smashed the little orgi's testicles between the slabs. She worked skillfully, knowing exactly where and how hard she had to strike to stop his hormone flow without causing major damage. I cringed, feeling the need to protect my own private places. *It must hurt terribly*, I thought, but I didn't feel too much compassion for the orgi. I regularly saw animals slaughtered, their bright red blood forming small, flowing rivers across the dry earth beneath my feet. I watched goats thrash about, flailing their legs as their lives were snuffed. Part of me wanted to step out of the shadows and ask why she was doing this, but the threat of being "twigged" was enough to keep me back. Instead, I stealthily continued to watch.

Shortly thereafter, the stunned small orgi rejoined the herd, moving slowly and painfully. When he encountered the females in heat, there was not a peep from him. He stood apart from the herd, as though his thunder had been ripped right out of him. In time, I was taught that this technique of neutering was used to selectively breed stronger offspring who could better weather the harsh conditions of jilal. Having larger goats to sell also allowed us to buy more of the things we needed from the city, such as tea and sugar.

It seemed as if those noisy goats could smell the rain coming, and they proclaimed its return lustily. Even the dry, red desert can birth green growing things and breathe new life into its inhabitants within just a few weeks of the rain's blessed return. Every

corner of our world crackled with life once again. Gu was good
for all: baby goats soon frolicked about, meat became plentiful,
children gained weight, and renewed energy was infused into the
adults. Once again, stories and poems were told around the fire,
and teens gathered and danced under the moon. Responsibilities
and danger eased a bit since we could stay closer to the huts with
our animals. During the time of gu, it was as if we had a sacred
reprieve, a time for rejuvenation, which we appreciated even more
because we knew that jilal would come again and the red desert
would turn ominous once more.

While the adults were in this festive mood, I gathered my
courage and tried to get answers to some of my nagging questions.
Abti Qoodaar never minded my curious nature; in fact, he was the
only adult who went out of his way to answer me. One day, I asked,
"Abti, have you ever seen a hyena?"

He laughed and said yes.

This was, of course, a silly question to ask. My whole life, I
had been warned about hyenas, heard their sounds at night, and
seen their eyes shine in the darkness, but I had never seen one up
close. Lately, the herders had been reporting many sightings of
hyenas, so I was sure it would not be long before I ran into them. I
wanted to know exactly what hyenas looked like, in case they tried
to attack my goats.

The next day, around midmorning, my uncle called me out
of the hut and said, "You are the one who wanted to see a hyena,
right?"

"Yes, Abti," I said in a timid voice.

"There is a hyena under that tree waiting for you." In that instant, I could hear the deafening pounding of my heart in my ears as I thought of seeing a live hyena. My uncle, perhaps noticing the shift in my energy, said, "I killed him for you already."

I felt guilty. I did not want the hyena to curse me. I had heard stories of people killing animals and then turning into the very animal they had killed. In fact, the previous year, I heard my Abti Qoodaar had turned into a hyena one day. Reportedly, he walked up to a group of men and began running around and making noises like a hyena. This was confusing to me. The men recognized him and read the Quran over him and they claim that was how he got better.

Alone in front of my ayeeyo's hut, I mustered enough courage and set out toward my dead hyena. I looked quickly at his lifeless limbs and gaping mouth and hurried away, convinced he was about to come to life. That was the last time I asked to see any wild animals up close.

SOMALIA IS KNOWN as the nation of poets, and creating poems is considered a sign of intelligence in our culture. Generations of Somalis committed countless poems to memory and repeated them to their children, creating an enduring legacy. During my ayeeyo's time, poetry was a major form of communication among the nomads. They gathered under the light of the moon and created rhythmic, complex, and well-articulated poems. Young people courted through poems, clan men insulted each other through poems, and women with sharp tongues and minds told their no-good husbands they were done with them through metaphorically complicated poems.

My ayeeyo was a well-known and respected poet in her time. Even today older poets remember her and can recite some of her poems. Her family name was Halima Hirsi Bille, but she was also known by her poet name, Xadiya Ooga Xardhanley, meaning "the one decorated with the telling art." Most men respected her, but at the same time were threatened by her quick poet's tongue, which often bruised their egos. She composed poems about daily life, praising a prolific goat whose udders stayed wet through the end of jilal or the beauty of the desert in gu.

My ayeeyo's poems also drew attention to the shame or weakness of enemy subclans. She would say things like, "Don't marry into this subclan because they make you ride a donkey" and "Don't marry into this subclan because they beat their wives" and "For sure, don't marry into this subclan for you will go to an early grave." The only clans my ayeeyo spared from her scorn were her mother's subclan, Macherten, and her own subclan, Wagardha. She only stopped insulting other clans when two tragedies befell her family.

First, one of her daughters, Aarey, became disabled as an infant. A crazy woman they encountered one day grabbed baby Aarey by the leg and took off running into the desert. As she ran, Aarey was shaken back and forth, her head jostling dangerously. My ayeeyo ran after the woman and took her baby back, but Aarey was never the same after that day. I was only a baby when she died in the severe drought of 1974, but my sister Abshiro remembers her well. She said Aarey remained very simple in her speech and comprehension, reacting to things with a child's delight and sadness.

The second tragedy occurred approximately five years later, when my ayeeyo lost her youngest son, my abti Duran. Our men had just returned from a war between two subclans, Wagardha and Saleeban. As the warriors were sitting around the fire cleaning their guns, one of the guns accidentally fired, killing my uncle instantly and wounding another man. My uncle did not yet have a family of his own. Somalis grieve deeply when someone dies without leaving children behind to remember them by.

Despite the fact that we were constantly at war, we understood that an accident was an accident. The family of the man who shot my uncle offered my ayeeyo compensation, knowing she had just lost her camel herder as well as her son, but she refused. But she never insulted another subclan with her poems again. She believed those subclans had put a curse on her family, and therefore, if she continued on that path, the rest of her blessings would be short-lived.

In my ayeeyo's time, not only poetry but traditional folk songs and dances, such as *dhaanto*, brought young men and women out of their huts and into open fields under the night sky. They danced and took turns creating poetry. Young men, moving with the speed of an unmated bird, would confess love for a chosen woman. In answer to this signal, women swayed in a most choreographed way, bringing attention to their earthly goods— mainly breasts and hips. Women knew they could not have sexual encounters until they were married, but these nightly interactions created a healthy venue for young teens to test the waters and get to know each other, like some kind of Nomad Mingle. Single women showed their availability by parting their hair right down the middle, and then either leaving it loose or braiding it into many long, thin braids. Married women covered their hair with a simple, colorful scarf knotted in the back.

My ayeeyo's youth was summoned from the past as I worked alongside the women of my family. The rhythm of their voices as they sang, recited poetry, and reminisced not only kept me in the rhythm of the work but also provided a living history lesson. A sense of excitement loomed in the air whenever we prepared to make yogurt, as I knew we would soon sit in a circle and I could further feast on the stories and songs of the past that so capti-vated me. First, Ayeeyo milked the goats into a woven milking bowl, and I emptied this *hadhuub* as it got full. I poured milk into each family member's dhiil and capped it with another hadhuub so they could carry it with them as they herded. The rest of the milk I emptied into a *haan*, an even larger woven basket we used to make yogurt and butter.

Yogurt-making was its own ritual, played out when milk was plentiful, most often in gu. We sat in our circle, each with a full haan in front of us, now secured with an animal skin and sup-ported by a frame of sticks. My ayeeyo sat with one leg extended and one folded in, rocking her haan back and forth in front of her. I listened attentively as the women laughed, gave each other advice, and as always, talked about rain and water. A sense of pride filled me when my ayeeyo gave me a smaller haan of my own, and as I worked we all began to sing:

Haantaydiyee heedhe,

Mafiyoobidoo ku arkay,

Marfurkaa lagaa dhuuqay,

Naa ma lagu fandhaalaystay

This song was sung directly to the haan, asking it if anyone had contaminated its milk.

O my beloved haan,

Have you been tampered with?

Has somebody spoiled your milk?

Has somebody ruined your milk?

Our goats grazed nearby, their little ones frolicking around as the sun changed direction, cooling the desert a little. The sounds of contented goats, singing birds, and the cadence of milk swishing in the rocking haan provided a musical backdrop to our songs. A sense of harmony flooded over me. I felt connected to all the women in my family. No one was shooing me out of this adult ritual, even though I was not more than seven. Not only could I herd on my own, but now I could make yogurt, too.

After we made yogurt and butter, I helped cut goat meat into long, thin, pieces that were hung from a rope to dry in the sun. The dried meat was cut, cooked in fat, and stored for the next jilal. I always kept a close eye on whoever was cooking the meat, because my favorite thing was to lick the pot when they were done. It was salty, crispy, a little sour, and I loved it.

Although I felt like a big girl after making yogurt with the women, I knew there were some chores that were too dangerous for me. But my ayeeyo's skills had no limits. Her every movement was poetic, whether she was building a hut, neutering animals, taming headstrong male camels, or milking female camels. She was a true camel whisperer, uttering low, soothing words from time to time to calm an animal or pushing on its legs as she milked it. I thought all women did all of these chores, because my ayeeyo did them so effortlessly. In fact, it wasn't until I was writing this book that my sister Arafo pointed out that women did not usually take care of camels—it was men's work. I gained even more respect for my beloved ayeeyo when I realized that she did not live within the societal norms but instead took care of everything herself. She did not need a man to save her.

One day, my ayeeyo led one baby camel away from the rest of the herd and tied him to a tree. Baby camels are really cute, with extra-fluffy, almost white coats. Adult camels have smooth fur that is the color of reddish tea with milk, almost as if the red dirt of the desert stained them over time. I busied myself around the yard, but from time to time, I caught sight of him out of the corner of my eye, pulling on his rope and trying to get loose. His big brown eyes and long eyelashes flickered nervously as he called to his mother. The rest of the camels were being led out to graze and he didn't like being left behind. His mother didn't want to leave him any more than he wanted to be left, and she required a lot of coaxing from my Abti Qoodaar and his stick. She continued to bellow mournfully, even after they were out of sight, and he continued to cry after her.

I didn't see my ayeeyo actually slaughter the little camel, but my attention was caught when I saw her holding the camel's head and neck, which she had separated from the rest of his body. I immediately went to investigate and watched, mesmerized, as she carefully slit all the way up the front of his neck to his mouth, then meticulously peeled back the skin from his neck and head, making sure she did not destroy any of the outer layer. *Why is she being so careful?* I wondered. *It's dead already, and that part of the skin is not used for carpets or hut covers.* She painstakingly removed everything inside his neck and head that could rot, including his tongue and his beautiful eyes. Finally, when all soft tissues had been removed, she carefully stuffed the neck and head with dry twigs, leaving one stick protruding from the bottom. She leaned the head against our hut, then went on to her next task. Watching this process was like watching a story being told, but without knowing the ending.

The next morning, while Ayeeyo was milking the camels, I saw that mother searching for her baby. She frantically scanned the crowd of babies and bellowed with great concern, but no baby responded to her pleas. She even smelled a few, only to grow more disappointed. Then my ayeeyo brought the stuffed head to the panicked mother. She smelled it while my ayeeyo waited with the milking bowl for her to respond. The mother camel fell for the trick and spread her legs to let him nurse and be milked. As

I watched, I wondered how long this false interaction would go on, and in truth, it went on longer than I expected—for weeks rather than days. This was a rare instance of nomadic life where it was worse to be male. That baby camel was a male, and therefore expendable. We only needed a few males for mating and carrying our huts and water. Otherwise, we valued our camels for their milk.

2 Galkayo

Dad iyo duurba wax walbaa laga fishaa.
Of both man and an unknown forest, anything is to be expected.
—Somali proverb

IN THE YEARS before I was given to my grandmother, I lived with a foot in each world. I clearly recall that one moment I would be chasing my little waharo around the desert and the next I was abruptly dropped in the city of Galkayo where my father lived. Galkayo seemed like an endless city to me, but in reality it was only medium-sized, with schools, government offices, stores, and a large open-air market. Typical houses were made of cinder blocks finished with a thin layer of cement to give them a smooth appearance. Rooms were arranged in a U-shape, with flat roofs, and surrounded a large open space with a packed-dirt floor and no roof. Most families had kitchens and bathrooms outside. Poor people lived in corrugated metal houses or houses made from branches and finished with a mixture of grass, mud, and manure.

Our house, designed by my father, was near the edge of the city and very different from any other house around. My father had traveled to Ethiopia, worked in a British camp, and spent time in our capital, Mogadishu, which itself was influenced by Italian colonialism. I suspect these travels affected his architectural design. The first thing you noticed was that our house sat taller than all the other houses and a high wall protected the front yard from view. Behind it was our large cinder block house, the only one with a peaked roof. Another unique feature, which I think not only set us apart from the people in the city but from all of Somalia, was that my father built beautiful, apartment-style pigeon houses just under the eaves. This made us stand out and attracted gossip—nobody in Somalia kept pigeons. Their perpetual calls provided an agitating symphonic backdrop to our childhood. Every evening, all of the pigeons of Galkayo flew toward our house, leaving feathers and droppings in their wake. My father provided them with shelter and food, and they showered us with feces in return. Even worse, my father used to eat the pigeons. I have never seen any other Somali eat pigeon in my life. This was a whole different level of oddness and I'm embarrassed to confess it even now. Luckily, my father was so well-educated and respected that people thought, *perhaps he knows something we have yet to find out*. That protected us from being shunned, although his own brothers thought he was cursed with pigeons.

The house itself had two bedrooms in the front, which were our main rooms, and two back rooms used for my father's school. A hallway, another rare element, led from the front to the back and had a door that could be closed when my father was teaching. Our center living area was roofed and even had an attic and was finished with a cement floor instead of packed dirt. For special occasions such as Eid, we cleaned the floors with benzene. Even now, every time I fill my minivan with gas, the smell instantly reminds me of how our whole house reeked when we cleaned. The feelings it evokes are mixed because this memory holds two powerful images in my mind: I see my mother cleaning excitedly, see her body language and colorful clothing. It is the clearest picture of her I ever get. On the other hand, the smell triggers the extreme nausea I suffered from the odor. It still makes me feel ill, but I have come to lean into that smell and perhaps even love it because it carries that image of my vibrant mother.

That large central space had bare walls and only a few mats on the floor, so it was very echoey. My sister Arafo and I loved the sound effects in that room and would imitate our father's calls to prayer as loudly as we could. We ran around the space, trying to create different echoes, periodically checking the windows to see if our father was returning. But the most memorable part of that room was the shiny metal pasta machine in the corner.

The high wall that ran across the front yard encircled our outdoor kitchen, bathroom, and chicken coop. The wall dropped to about three or four feet when it reached the side yards and continued all the way around the house. My father planted trees throughout the yard, giving us shade and places to play in the sandy soil. One of our side yards contained our well, which my father shared with those in need. Sometimes I would look out and see a camel herder watering his herd or performing dhaan and knew he had come a long way in search of water. The water from the wells in our area was heavy with minerals and smelled slightly like rotten eggs. Over time, it left permanent dark stains on our teeth. But if the stain happened to create a perfect line across our front teeth, it was considered a sign of beauty.

My older sister Abshiro, who was very protective of me, never let me play near the well, so one of my favorite places to play was under a tamarind tree in the other side yard. I would sit and break twigs into three sections, leaving them partially attached so I could bend them into animal shapes. By sticking the two "legs" into the ground, I could create a herd of goats, including babies, complete with a twig fence to protect them at night. I then broke a twig from the *adey* tree, which we made toothbrushes from, and chewed one end, fraying it until it looked like hair. I tied two pebbles to my stick with a scrap of cloth to create breasts and wrapped another scrap of cloth around it to create my own little female goat herder. I spent hours herding my stick goats—singing to them, tucking the babies and moms into separate pens at night so the baby goats wouldn't take all the milk, and especially keeping them safe from predators.

As I vigilantly watched for foxes or guduudane who might be stalking my imaginary herd, increased activity and more urgent calls coming from the pigeons above me pulled me out of my reverie. I knew immediately that something was stalking them. Looking up, I saw not a guduudane, but a feral cat. This scene melded with my own pretend play, enriching my story. I soon shifted my attention completely to the pigeons as they fended off this predator and protected their babies. I was so used to being in tune with nature that in the absence of warthogs and foxes, pigeons and chickens filled that void.

Our chickens, which we raised for both eggs and meat, roamed around our yard during the day. After studying them carefully, I discovered that when a hen cackled, she was moments away from entering the chicken coop to lay her egg. When I felt the smooth, warm shell of a newly laid egg, I thought, *How about if I crack and swallow one raw?* I liked it, and was soon eating nine raw eggs a day, leaving our family without breakfast. They were convinced some kind of rodent was eating the eggs, until the day I was caught in the act. I was punished, and was surprised to learn I had been causing a problem. In my mind, I thought there were plenty of eggs. I wasn't trying to be sneaky either, I just happened to do my egg eating during a time when everyone else was busy with their duties so they didn't notice. After I got in trouble, I never ate raw eggs again.

But I still had more questions: How did the big, broad-shouldered rooster that chased the hens around figure into the picture? I often saw the hens running from the rooster, which initially I thought was a game. But when I saw him trap a hen in the corner, hold her down with his claws and grab the scruff of her neck with his beak, I began to doubt my game theory. *Was he trying to kill her?* Suddenly the image of an orgi in heat getting on top of a female goat flooded my mind, merging my two worlds. I realized it had something to do with babies.

In the city, I never thought about how food got there. One minute I would be playing outside and the next minute I would be

sitting in the front yard with my family eating our meal. I knew
we got eggs and meat from our chickens and that my mother or
older sisters went to the market, but I didn't have any of those
responsibilities. Unlike the nomadic world, where a great deal of
our time was spent talking about or obtaining food and water,
in the city our well was just a few steps away. I do recall that my
mother had a metal can that held dried meat soaked in butter,
which I could snack on. She must have brought it back when she
visited my grandmother. This oodkah was familiar and comforting to me because it reminded me of being home with my ayeeyo.

The only food-making process I watched in the city from beginning to end was making pasta. I was fascinated by the smooth,
shiny, metal surface of our pasta machine and was allowed to
turn its large handle if someone was supervising me. But when
no one was watching, I used to play with it. People treated what
belongings they had with great care, and I knew I must hide my
play from the adults. I would sneak little scraps of dough into the
machine and watch eagerly as it came out in different shapes. I felt
important "working" with this big metal machine. As I played,
the flour covering the table caught my attention, and I traced my
finger through it, drawing pictures in its dust just the way I doodled in the desert sand while waiting out the midday heat.

In the desert I had a lot more freedom, and I also loved the
feeling that my help was truly needed. Even when I was not old
enough to herd alone, I was still responsible for the waharo. I
felt as important as an adult when I put on my little tunic and

watched the baby goats prance around me with excitement. As I herded my little goats around our huts, I kept one eye on the waharo and one eye on the horizon, just as my ayeeyo had taught me. Every day, when the sun was at its hottest, I ushered my goats to the shade of an acacia tree, where they dropped to the ground, panting. I settled next to them and scanned the land around me, knowing I never had to look far for something to engage my curiosity. When a group of warthogs grazed by, I wondered why their heads always moved up and down, but their tails stayed up as they trotted past. *Is it true that it's because they are constantly putting curses on Somali children for chasing them?* I thought to myself. I often saw flocks of *digiiran* running around, but no matter how hard I chased them, those little spotted brown birds never flew away, they just ran back into the bushes. I kept waiting for them to lift to the sky in one giant herd. *All the other birds know how to fly, and you do not look injured. Why won't you fly?* Despite the fact that I saw these birds everywhere I went, I never saw them leave the ground. At the end of the day, I perched on top of a dudumo or tree stump, listening for the bleating of mother goats that marked Ayeeyo's return from herding.

In the city, I lived in the shadow of my older siblings, so most responsibilities shifted to them. My only real duty was to accompany my older sister Arafo around our dark house when the power was out because she was afraid. I felt a sense of pride when my siblings praised me for being the braver one.

As I got a little older, Arafo and I were given a little more freedom. We ran around with a different kind of herd—the neighborhood kids. City kids had to find things to do, and they often entertained themselves by tormenting mentally ill or physically challenged people, or stray dogs. This felt wrong to me. It wasn't something I ever saw nomads do, either because we were so connected or because the disabled didn't survive the harshness of the desert for long. I recall an accident where neighborhood kids pushed Arafo into the lap of a man who was sleeping against the wall of a house. Her hand landed right on his private parts and the other children began chanting and laughing. The man just lay there, a haunted look in his deep, black eyes. I felt instant sadness. I had seen this man many times, walking around with a white piece of cloth thrown around his deep-black skin like a Roman senator. He looked like a visitor from another world. He shuffled around with an unsteady gait, although I never once saw him fall. I don't know what his real name was, but everyone called him Qaataaquble, a demeaning name created to make fun of the way he walked. Nobody knew where Qaataaquble spent his nights, but I have a clear memory of watching him walk away from the city after that incident. As darkness gathered, the orange sun swallowed his silhouette, deepening this mystery. *Where is his family?* I thought, as I imagined a better life for him beyond the city border. But the next day he would appear again, only to endure another day of torment. His memory still haunts me. In retrospect, I think, *How did the adults let this go on?* but in reality, people in that time and place were not awakened to mental health issues and no one reached out to help him.

A CONSTANT STREAM of nomadic cousins and traveling friends and relatives filled our house in the city. Hospitality is very important in Somali culture, and we received all guests accordingly. One of my mother's cousins liked to make little girls look pretty and display them like dolls. During one visit, she spent a long time fixing my hair, which I found irritating. She then put a fancy dress on me and told me to sit still. I was already antsy from sitting while she did my hair, and my new braids felt tight and confining. She kept checking on me, watching closely so I wouldn't do anything to disturb the perfection of her work. For a child used to wearing a simple tunic and having the freedom to move, this was too much and I finally snapped.

"*Shidadaada iga daaf!*" I screamed at her over and over: "Leave me alone!" (literally, "Don't trouble me with your trouble!"). I ripped off the dress, pulled out my braids, and tossed the shoes from my feet. She never tried to make me look like a lady again.

While the rhythm of nomadic life was based on nature, in the city, the five daily calls to prayer gave structure to my day. I did not see nomads praying or celebrating religious festivals, but Eid-al-Fitr was a big celebration in the city to mark the end of Ramadan. The day before Eid, we cleaned the whole house. On the morning of Eid, all the children put on new clothes or their finest garments and went around the neighborhood, wishing everybody "*Eid wanaagsan.*" In return, we were given candies, pastries, or money. Family and friends visited each other throughout the day, socializing and sharing tea and treats. People slaughtered goats and had large feasts, sharing with those in need.

When I lived in Galkayo, Abshiro took a maternal role with me, favoring me over my other siblings. I never cried for my mother if I was hurt or scared; I cried for Abshiro. My older brother Aadan, however, constantly tormented me, especially when Abshiro wasn't looking. One of his favorite ways to irritate me was to call me *"Eel, Eel."* This phrase was used by neighborhood teens to taunt a mentally ill woman who roamed the neighborhood. People claimed that if you said "Eel, eel" ("Well, well") to this woman, she would jump into the well. I didn't understand how she could jump into so many wells and still live to be teased. I resented being compared to a woman who had lost her mind—a woman society had discarded. My hurt at being called "Eel, eel" was deep and instantaneous, and my behavior turned animalistic. I threw myself down on all fours and scratched at the floor and the walls, screamed, cried, and banged my head against the cement wall in frustration. My reaction excited my brother and he teased me even more, which only amplified my head banging. Now that I know more about human anatomy and head trauma, I am convinced that my migraines and occasional word recall issues are lingering effects of self-inflicted concussions.

ONE CONDITION OF my parents' marriage was that my mother remain in the cities that bordered the nomadic lands so she would be relatively close to her family. Instead of taking my mother to his hometown of Galkayo, my father established her in a small city, Dhabad, closer to the nomadic lands, and he traveled back and forth between the two cities. He kept his daughters from his previous marriage, Sofiya and Khadra, with him in Galkayo when school was in session and took them to be raised by my mother the rest of the time.

When my siblings and I were old enough, my father took us to Galkayo to go to school as well, sending us back to our mother when the session was over. Eventually, when more and more of her children were living in the city part of the year, she decided to move to Galkayo and live with my father so she could spend more time with her children.

Perhaps the hardest adjustment each time I came to Galkayo, either from Dhabad or after time with my ayeeyo, was living with my father's strict rules and punishments. I was terrified of his temper. He was so serious about his teaching that he forgot I was just a preschooler. Every day, he woke my siblings and me at 4 a.m. to teach us Arabic. It is one thing to get up with the sun when you are a nomad; it is entirely different to get up before the sun and be expected to learn a difficult subject. I hated the class and was too tired and afraid to understand anything, but I couldn't utter a word about my discomfort because I knew my father would punish me harshly. He believed well-disciplined children should get up early and that this would set the tone for the rest of their lives. It didn't work. To this day, I'm not a morning person. Perhaps I hated those morning sessions so much that I subconsciously willed my internal circadian rhythm to change.

One early morning, my siblings and I sat in a row as usual, facing my father. At first, I sat at the end of the bench next to Arafo, but then I realized it would be harder for him to deliver a direct knuckle rap to my head, one of his favorite attention-getters, if I was more in the middle. I wedged myself in between Arafo and my half-sister Fowsiyo. My father started asking questions about yesterday's lesson to see what we had retained. I, of course, had retained nothing. When he moved toward me, I panicked and peed on myself. My urine began flowing toward him over the uneven cement floor. Terrified, I tried to stop the pee with my feet, while avoiding his attention at the same time. If the urine touched him, it would ruin his preprayer wash and send him into even more of a rage, because he would have to cleanse himself again.

Just as I thought I had escaped unnoticed, out of nowhere my father slapped me so hard that for a few seconds the light went out of my head. Despite my precautions, he had seen the whole incident. He grabbed me by the ear and trotted me toward the bathroom, where I was smacked a few more times and ordered to clean myself up. I washed and changed clothes, all the while afraid of what would happen when I came back out. When no further punishment followed, I realized that I got off pretty easy that time; he often left us near death.

After that, I vowed to avoid him and his anger at all costs. In the end, I guess his punishments did cause me to be a better student; I studied hard because I did not want him to ever touch me again. I also became more vigilant and monitored his every move around the house. Luckily, he was a devout man, so the calls to prayer helped me to track his whereabouts throughout the day. Arafo was certain I was smarter and braver than she was since I rarely got hit by our father. In reality, however, I was not smarter nor braver; I was just more terrified of him. I created a fantasy world in which he was not my father but had stolen me from my real father, who would one day show up and rescue me. I even convinced myself I didn't look anything like my siblings. My imaginary father was kind, gentle, playful, and cared for me a great deal.

My mother was very protective of us and made it clear to my father that she did not agree with his disciplinary methods. "I gave birth to these kids; you have no right to touch them," she said. She wasn't always there to protect us from him, but when she was, she stood up for us fiercely.

I remember this next incident so vividly that I honestly can't remember if I saw it myself, or if Abshiro relayed it to me with such detail that it lives in my memory as if I saw it. On this day, my mother came upon my father beating Aadan with a stick in our front yard. She fired off a serious Somali curse, warning him to leave her son alone. But my father was well into his beating mode and failed to respond. Out of desperation, my mother picked up some stones and threw them at him as hard as she could. She hit him a few times before he noticed and released Aadan. My mother shielded my brother with her body, but my father, still in striking mode, accidentally hit my mother with the stick. My father may have believed in corporal punishment for children, but he never, ever touched any of his wives. My mother was now enraged; in her mind he had crossed a line. She began stoning him even more vigorously as my father ran through our yard, trying to escape her wrath. My mother chased after him and did not stop throwing stones at him until he was out of our main gate. This was a turning point: he stayed clear of her children after that, at least when she was present. When she wasn't present, we did our best to stay clear of him.

3 Ageless Desert Flower

Hooyadu waa lama huraan.
Only a mother is indispensable.
—Somali proverb

EVERY TIME I dream about my mother, it is always the same. All I can see are her lower limbs and torso. The moment my gaze approaches her face, she completely disappears from my view. Over time, my memories of what she looked like have faded and I feel like I am chasing a mirage that refuses to give the promise it once held. My mother passed away when I was about six, and now it feels like I have never laid eyes on her. This realization frightens me. How is it possible to forget the face of the woman who once gazed into my eyes as she breastfed me?

I desperately want to retrieve the image of my mother's face, but it is buried so deep beneath trauma, loss, and time that I can't access it even if I try my hardest. I have a fantasy that one day I will be describing her looks to someone and they will draw her just as she was. I can even imagine the emotions that would overtake me to see such an image: joy, grief, happiness, and deep sadness all at once. My own children constantly prod me for information about my mother and what she looked like. I have told them everything

I remember—her deep dimples when she smiled and her kind, deep-set eyes—but even these images are fleeting and only exist because they are reflected in Abshiro's face.

My obsession with remembering my mother's face and learning more about her life grew more intense when my oldest daughter turned six—the age I was when my mother passed away from malaria. Suddenly, I wanted to know more about her. Did I look like her? Did my children? Who were her friends? What was it like to grow up as a nomad, and then at fifteen marry an older man and be taken to the city? I wanted to know what made her laugh, what upset her, how she thought her life would turn out. I also wanted to know silly little things about her: what she named her goats, the little boys who teased her, the older ones she had crushes on.

As a child and young woman I hadn't had time to think about any of these things; just getting through our days took a lot of energy. As an adult, however, I started searching for a picture of my mother. I contacted my sisters, aunts, and every other relative who could possibly have one. When that proved futile, I recalled a British man visiting my parents' house and clung to the hope he might have taken a picture, because in my mind, Europeans were the sort to carry cameras. Again, I questioned my siblings, but none had any recollection of this visitor. After a long but ultimately fruitless investigation, it became clear that no one had ever taken my mother's picture. This truth devastated me. *How can this be?* I asked myself. *How could this beautiful, strong, intelligent woman have walked this world, worked hard every day, given birth*

to ten children, and yet no one cared enough to take her picture?
Not even my father, who was married to her for twenty years until
her death, had a photograph. Over the years, I have seen various
pictures of my father but none of her. Was she not important
enough to him to have a simple snapshot?

Without an image, I sought out the stories. The stories my
nomadic relatives used to tell around the fire every night painted
vivid and complete pictures of my ancestors, and so I called my
relatives, expecting them to be able to bring her to life. Sadly, these
conversations were too superficial for me and always ended with,
"She was a good wife who cared for her husband," as if being a
good wife was all she was, or all she needed to be. Most ended
abruptly with "Pray for her." It became harder and harder to get
any history from my Somali relatives without them invoking God
or prayers. Countless times I hung up the phone more than a bit
confused, finding it difficult to reconcile the religious bent of
these conversations with the storytelling world of my childhood.

I was excited when my *eedo* (aunt) Maryan offered to help me.
She not only was my father's sister but had married one of my
mother's relatives and been my mother's best friend from childhood. Eedo Maryan was a poet and held a deep understanding of
Somali storytelling. When I asked her for stories about my mother,
she said, "I will record it for you and find a way to send it to you."

She was in Dubai getting treatment for asthma when I spoke
to her, but I was so eager to hear what she had to say that I hatched
a plan. When she had recovered and returned home, I would call
and have her give me the information over the phone instead. I

got her phone number in Somalia from her daughter, and eagerly waited for our call. But to my dismay, I learned that, within a week of returning to Somalia, my eedo had died from complications of asthma. This news brought a double blow. I was not only mourning the loss of Eedo Maryan, but the loss of my mother all over again. I had been ready to dig up the story of my mother's life, but sadly, her tale died with my eedo, leaving me feeling like an archaeologist without a tool. I lost any hope of really knowing my mother. It took many years for me to reopen my heart and mind. Most of what I now know has been cobbled together from my own fleeting memories and the various statements, comments, and stories from my siblings and other relatives.

MY MOTHER WAS short and light-skinned, born with a rare beauty and never-aging features. Like most Somali women, she had a generous backside and hips, but in all other ways looked more like her father. My mother would have lived her entire life as a nomad had it not been for my father, who saw her for the first time when he came to visit his sister. He was instantly overwhelmed by the sight of the beautiful young woman tending goats. When he asked my ayeeyo for her daughter's hand, however, she flatly refused. She was concerned about their age difference; my father was in his forties, and my mother was only fifteen. While that was generally not an issue in my culture, it bothered my ayeeyo. Not only was he about the same age as my ayeeyo, but he was divorced and had two daughters scarcely younger than my mother.

In Somali culture, fathers traditionally give away their

daughters, but since my mother didn't have a living father, my ayeeyo was responsible for choosing her daughter's husband. She did not want to make a mistake. When her clansmen heard of her refusal, they tried to persuade her to change her mind. "This man is *waadad*, a devotee. Do you want to risk a curse being put on your child?" they demanded. They pressured her until she allowed my mother to marry my father.

After their marriage, when she was settled in Dhabad, she did not know how to read or write. Village life was an unknown galaxy to her. But she quickly learned the routine and hatched a unique business idea. She became a trader, selling goods from the city to the nomads, and vice versa. She bought sugar, flour, tea, and other things nomads needed in exchange for butter, milk, goats for meat, animal skins, and other commodities people in the city needed. She quickly learned basic math and whatever reading she needed to make her business a success. Despite his obsession with education, my father never bothered to teach her; everything she learned, she figured out herself.

My ayeeyo supported my mother's business ventures by taking care of her children when she traveled as well as looking after any goats my mother bought to breed. As her business expanded, my mother built a hut on the nomadic lands outside Dhabad that functioned like a *dukan*, a store. She bought camels with the money she earned from her business. The money she made benefited her entire family. Nomads took care of their own and shared with anyone in their subclan who needed help. In fact, my mother's herd of camels and goats is still reproducing, and despite having many siblings, I have an inheritance to claim anytime I wish. I think it would be funny to show up on my ayeeyo's nomadic lands and say, "I need to buy my son a wife. I've come for my camels." I also had some goats I was given as a child, and technically all their offspring are mine as well. My foreign investments keep yielding!

My mother never met her father; he died when my ayeeyo was still pregnant with her. Still, she inherited his bravery. When my mother was about thirty-five weeks pregnant with her first child, my sister Saada, she decided to visit my ayeeyo, whom she hadn't seen in a year. She thought she knew where her mother was, but after walking endlessly, it became clear she was lost. Night was coming on fast. Heavily pregnant and tired, she knew she could not sleep out in the open, so she pressed on, even though she could hear hyenas giggling up ahead. As she got closer, she heard a loud commotion coming from a fenced-in area where nomads kept goats and sheep. Wondering if a family had left an animal behind, she entered the enclosure, only to find herself standing in the center of a group of feasting hyenas. Her sudden appearance startled the hyenas, who began jumping over all the sides of the fence. My mother, equally surprised, tried to utter a curse: *"Awoow giin la'adaab"* ("May your forefathers go to hell"), but she was so startled she couldn't get the words out. When her confusion cleared, she realized the hyenas had been eating a dead sheep left behind by a nomadic family.

According to Somalis, hyenas size up their prey before attacking. As children, we were taught to stand tall with our arms straight up in the air if we encountered a hyena, so it would think we were too tall to attack. Perhaps her protruding belly made my mother look larger than she was, but in truth, the hyenas were lucky they didn't attack her. She would have fought back with a warrior's spirit.

In her later years, people often saw my mother pregnant, carrying one child on her back and another on her side, while going about her business. She did not stop having children until she died. In all, she gave birth to ten children over a twenty-year span (one died as an infant), with me in the middle of the birth order.

IN THE MUSLIM religion, men are permitted four wives at a time. Not all Somali men choose to be polygamous, but five years into my parents' marriage, my father took on another wife, Faduma. In the Somali culture, a man with a beautiful young wife tended to her and waited before taking another wife. To my knowledge, my father married a total of seven women, although he divorced five of them. My parents' living arrangement, and the fact that my mother's first two children were girls, may have rushed my father's decision to take more wives. My mother was generally civil to his other wives, displaying hospitality and burying any outward signs of jealousy like any dignified nomad. What it did to her internally, I can only guess. But my mother's family felt my father dishonored her. When my father went back to them after her death and asked to marry one of my young cousins, they refused him outright, despite the fact that he was a holy man.

Faduma moved into our house in Galkayo while my mother was going back and forth to Dhabad, which is where I was born.

While my mother was busy raising her young children and helping my ayeeyo, my father had two children with his new wife. My
half-sister Fowsiyo is about my age, and her brother Abdifitah is
my younger brother Guleed's age. Faduma was dominating and
temperamental and made it clear from the beginning that she and
my mother were enemies. Whenever my mother came to Galkayo,
she was treated like an unwanted guest, manipulated into a subservient position by her husband's new wife, who acted like she
owned the place.

I will be honest: excavating my mother's agony was not easy,
and when I first came to understand this part of her life, I broke
down crying, feeling visceral pain for my mother. For a minute, I
hated Faduma for causing my mother grief. Then it dawned on me;
my father was the one who had most hurt my beautiful mother.
It is easy to feel the injustice of the situation now, but theirs was a
complicated world. Living my current life in California, I am so
far removed from that mentality that I cannot decipher it. Yet I
cannot help but become angry about how women, including my
mother, were treated then. The ironic thing is, had I remained a
nomad I would not have thought twice about it. I would have just
accepted my fate.

Faduma was the quintessential evil stepmother, rivaling
any fairytale version. She made my older half-sisters Sofiya and
Khadra from my father's first marriage work all day, beating and
abusing them regularly, and she found ways to get them in trouble with my father, knowing full well he would inflict even worse
punishments on them.

Sofiya told me recently that during a beating one day, she looked at our father with sad eyes and said, "Father, why do you beat me so badly? Don't you love me at all?"

But my father continued to beat her.

Years later Sofiya, who was living in Italy at the time, became paralyzed as the result of meningitis. When my father heard the news, he was overcome by sadness. "If Sofiya is paralyzed, I am, too," he lamented. My father's deep grief at that moment showed the complexity of his character. As tempting as it may be, I cannot simply vilify him as a womanizer and abuser of children. My father was a man of his time. I have more compassion for him when I look at the big picture, taking into account the time, place, and culture as well as his past and his determination to provide us with a good education. Faduma eventually demanded our house for herself, but my father refused, saying it belonged to all his wives and children. He finally divorced her, giving her land and a house nearby.

My mother found out about another young wife of his quite by accident. She had traveled to Mogadishu to save my younger sister's gravely infected arm. She showed up on Sofiya's doorstep, carrying little Hamdi, whose upper arm was ballooned up to the point of cutting off the circulation to her hand. My mother had taken her to all kinds of healers and wadaads, who suspected she had been bitten by a snake or insect but had been unable to help her. They all agreed that the only solution was to cut off Hamdi's arm, but my mother said, "I won't leave a girl without an arm."

My mother went to Sofiya's house to see if she knew where our father was. To my mother's surprise, Sofiya informed her that my father, who by that time was in his sixties, lived with his beautiful young bride. Determined to save Hamdi's life and arm, my mother asked him to come to Sofiya's house. Their conversation was minimal, and after he read the Quran over my sister, he felt he had done his duty. Little Hamdi remained on the brink of death, however, so my mother finally took her to a Chinese doctor in Mogadishu, who saved her.

AS A CHILD, I overheard some female relatives talking about the time my mother was caught by *rohan*, demons, after she gave birth to Abshiro. I pulled a low stool to a hidden location and pricked up my ears. They said the demon possessed her and tossed her around like a rag doll and also caused her newborn to have constant diarrhea. The women wanted to help her, but my father was convinced he could drive away the demons by reading the Quran over her. Every time he was in the middle of a long verse, the demon distracted him and he had to start over. Frustrated, he performed his preprayer ablutions countless times. "He was no match for that rohan," one woman scoffed.

I was unsettled by that story. *What could have caused such a scene? Why did it happen to my mother?* I bore those questions for thirty years before I could begin to unravel the mystery. It took a nursing degree and my love of human psychology to make sense of it, although I still don't fully understand. My best guess is that she suffered from postpartum psychosis, which is different from postpartum depression and has symptoms that include delusions and hallucinations. My conclusion is based on two main factors. First, the timing of her "possessions" always followed the birth of a child. Second, I got the impression she was hallucinating because she was reacting to something only she could see. As for the baby with diarrhea, that is a common occurrence in Africa.

Proud that I had it all figured out, I called Sofiya to let her know my brilliant diagnosis. But she puzzled me all over again when she described her own memory of the episode. Sofiya remembers our father physically fighting a strange force with all his might while screaming verses from the Quran.

"What?" I asked, more confused than ever. "He was physically wrestling with an unseen being?"

"Oh yes," she replied, "He was battling not a rohan, but a *jin*!" She explained that my mother believed her condition was caused by rohan, demons that inhabit you but don't do bad things unless you fail to appease them. My father and Sofiya believed it was caused by jin, evil spirits that can possess people. "You are burning us; stop reading the Quran on us! Do as we want, and we will leave your family!" my father heard the jin scream. My father, of course, would not give in to their demands and just kept reading the Quran. In the end, both my mother and baby Abshiro were left lying unconscious on the floor, and the demons were gone.

I hoped my medical explanation would influence my sister. "What do *you* think it was?" I asked.

"Oh, it was jin," she answered instantly and with conviction.

Most Somalis believe in jin and have rituals to avoid them. People utter words to ward them off before entering bathrooms or anytime they feel uneasy. In some rural areas they do not like going out in the evening or at night for fear of being possessed. Stories I heard about jin were an elaborate mixture of religion and culture. "I dumped my garbage on the pile, and it was thrown right back at me," I heard people claim. And they believed the culprit was jin and could not possibly be the wind. The jin had their own families and children and lived in huge castles in a big city that was invisible to humans and could be anywhere. Like a beautiful storybook tale, jin both intrigued me and frightened me.

My mother, like most Somalis at the time, practiced Sufism, a mystical branch of Islam characterized by rituals and spiritualism. My father was one of the few men who did not practice Sufism. His version of Islam was more conservative and restrictive than Sufism, yet he was liberal when it came to women's dress; he believed they could be modest while still wearing functional clothing. He was also tolerant of others' religious practices, focusing more on spirituality and compassion.

MY MOTHER DIED in Luuqjeelow in 1980. The word *town* is really too generous for the place. Once, when I described it as a town, my older brother corrected me: "That was no town, Shugri. It was just a place with huts and bushes." It was a full day's bus ride from Galkayo, but a world away in terms of development. Although I referred to it simply as a town, I'd like to add a few adjectives: destitute, forsaken, primitive, impoverished, clinging-to-life. Even as a six-year-old, I thought, *This is not my mother's clan land. No one else from her family lives here.* I was perplexed. *Why would she move here?*

At the time of her death, my mother was earning the majority of the family income and supporting not only her immediate family but her extended family as well. She moved to Luuqjeelow with my four youngest siblings when she became aware of an untapped opportunity for business there. As my brother Aadan once asserted, "She could make something out of just dust."

Luuqjeelow was certainly the place for that. Most of the people who lived there were refugees from the Ogaden region of eastern Ethiopia. Ownership of that patch of land, about the size of the state of Nebraska, has been disputed longer than I have been alive. Conflict increased after Somalia gained its independence in 1960, and war finally broke out in Ogaden in 1977, when President Barre sent in the Somali army to retake the land. Initially, the Somalis were winning, despite being outnumbered, but the tide turned when the USSR saw Ethiopia as an important geopolitical concern and provided weapons and manpower to bomb and invade villages in an attempt to drive the Somali army out. This caused 1.5 million refugees, mostly women and children, to flee to eastern Somalia. These refugees received foreign aid in the form of rice, oil, corn, flour, and other staples. My mother realized this was only a partial diet; the people still needed meat, milk, vegetables, and fruit. The refugees did not have any money at all, but my mother did. She bought their extra staples and they used that money to buy the fresh items they lacked from her. She planned to eventually take the purchased staples to sell in Mogadishu for a greater profit. Unfortunately, death interrupted her plans, coming about a year after she moved to Luuqjeelow, so she never sold the dry goods she had amassed. She had so much flour, rice, corn and oil stored up that it fed our entire family for a year after her death.

I visited my mother in Luuqjeelow when I was about six years old, which turned out to be the last time I ever saw her. Dust swirled around me as I climbed out of the open cargo truck that delivered me, but when I saw the river that ran next to the town, my hopes soared. The Shebelle River was beautiful; the wind created little ripples on the surface that sparkled in the sun, and lush vegetation grew along the opposite bank. As I stood gazing at this plentiful, peaceful-looking source of life, a cool wind blew across the water and brought freshness to my overheated face. I was admiring its beauty when a log some distance from shore suddenly turned and swam away. *Strange*, I thought. A few moments later I realized the sun was not only reflecting off the water, but also off eyes that were sticking up out of the water. Now I was alarmed. I glanced wildly around, and a short distance from the path the villagers used to fetch water, I saw crocodiles sunbathing, mouths agape. Creatures that lived in the water were new to me, but I knew enough about wild animals to understand that these things could eat me. I had no desire to test them the way I had tested the warthogs.

The area between the flowing river and the desolate town was a wasteland. The sand was covered with dried silt from the river, and the same wind that created such enchanting patterns on the water caused swirling dust storms on the land. The people living there had a grayish-black skin tone from the silt, and their eyes were perpetually crusted over. They used part of that wasteland as their garbage dump, which was infested not with rats but with donkeys, which hung around the garbage, mating without regard to the season.

We lived in a *mudul*, a circular hut constructed of sticks, mud, and manure, with a thatched grass roof. This dwelling was a couple of steps up from a nomad's portable hut and was considered a high-end house in that town. We even had bunk beds made of wood and finished with animal skins. Our large yard had a real fence running around it, made of wood instead of bushes, and there were three mudul houses inside the fence. Our outhouse, however, was the bane of my existence. The minute I squatted down, a swarm of flies would fly up from the black hole below. I was terrified they would end up in my private parts. I fought them from the second I entered the outhouse until I finished my business. The only thing that made it bearable was that our bathroom was situated quite close to the fence and I could distract myself from the fly battle by eavesdropping on people as they passed by. I heard many interesting conversations that were not meant for children.

One morning, when we were sitting down for our breakfast of *anjeera*, a Somali flatbread, and tea, a hungry family walked in and asked my mother for food.

"Give these people your breakfast," she told us. We must have looked at her with a mix of confusion and hunger, because she added, "We need to share because they don't have any food. I can make more for you."

My siblings and I got up, handed over our anjeera and sat back down to wait for more. I had never seen anyone beg before, but I didn't grasp the dire situation most of the refugees were in until a second beggar, this time an older, thin man with a walking stick, came and asked for breakfast. The war between Ethiopia and Somalia was having a profound effect on everyone.

The last image I have of my mother is of her building a mud house with her Bantu friend Madlan. The Bantu are Somalis who live near the Shabelle and Juba Rivers in the southern part of the country, and are discriminated against. Even as a young child I knew that it was unusual for my mother to work along-side Madlan and treat her like a friend. I heard the way others spoke to and about the Bantu, and I felt proud that my mother was kind to Madlan. I watched them as they squatted on the floor and splashed mud onto the wood supports of the walls, laughing, singing, and talking as they worked. The Bantu spoke in their own dialect, and I loved to listen to the sweet, soft, melodic sound of their voices. Their laughter echoed throughout the yard, joyful and contagious. Madlan helped my mother build her house, and in exchange, my mother paid Madlan in rice, flour, oil, and sugar. Madlan's family were river people, so she brought my mother fish, vegetables, or anything else they could grow or catch.

PEOPLE DESCRIBE MY mother as being her usual vibrant self right up until her last days. I wouldn't know—I was far away then, living in a different world, happily herding animals with my ayeeyo. My mother was a true nomad until the end: tough, resilient, uncomplaining. Malaria is not a common illness among the nomads, but it was prevalent in that pathetic town, whose river was infested with mosquitoes. I suspect my mother was sick long before anyone knew; nomads never went to a doctor unless they were in a dire situation. Who knows what kind of medical care was available in Luuqjeelow? She got sick on a Tuesday, went to the doctor on Wednesday, and died on Thursday night. Sometime in the night, as the wind blew ripples across the river and swirled dust through the village, my mother's soul soared up with the wind. And just like that, everything changed dramatically.

Early Friday morning, my five-year-old brother, Guleed—the first child out of bed as usual—went to the fire to get his breakfast. He and my mother had a deep bond, and early morning was their special time before the rest of the house was awake. That Friday morning, as Guleed recounted to me many years later on a snowy day in Canada, he immediately knew something was wrong. Our mother was not making anjeera by the fire. In fact, there was no fire. Guleed felt a sense of foreboding, as if the air was telling him, "Remember this moment. Your life is about to change." Frightened and bewildered, he scanned the room for any sign of his mother. He saw a group of men hurrying out of our house, carrying what looked like a long sack of corn.

"What are you carrying?" he demanded.

The men were startled; they didn't expect to be confronted by a child that early in the day. They tried to trick him. "It's just a load of food."

When Guleed demanded to see what they were carrying,

they ignored him and attempted to scurry away. Frustrated, he
followed them outside, picked up all the stones around him and
started stoning them until they finally let him see what they were
carrying. My little brother saw our mother's body, once so full of
life, frozen in a state of rigor mortis, her mouth agape.

Guleed never fully recovered from that trauma. From the time
he saw her dead body, his grief took the form of anger, acting out,
and risk-taking. He frequently swam in that crocodile-filled river,
as if taunting the crocodiles, "Go ahead and eat me, I want to join
my mother." Anyone who tried to intervene was hit with flying
stones.

A day later, a telegram bearing the news of our mother's death
was sent to my father, who was living in Galkayo with my four oldest siblings: Saada, Abshiro, Aadan, and Arafo. Arafo tried to read
the telegram after my father abandoned it on the table. Although
at seven years old she didn't understand all the words, she knew
something had happened to our mother. In fact, in the days leading up to our mother's death, all my older siblings say they experienced a sense of impending doom in one way or another.

Saada, who was about seventeen, kept asking our father for
weeks, "Please take me to see *hooyo*!" But he was too busy. She
later told me that she had a dream a week before our mother died
in which it was early morning. She was standing with our ayeeyo
when they saw my mother's brother, our Uncle Duran, who had
passed away years before, walking toward them. The red-orange
African sunrise shone behind him, creating a beautiful image of

my uncle, but making it hard to see his face. "Abti, where are you going?" my sister called.

"I am going to get Ruqiya [our mother's name]," he replied and headed off into the distance. That dream intensified her desire to see our mother, but she didn't get the chance.

That morning, Saada saw our father walking toward her, wearing a traditional male *ma'awis* (sarong) striped in gray and purple. As he approached, she noticed that his face looked as purple as his ma'awis. "What happened, *aabo*?" she asked.

"Hooyo died," our father said matter-of-factly.

Thinking he was talking about his own mother, Saada said, "I'm sorry your hooyo died."

He realized she did not understand, so in a very direct tone he said, "Aabo, *your* hooyo died, not mine."

Saada screamed until her lungs ran out of breath. Despite her premonitions, she hadn't truly expected this. She ripped off her clothes and ran out of the yard, screaming and crying. When that was not enough, she shaved off all her beautiful hair, as if her anguish transformed her inside and out. My father let her grieve. Saada was still crying when she arrived in Luuqjeelow the next day.

My oldest siblings all wanted to go to Luuqjeelow right away, but our father felt he could only bring one with him initially. "I know you are all grieving, but I can only take Saada now," he said. Abshiro and Aadan resented her for that, but the oldest usually got priority. My father needed to find transportation to

Luuqjeelow in a hurry, and his respected position in the community helped in this regard. By then, it seemed as if the whole city knew that Ma'alin Sa'iid's wife had died. The governor of Galkayo ordered all cars to be stopped at a checkpoint until a car heading for Mogadishu could be commandeered to take my father and Saada to Luuqjeelow.

When they arrived, my sister sat at the head of my mother's grave, a small rise of dirt the length of a human, and wailed, the way a child does in the deepest pain. The next day, she went back to our mother's grave and planted a tree, an uncommon gesture, since traditionally Somalis don't mark graves.

On the day of our mother's burial, the whole town of Luuqjeelow came out to pay their respects. The poor cried her name, saying, "Who will take care of us now that she is gone?" Even the feral dogs, who were constantly twigged, stoned, and chased away by everyone else in the village, seemed to feel my mother's loss. On Thursday, hours before she passed away, all the dogs in Luuqjeelow had begun crying and howling, as if they knew something the humans hadn't sensed yet. Their mournful cries had continued until my mother was buried the next evening. The townspeople were convinced the dogs knew they were losing the only person who had ever fed them or shown them any kindness.

When our father told Abshiro of our mother's death on Friday, it was as if the impossible had happened. Without knowing why, she had not been able to stop crying the previous day, the day our mother died.

My father had noticed then and had asked, "Aabo, what happened? Why are you crying?"

His question had only brought more tears.

When he told her the news that Friday, she did not yell or scream like Saada. "I had not one drop of tears left," she explained. She simply buried her sorrow and went about her routine of helping her siblings, feeding them and getting them ready for school each day. When she joined our father and Saada in Luuqjeelow several weeks later, she could not bring herself to visit our mother's grave. Instead, she kept herself busy taking care of our four youngest siblings, who were in a state of disbelief and despair, despite the fact that one of the local refugees had sent his teenage daughter, Sureer, to help him with the children.

Just when Abshiro thought her grief could not get any worse, my father told her he was going to marry Sureer and asked her to cook for his wedding. Abshiro thought she had misheard. *How can a father do this while his children are distraught with grief?* she asked herself. A wedding barely more than a month after our mother's death seemed cruel and disrespectful. In all fairness, Sureer, my father's wife-to-be, was probably just as shocked and dismayed when she found herself about to be married to an old man with eleven children, some of whom were older than she.

Abshiro cried and pleaded with my father not to make her prepare for or even participate in his wedding, but he did not care to listen. My father's twin sister, Eedo Sa'iido, arrived in Luuqjeelow shortly before Abshiro, and when she got wind of his plan, she was livid. "These kids are grieving for their mother. Do not bring another woman into their lives. They need their father's care and attention."

He did not listen, and Abshiro cried the whole time she prepared the food for his wedding.

In direct defiance of my father, my eedo held a *madah shub* ceremony for our mother on his wedding day. Madah shub is the act of feeding the poor on behalf of a loved one who has passed away. On my mother's madah shub day, not only were the poor of Luuqjeelow fed, but people gathered to give eulogies about her as they drank tea and ate popcorn and dates. My sister was kept too busy to attend this remembrance-day ceremony, but she felt relieved that her mother's life was being honored.

Abshiro visited Luuqjeelow every time school was closed and was shocked by how destitute her younger siblings looked. Sureer was inept when it came to domestic responsibilities. She did everything in a haphazard fashion; she couldn't clean, cook, or take care of children very well. In Somalia, a sixteen-year-old girl is expected to run a household efficiently. Even my sisters, who had been going to school full time, had better domestic skills than Sureer. It was *haram*, forbidden, for a single woman to live with a man, even if that woman was sent to help him domestically. My father may have thought it would fix things to marry this girl, but in reality, it was the worst thing he could have done to his children. He now had to stay in that godforsaken town because his young bride's family lived there, and instead of moving everyone out of that hellish town, he brought more of his kids there.

Aadan and Arafo were brought to stay shortly after the wedding, and when school was out, all the children except me were brought to live in Luuqjeelow. When Aadan was forced to move to Luuqjeelow, he was at the top of his class in Galkayo and preparing to take his grade eight exit exam. The school in Luuqjeelow only went to eighth grade, and my brother was shocked when he saw that the school he had to attend was nothing more than a tree with a brush fence running around it and stones to sit on. Even the tree was so pathetic that they had to hang old shawls, blankets, and plastic in the branches to provide some cover from the harsh sun. He resented having to study by lantern for his exit exam; at times, even the fuel for the lantern was hard to come by. At least Galkayo had electricity most nights, even if it was unpredictable.

I DO NOT remember who brought the news of my mother's death to my ayeeyo and me, a month or so later. When I try to remember the sadness I felt for my hooyo, only my ayeeyo's sadness comes to mind. That does not mean I didn't feel the loss of my mother, but my ayeeyo and I were so deeply bonded that it pained me even more to see her in pain. My ayeeyo did not wail and sob out loud when she received the news; she remained stoic and carried out her daily duties as usual. But I could see in the way she walked and spoke that a deep sorrow permeated her body. The harsh reality of survival in the desert does not allow you to be swallowed by grief. We had no choice but to go about our daily life: herding our goats, gathering food, and preserving meat for the next jilal.

In our culture, people don't usually seek closure about someone's death. "God gives life and God takes it away" is about as far
as it goes. But for my siblings and me, sharing our stories recently
has brought us closer together.

Saada told me that on the day our mother died, there was a
solar eclipse, an event Somalis call *qorah madoobaad*. The eclipse
marked the day the light was snatched out of our lives, leaving in
its wake a darkness that engulfed all of us from that day on. It was
as if our mother took her light with her.

I wanted to know the exact day my mother died, so I looked
it up. I discovered a total solar eclipse occurred in Somalia on
February 16, 1980. *Could this be the day my mother died?* That
night I took a bath to let the weight of my discovery sink in. My
eight-year-old daughter was sitting on the floor beside me so I
could help her with her homework and enjoy her chatty company.
The loss of my mother hit me hard. I sat with this feeling and let
it take me. I began to sing an old Somali song for mothers, one
I heard as a child. As I sang, my voice turned from nostalgic to
mournful. I saw that my daughter had stopped her homework and
was watching me, her face bleak with a sadness I had never seen
in her before.

I wanted to stop singing for her sake but was powerless to do
so. I pleaded with myself, "You don't want to ruin your young
child! All this time you've protected your kids! You *must* get ahold
of yourself. Look at her face. She's an innocent soul. You don't
want to hurt her."

Still, I let my voice echo on the walls of my bathroom and

travel the hallways of my house, feeling like an imprisoned soul both physically and spiritually, singing an old freedom song from a forgotten era. My voice began to quiver and crack as it transformed into full-blown crying along with the singing. *What was going on? Was I possessed by jin?* I was horrified at what was happening to me, but also enamored with the freedom I was finding.

My daughter jumped toward me and hugged me hard, holding me as I hugged her in return with gratitude and compassion. She offered me the kindness my younger self once desperately needed. Naked in that bathtub and singing my sorrow out, my little girl in my arms, I felt I was being born again. The song only stopped when my body decided it was time. I suddenly felt much better, as if I had truly grieved for the first time in my life. That song was my eulogy to my mother, and now I was finally free.

I hugged my daughter deeply and said, "My mother would have loved you very much. She was a very loving person!"

She held out her hand tenderly, as if holding a delicate soul she needed to let go. She echoed the usual sentiment: "I wish I could see her picture, Mom. How come there is no picture of her?"

I could see she longed to see my mother, her ayeeyo. At that moment, I realized my daughter is my mother's grandchild. Since my mother was only thirty-four when she died, I had only tried to picture her as a young woman. Never in my life had I pictured her as an ayeeyo, but of course she was a grandmother many times over—a young and vibrant ayeeyo, who died with her ageless beauty.

That night, after I'd hugged my daughter goodnight and

tucked her in, she awoke around 2:30 a.m. and stumbled toward
our bed. I opened my blanket like a mother hen opens her wings
for her little one, and she planted herself between her father and
me. I wrapped my warm body around her, and she slept, content,
in an embrace.

As my own mind descended into sleep, a thought floated
through my consciousness, *Would this be my life had my mother
lived? Would I be holding this same precious child in my arms
right now?* But my mother had to die for the trajectory of my life
to change. I feel a twinge of guilt when my imagination wan-
ders there, but another part of me believes my mother would be
delighted to see me now. She was a curious person by nature, and
so I have no doubt she would love hiking with me in the rolling
hills of Sonoma County, asking about Californians and their way
of life.

Dear *hooyo*, I am sorry your radiant life was taken away pre-
maturely in that dusty corner of Somalia. My only wish is that the
river that flows beside your grave has assuaged your wounds. I am
bothered by the fact that you are not buried in the red desert you
sprang up from, the land where your forefathers died. I see now
that you sacrificed deeply for your children, even moving where
no clan member of yours ever lived or died, just to support us.

When I think of your burial site, I see a rare desert flower
planted in the wrong place. I see dust dancing around your grave,
and amid the dust, a raised dirt patch that marks the spot where
your body is buried. It saddens me that I may never be able to visit
your grave, for I have a lot of stories to tell you. But Somalia is not

the same anymore, *hooyo*. It is now run by religious fanatics and a new type of madmen. Our beautiful culture is under attack, and our way of life is threatened. If you were alive today, you would cry over the cultural genocide our people have suffered.

Dear *hooyo*, now that you have had time to reflect as you lie in your grave, I hope you are at peace with the demons that once unsettled your spirit. Goodbye, *hooyo*, you ageless desert flower. Sleep now; all is well.

4 Carrying Out Tradition

Wixii xunba Xaawaa leh.
Men still blame Eve for everything.
—Somali proverb

ONE DAY I returned from herding my goats and found that Arafo had come. I was happy, thinking she was going to live with us now, but I soon learned that she was there so we could both undergo an important ritual. Now that our mother was gone, the responsibility for circumcising us shifted to my ayeeyo. At seven and eight, we were on the older side to be circumcised; some girls have it done as young as four or five. Female circumcision is a normal part of Somali culture. What's more, we looked forward to this rite of passage, when we would join the ranks of "clean girls." The belief that uncircumcised girls were dirty and not worthy of respect permeated every aspect of Somali culture. It began with mothers publicly shaming toddler girls for accidentally showing their uncircumcised parts and continued with the open praising of young women for being circumcised, subservient, and obedient.

Female circumcision is believed to have been practiced by the ancient Egyptians and perhaps even earlier than that. The custom was adopted in Somalia centuries ago and is still performed to this day. The Somali word for the procedure is *gudniin*, which is a very innocent word. It just means "circumcision," with no allusion to the horrifying implications. Medically speaking, circumcision refers only to the removal of the outer skin of the clitoris or the penis, and while that is a true description of what is done to Somali boys, the girls' procedure goes beyond mere *gudniin*.

Throughout the world, anything more than the removal of the outer skin of the clitoris is regarded as *female genital mutilation*, or FGM, and not circumcision. However, the term female genital mutilation or anything remotely similar is absent from the Somali language. Medically, FGM is categorized into four types. Type IV is for miscellaneous types of genital mutilation, such as piercings. The remaining three types are still practiced in my country. FGM type I is called a *clitoridectomy* and involves a partial or total removal of the clitoris. In Somalia, the clitoris is blamed for all humanity's troubles—the root of all evil, so to speak. In FGM type II, both the clitoris and the labia minora are removed, and sometimes the labia majora. FGM type III is the most drastic type of genital mutilation and is the standard procedure done to young girls in my country. Sadly, Somalia has the distinction of having a higher rate of type III FGM than any other country in the world. This procedure involves removing the clitoris and inner labia and then sewing the outer labia shut, leaving only a small opening for urine and menstrual blood to pass through. At times, this hole is left too small, causing all kinds of gynecological issues, including death. A woman is left with this small hole until her wedding night, when it is her new husband's duty to tear the hole open enough for intercourse, basically using his penis as a battering ram. The hole is made larger again during childbirth, either by the baby's head or, if a woman is lucky, a midwife's blade.

In Somalia, no man would marry an uncircumcised girl, and no self-respecting woman would let any girl in her care go without the procedure. How did such a barbaric ritual become so ingrained in a culture? The short answer is that it has been done solely for the benefit of men, based upon the fact that women were considered and treated as a commodity. This is true, but only part of the more complex truth.

Long ago, the Somali clan system and the harshness of the environment made alliances with other clans necessary for survival. Virginal daughters were given in marriage to seal these alliances. Forming alliances through marriage was crucial to ensuring your tribe's safety and peace, but the alliance was forged only if the girl's clan delivered an untouched daughter. Clearly, women were not trusted with their own morality, even though they had long known its importance to their tribe's well-being. At some point, the way to ensure that a girl remained a virgin until marriage became to cut away her clitoris so she wouldn't become aroused. Sewing the vagina shut until her wedding night was further insurance.

If, on the night of her marriage, her vagina was not found to be sealed shut as expected, it brought dishonor to her father, brothers, and male cousins. The men were shamed for providing "spoiled goods," and their social standing was disastrously devalued. In the Somali clan system, social standing is everything; a man is literally nothing without it. It is of such importance that girls are groomed from birth for a subservient role, and it is drilled into them that they must never do or say anything that would affect the social standing of the men in their family.

As a result, girls are taught by the females of their family to guard their virginity with their lives. I remember being as young as eight when I was taught maneuvers to perform if a young man tried to rape me. Older women told me, "Twist his testicle and don't let go until he loses consciousness." They said the testicle was a man's weak point and we must not forget that when men attack us. If a girl got raped, the blame was always put on her because she failed to protect her virginity. "Who gave birth to this daughter?" her clan members would demand, and the girl's mother would be shamed even more for the crime of giving birth to such a girl.

When my mother died, she left behind nine children, six of whom were girls. Our circumcision experiences were different, depending on whether the procedure was carried out in the city or with the nomads. One thing was similar, however: we were always circumcised in pairs. My mother had a pattern, giving birth to two girls in a row, then a boy. This meant that at least we each had a sister to go through the procedure and sympathize with. Arafo and I were to be circumcised together under our ayeeyo's watchful eye.

The day of my circumcision is well engraved in my memory, as crystal clear as if it took place yesterday. It was the season of plenty, and our huts were set up near a natural reservoir. Our ayeeyo slaughtered a young goat for us in preparation for

the ceremony, and as was customary, a medicine woman from
an inferior clan came to perform our gudniin. The sky was clear
and blue, with just a few wispy white clouds. I heard the sounds
of nature in the distance and watched as birds began to gather
overhead, circling around in anticipation. The African sun was
extremely hot that early morning, and I instinctively wanted to
shelter under a tree instead of being in the open. The bushes surrounding our compound had a distinctive herbal smell, and on
that day, their smell seemed to intensify in my nostrils, as if the
bushes knew they would be a portal to my memory from that day
on. I did not want to do anything that would ruin this important
rite of passage. Although it may sound as if I am setting the scene
for an idyllic childhood memory, it is quite the opposite. Reader
discretion is advised: graphic content to follow.

Ayeeyo thoroughly cleaned our private parts in preparation.
She always showed her love through her actions, and I trusted her
fully, knowing she would take care of me throughout the procedure. About seven girls were brought to be circumcised that day,
and we were lined up like goats going to slaughter so we could
see the fate of each girl in turn. The cutting was done out in the
open, in the center of the village, surrounded by the women who
were performing the ritual. My attention was drawn to a girl who
was much older than the rest of us. Her hair was unkempt, her
white guntiino was covered with red dust, and a look of impending doom covered her face. She must have tried to run, because
several women were standing guard over her. *What a coward!* I
thought. *You're a big girl. What are you afraid of?* Others tried to

run as well, but the women were ready to catch fleeing girls. No one was going to escape the medicine woman and her blade.

Two emotions rose up spontaneously as I stood stoically, the first in line. I felt scornful of the cowardly behavior of those who tried to run. At the same time, it pained me to see my sister Arafo's fear. She was one of the runaways, and they brought her back by force. Arafo had told me she would rather be eaten by a lion than to go through this procedure. She and I were very close in age but had different ways of showing our emotions. I had that Somali tribal pride, almost arrogance, when I thought about my ancestors, some of whom had fought with lions and won. I would not show fear and disrespect my ayeeyo's strong and dignified legacy.

When my time came, I was lowered to the dirt, as the medicine woman, whom I had never seen before, sharpened her knife, striking its well-used blade against another knife. Two women pulled my skinny legs apart so the woman with her shiny blades could have direct access to my private parts. I studied her face intently. She was a small, thin middle-aged woman, her face shiny from frequent prayer washes; she had a calm demeanor about her. She wore a colorful garment, with a light, soft shawl over her shoulder and a netted black scarf on her head. I imagined she was a witch who could utter a bad curse if I did not do what she said, but I was not scared or even intimidated by her.

I glanced at the women restraining me. The woman on my right was holding my right leg firmly open, but her body was angled toward me so I had a direct view of her face. She was squatting in a way that unwittingly revealed her vagina to me. Shocked by what had just flashed into my view, I studied her more closely in the few seconds I had before the knife cut me. Her genitalia were completely butchered. It appeared as if someone had chopped her with a knife held perpendicular to her vagina and cut her up like the rungs of a ladder. Pieces of skin that looked as if they had been fried in hot oil hung loosely from her vagina. Within this series of cuts were random holes that created a maze of confusion that reminded me of a network of meerkat burrows in the desert.

As if she noticed my gaze, she quickly pulled her garment closed. I was confused by what I had seen. *Is that what my private parts will look like when I get older?* As the medicine woman approached my vagina with her blade, the woman on my right tightened her grip on my leg. With her knife parallel to my body, the medicine woman abruptly sliced down, cut my clitoris off from its root, and tossed it away. A bird, who was circling the sky above me, suddenly swooped down, snatched my womanhood from the ground, and soared back into the sky with its prize. African birds are smart, and a group of nomads clustered together usually means something is being slaughtered, so they were keeping an eye out for scraps. Food is food in the desert, whether a discarded clitoris or a piece of unwanted goat meat.

As I felt the strange sensation of a knife cutting my flesh, I winced but held myself rigid. I stared straight at the witch woman as my blood spurted in a projectile stream away from my body, right toward the women holding me down. The one to my left cursed me, as if this was my fault, and scooted away to avoid getting splattered by my blood. I saw the stream lose its power and dribble down to the hot, dusty sand below me. I must have gone into shock, because I don't remember feeling pain. I glanced at my grandmother, who was standing beside me looking proud. She liked the fact I was brave in the face of this infliction.

I said, "Ayeeyo, I don't want anyone to hold me. I will not run."

My grandmother ordered everyone to get off me, which caused a ripple of shock around the circle. I felt respected and felt I had a little bit of control over my life.

I withstood the rest of the circumcision with no one restraining me. Not a peep came out of my mouth, and my body remained stiff and motionless. The medicine woman looked at me as if I had been bewitched, and I stared back at her like an unbroken warrior. Whispers of my bravery traveled the circle around me. She continued to meticulously cut away at me, as if to make sure no feeling ever arose from the land she had just decimated. She scraped the inside surface of the labia majora and minora with the edge of her knife, and then pulled them closed over my vagina and sutured them shut. Using three thorns from the *qurah* tree, she pushed each one through my closed labia and secured them with thread. The thorns would be left in for weeks, until the skin began to heal together. She then pulled my legs, now in a state of near rigor mortis, together and wrapped them from my ankles to my hips in a soft red scarf. The thorns stabbed painfully into my thighs.

Later, I found myself under the shade of a tree with my sister, sitting with our legs straight out in front of us. We would sit in this L-shaped position for a week or so, until we had healed enough to move without the risk of undoing the crude sutures. Our ayeeyo came to us with words of encouragement and advice. She told us we were clean girls now and could marry an honorable man. I think my sister and I were too exhausted from the war our female organs had just been through to listen. Arafo was broken and sad. She looked defeated. She really hated pain, and this was far too much for her body. I hurt for her and hoped we would both get through the rest of this ordeal alive. We had survived the cutting and sewing, but infection was an even greater danger. The medicine woman had used the same knife on all of us that day, merely wiping it with a cloth and sharpening it between procedures.

Our ayeeyo gave us one serious piece of advice that day: we must pee, even though it hurt. The way she stressed it made us believe our lives depended on it. Then she left to look after her herd, and we were alone. Time passed and the mirage-inducing African sun marched across the sky, finally finding us under our tree. It warmed our bodies, but perhaps too much. I looked down at my hips and thighs and saw fresh blood dripping onto the hot sand below me. The same thing was happening to my sister, so I told her we needed to scoot to the shady side of the tree. We painstakingly made our way to the shade, and when Ayeeyo came back from animal herding, she headed straight to us. She asked if we had peed, and we shook our heads in unison.

Peeing proved to be the hardest thing I have ever had to do. Every time a drop came out, it was like acid was being poured onto my raw, wounded flesh, and my body launched into the air with pain. I fought tears as I became nauseated and the pain became unbearable. After what seemed an eternity, I finished, and the pain began to subside. *I am never doing that again,* I vowed, even though I knew it wasn't true. I looked over and saw my ayeeyo still trying to coax Arafo.

"Arafo, bear the pain and pee," she pleaded.

My ayeeyo checked us every day, using several natural remedies to help us heal. She dug a hole in the ground and filled it with *bil'il* plants and herbs, then lit them until they smoldered. We sat over the top of the holes, and the medicated smoke felt soothing as it rose up to our mutilated privates. We could not walk much, so our ayeeyo carried us to the hut one by one, keeping our bodies as still as possible. After a week or two, she removed the thorns. The scarf around our legs was loosened so we could walk with baby steps, but there was still a fear that we might rip open the freshly sewn flesh.

Eventually, after a long convalescence, my sister and I got better. It felt good to be free of the restrictive scarf, although we were still not allowed to walk normally. We were instructed to take tiny steps because we were still at a delicate stage. At night, our ayeeyo still wrapped our legs with a scarf to make sure we didn't open our wounds by flailing around in our sleep or getting up in the night to go to relieve ourselves and forgetting to take baby steps. She also told us, "No running, jumping, or climbing trees." This instruction was aimed at me. She knew I had a strange relationship with trees or anything that stood more than a foot above ground. I must climb them. I still do, even as a grown woman. But for the time being, they were off limits. "You are not fully healed yet," she warned. Even when we had recovered, we were advised to never open our legs widely or participate in any activities that might open us up too much.

AFTER A MONTH or two, Arafo was sent back to Luuqjeelow, but my father had finally given in to my mother's final wish, and I was left to live permanently with my ayeeyo. She continued teaching me her way of life; I still had a lot to learn in order to survive and become a good wife.

Most of her lessons focused on food, either gathering or cooking it. One day, my ayeeyo taught me how to make *bur iideed*, a flatbread similar to pita bread. We herded our goats to a grassy area, and she set to work while they milled around, grazing peacefully. Since it was gu, the rainy season, many babies frolicked around as we worked. My ayeeyo began by creating a large dome of sand and surrounding it with rocks. I busied myself collecting twigs. She lit a fire on top of the sand dome, and when the sand below was hot, she took out a dough made of a simple mixture of flour and water, broke off a small piece, and flattened it with her hands. She thrust the dough patty into the base of the sand, below the fire.

"Don't burn yourself, Ayeeyo," I warned. By this time, I had received my share of burns and felt the need to caution others, whether they needed it or not.

After a few minutes, she inserted her hand into the hot sand and took out the baked flatbread. Sand coated every surface, but she easily brushed it off, and I did the same when she handed me the delicious treat.

We sat under the acacia tree, eating our meal with fresh goat's milk. It was a relaxed day with the goats, but occasionally my ayeeyo ordered me to circle the herd to make sure no guduudane or fox was eating our precious goats. On one of my rounds, I saw the legs of one of our goats thrusting up in the air just beyond a small hill of sand. *Something got her!* I thought. I moved closer to see what was going on and discovered that she was giving birth. She grunted from the pain but pushed determinedly.

I tried to help, but I really didn't know what I was doing. I played carelessly with the baby's legs, which were sticking out, and the goat moaned louder. I must have interpreted this as some sort of game, like "when I push her, the goat makes a weird noise." I did not fully understand that she was laboring. I finally became helpful and grabbed the protruding legs, pulling the baby out. Through the half-intact amniotic sac, I could see the baby goat's black head and white body. The mama goat jumped up, licking her slimy, bloody baby clean. The baby goat struggled to gain steadiness on its feet, so I picked her up and headed to my ayeeyo, her mother bleating close at my heel.

"Look, I helped the goat to birth this baby," I said proudly.

My ayeeyo lifted the little goat's leg. "It's a girl," she said. "This one is yours."

We named the baby Gorodo Madow, "half-black." I was happy and proud because I knew that not only was this baby mine but all her offspring would be mine as well. As the sun went down, we led our herd to the huts. I carried my baby goat all the way back, her mother still bleating at my heels.

While I was blissfully living the nomadic life, however, a storm was brewing in the city. All of my siblings except the two oldest were living in Luuqjeelow and suffering in one way or another. Saada and Abshiro became more and more convinced that our father and his new wife could not provide a loving, safe, and stable home for their younger siblings.

With the help of Abshiro and Sofiya, Saada spearheaded a campaign to help my siblings escape that dying town. Saada and Abshiro were living in dormitories in Mogadishu while they attended university, and Sofiya was now divorced and working in the capital as well. The three of them decided it would be best if the younger children were brought to live in the city so they could keep an eye on us. It wouldn't be easy to secure housing for us all, but Saada knew the biggest hurdle would be convincing our father to go along with their plan. She was prepared for both his anger and a beating when they finally got up the nerve to approach him.

His initial reaction was, "There is no way I am letting my children go."

My sisters knew better than to reveal that their motivation was to get us out of his house, safe from his beatings and his neglectful wife. Instead, they pleaded from their hearts, "We need to keep our siblings together. Hooyo would have wanted us to take care of the younger ones. We need them to be close to us in Mogadishu."

Miraculously, our father finally agreed, but only if all his conditions were met. He dictated that we all must be kept together, and we all must go to both regular school and Quran school. I'm sure he was convinced his demands could never be met, and he would win the argument. My sisters, however, were undeterred, determined to meet his conditions and save their siblings.

After searching for a year and asking everyone they knew for help, my sisters were finally able to find an agency in Mogadishu with a good reputation that helped needy children by providing shelter, food, and clothing. It was an orphanage school operated by a Canadian nonprofit organization called Families for Children, or FFC. Even though we had a father living, they were willing to take us as orphans. The problem was that the maximum number of children they accepted from one family was three, and we were six. My sisters approached a high official they knew from my mother's tribe and asked for help. After a long, grueling process of completing paperwork and bribing people, the official signed the final papers that would allow all six of us to be placed together.

As this was happening, my ayeeyo was also having a change of heart about her decision to keep me permanently. She noticed that in the year or so since my mother's death, none of my siblings had come to visit me. My mother had been the cord that held these two worlds together, and now she was gone. My ayeeyo figured that because my siblings were all being educated in the city, I would always be different from them. "I don't want to leave

Shugri without her mother, her siblings, and an education," she decided.

Aadan came to the nomadic lands and took me to Luuqjeelow, although he had strict instructions from our father that he could only take me if my ayeeyo offered me up. He was not allowed to ask for me. But my ayeeyo had already decided it was time for me to go and be raised with the rest of my siblings. With her blessing, I was taken from the nomadic life I had come to love.

5 Orphanage

Waxaanad hurayn horaa loo yeelaa.
One must surrender to the inevitable.
—Somali proverb

I WAS ABOUT nine years old when Arafo, Guleed, Hamdi, Hubi, Liban, and I arrived at the Families for Children compound. Overwhelmed and bewildered, I walked through the gates with my siblings, guards in military uniforms staring down at us. The whole scene was so foreign to my experience that I could not even process what was happening.

A car came rumbling out of the compound toward us, down the long driveway, and I gazed up at it, stunned. It was driven by a white woman with blonde hair! Imagine your reaction if an alien landed in front of you, looking completely different from anything you had ever seen. This was the first white person I had ever laid eyes on in my life. The closest thing to a white person I had ever seen were the Chinese workers who built roads in Galkayo. The guard who had opened the walk-in gate for us rushed over and swung open the big, green metal gate for the white woman. He smiled at her as she neared the gate, and to my surprise, she turned her head and smiled right at me.

I watched her drive away and then I turned to face this foreign place, startled to see a huge picture of a man staring back at me from inside a glass case. At the time, I had no clue who this strange man was, although I soon came to learn it was Siad Barre, the president of Somalia, whom I had learned about in first grade. I knew plenty of songs that praised him but had never seen his face before. Everyone called him Afwayne ("Big Mouth"), a nickname that was obvious once you saw his picture. At that time, all public places had his photo hanging on their walls. Anyone suspected of being antigovernment was imprisoned or killed.

Looking past Siad Barre, I noticed a long row of trees that stretched down the right side of the compound, separating two long driveways. These were not the scrubby, thorny, inhospitable trees of the desert. These were city trees, green and full. As I would learn later, their branches were particularly inviting for climbers like me. Someone appeared and led us off to the left, along a gravel and packed-dirt path, past clusters of low, white stucco houses. I followed along in a daze.

Most of that day is lost in a haze of new faces, unfamiliar surroundings, and uncertainty, but one thing stands out in my child's memory: white people. They seemed to be everywhere I looked. I couldn't understand them and I didn't know what they wanted with me. We stopped in front of a large house with stairs and a veranda in front, unlike any house I had seen in Somalia. They tried to get us to go inside with them, but we were too confused and terrified to comply. We had good reason to be confused. Our older sisters, following that strange Somali tradition of not telling

kids what was going on, had plied us with cookies and candy to
get us to go to the orphanage but had not explained that we were
to live here. In their hearts, they felt this was the best place for
us: we were together and close enough to their school lodgings
for them to visit us frequently. But we thought this was a temporary place we had been taken to, perhaps as a punishment of some
kind, although we had no idea why we were being punished.

Just outside the big house, which I later learned was the white
workers' housing, was an open area where the ground was hard-
packed dirt with a spattering of gravel. Since there was no way
we were going inside with these strange white people, my siblings
and I huddled together on that patch of ground and sobbed. We
didn't think we were supposed to be at this place and were determined to wait in this spot for our older sisters to come and get us. I
even believed my ayeeyo would come for me if I just stayed outside
where she could see me. It didn't matter that I was hundreds of
miles away from her—I was too young and traumatized to think
logically in terms of time and space. We clung to each other and
wailed as we waited for rescue. As evening approached, I began to
realize no one was coming. My take-charge spirit reawakened and
I decided I would be the one to rescue us.

I said to my siblings: "*Waan sii araabayaaye, iga soo daba
araaba,*" which loosely translates into "I will journey out of here;
you, too, should journey after me."

This was a typical phrase a nomad would use when trying to
get home before dark. I spoke with urgency, full of grief over my
siblings' distress as well as my own need for self-preservation. I

panicked. I had to get outside those brick walls that penned us in. I headed for the front gates, sure my ayeeyo would have a fire going in the distance so I could see my way home. It didn't even occur to me this compound was stuck in the middle of a large city.

As I was leaving, Arafo tried to stop me, saying, "Shugri, this is home now, there is no place else to go."

She had finally begun to see the reality of our situation. Not I. I took my meager belongings, ignored my sister, and marched straight to the front gate. I was immediately stopped by the soldiers on duty. They scolded me harshly, but when I stubbornly refused to listen, they chased me back, throwing sticks at me like I was a stray dog. Eventually, realizing they would not let me through, I returned to my siblings, even more confused.

When I reached them, still sobbing on that hard patch of ground, they had been joined by a Somali worker named Aboow, who served as a translator.

Arafo was upset because the white workers had told Aboow that our brothers were going to be separated from us and sent to different living areas. They wanted Guleed to go to the boy's dormitory, and most troubling of all, they wanted Liban to move into the toddler's quarters. Through Aboow, Arafo argued to let Liban stay with us girls.

"He is still traumatized by our mother's death!" she cried. "And he has nightmares unless he sleeps with me."

Aboow helped us plead our case to the white workers. In the end, only poor Guleed was separated from the rest of us. He subsequently suffered beatings at the hands of the other boys his age.

All of the boys had to test the new arrivals, so they got in line and he had to fight them to find his place in the pecking order. And that was just the beginning of his suffering. He was only seven at that time, vulnerable in so many ways. He was still grieving for our mother and was angry at the world. We tried to offer comfort when we saw him at mealtimes, but the separation of boys and girls at the compound, and the fact that as girls we had been raised to be terrified of a group of boys, meant we could not just go and check on him any time we wanted. The emotional damage that was done to him in those early years, not to mention in the years to come, would take the adult me to fully unpack.

Eventually, that first day, the white workers got us to come inside and settled us into a room together, with Arafo as Liban's main caretaker. But every evening after that, all six of us gathered together on that patch of ground outside and cried. This went on for a month, and soon other kids stopped by and asked why we were still crying. Instead of being sympathetic, they accused us of being spoiled rich kids. We were not rich, but the implication was that only rich kids would spend so much time crying for no reason. Most of the time Arafo would comfort us like the older sister she was, but sometimes she would be the one to start crying, and that would trigger synchronized wailing among us all.

I continued going to the gate every night, hoping to get out. I got the same reception from the guards every time. You would think I would have learned my lesson sooner rather than later. But I was persistent, and it took days for me to realize that no one was coming to get us out, and the guards were never going to let me just leave. After getting to know me well over the next four or five years, some of those guards probably came to wish they had let me out when I was a confused little girl.

IN TIME, I found out that the orphanage was operated by two women, whom we called Hooyo Kim and Eedo Ann, from Canada and England, respectively. Kim's mother, Sandra, who felt like a godly figure watching over us and visited us from Canada three times a year, was the real owner. I remember hearing that Sandra adopted a girl who had medical issues and took her back to Canada. After living in the orphanage for a few years, I used to dream of being swept away to a different world, too.

After about a month, I realized that things were not going to change. I stopped crying, and as if I was suddenly startled by a bee, jerked my head up and noticed there were other kids running, laughing, and playing all around me. I had been so wrapped up in our cacophony of grief that I had failed to notice them. It suddenly occurred to me, *Oh, I'm a kid. I should be playing, too.* And with that, I learned to run with a new herd. I began to make tentative friendships, to sort out friends from foes.

As I awoke to my surroundings, my curiosity about our white caregivers grew. We examined their blue eyes, blonde hair, and pale skin much the way a scientist would analyze an unknown specimen. I laid my arm alongside one of the white women's arms and marveled at the contrast. The blonde hair covering her arm was particularly intriguing to me. She admired my brown skin and said "Beautiful!" Her tone of voice and facial expression made her intention clear. We had a strong urge to touch each other, to examine the textures of our hair and skin, and fully understand each other despite our language barrier. At FFC, these strange white beings cared for us like we were their own children, and our ignorance and curiosity about them soon changed to affection.

When my siblings and I first arrived at FFC, very few girls lived there, but over time, more girls came and we were moved to our own building. When I walked into that house for the first time, I had no idea of the future that would unfold for me there. Like all the buildings in the compound, this was a low cement building with a rough cement floor. Five bedrooms surrounded a roofed common area. We had an indoor bathroom, although some of the other houses had only outdoor bathrooms. Our bathroom might be considered primitive by current American standards, but it was perfectly normal for that time and place: three stalls, each with a cement hole in the floor to squat over. The worst part about this bathroom was that it had huge cockroaches that flew at us out of nowhere—they ruled that bathroom like a king rules his kingdom. After we escaped the cockroaches and exited the bathroom, the common room had the sinks for handwashing.

When we approached the house on that first day, we walked up the path to a partially enclosed patio. To my left were tables and chairs, but to my right I was surprised to see an old blind woman who obviously lived out on that patio. It had a roof and was enclosed on three sides, but it was open to the view of everyone who walked in and out of the building. She must have been at least sixty. *That's strange. I thought only kids lived at this place*, I mused, but I didn't find her scary or threatening. Other than the white workers, she was the only adult who lived at FFC. The Somali workers came to the compound each day instead of living there.

After we settled in, our three oldest sisters visited us every Thursday or Friday (the Somali weekend) and brought us sweets and, later, pocket money for outings. On those days, we made sure to play somewhere near the gates so we could see who was coming. If we caught a glimpse of a colorful garment peeking through the walk-in gate, we kept our eyes glued to the entrance, only to grow disappointed if it was not our sisters. My sisters were well known for regular visits and for always bringing treats. We shared some of our treats with our friends since most never got visitors, and we locked up the rest in a plain wooden chest in our quarters, whose key either Arafo or I carried at all times. A few other relatives came to visit us, including my cousin Sandoon (a nickname meaning "looking for a nose"), who was my aunt Sa'iido's son. Even my nomadic uncle Qoodaar came to see us once and brought dried goat meat, sent by my ayeeyo.

These treats often sustained me, because I was a picky eater and had stomach trouble. I sometimes found dead worms in my food, and between the dead worms and nervousness that stemmed from fighting off orphanage bullies, I suffered from bouts of sickness, often having days where I couldn't keep food down. When I was too ill to eat, one of the white workers, Joselyn, usually took me to her quarters to care for me. She was a tall, thin woman with brown hair that was mostly graying, and her way of tending to me was very healing.

One evening, I was sick and feeling sorry for myself because all the other kids had gone to the monthly movie night in the kitchen. On this particular night, they were playing *Star Wars*. Even though the movies were in English and we didn't understand them, we loved going. I lay alone in the dark, the quietness around me punctuated only by the sharp chirp of a house gecko nearby. Through the blackness of the night, I heard Joselyn calling me. My name sounded so cute with her Canadian accent. I moaned to direct her to me, and her cool hand felt my forehead. Her perfumed scent hit me, and I inhaled deeply to take in more, but it was too strong for my queasy stomach. She gestured to ask if I had eaten anything, and I gave her a look that said, "If you give me any food, I'm going to vomit." She had come to take me to the movie, but when she realized I was too weak to walk, she carried me. The whole time the movie played, she sat next to me, explaining *Star Wars* in a mixture of English and broken Somali words, which was strange and confusing, but also somehow reassuring. The movie was hard to understand and connect with; there was just nothing in it I could relate to. It felt out of this world to me. Years later, when I saw it again with my own children, it struck me, *It actually is out of this world!* This time I thoroughly enjoyed the movie and watched the entire saga.

Living at FFC was like living in a world within a world. The compound was self-sufficient, with its own clinic, kitchens, and schools, so we did not venture outside our walls into Mogadishu very often. The townspeople called us "bastards" and later referred to FFC as the "handicapped kids' place," when they saw so many physically and cognitively challenged kids streaming out of our gates. But FFC took care of any child in need. At its peak, the orphanage was home to forty girls and over two hundred boys.

Because there were so many of us to feed, the kitchen staff started cooking breakfast in the middle of the night. One night, I was awakened by sharp hunger. I hadn't eaten my dinner that evening, thanks to finding yet another worm. Desperate for something to eat, I headed for the kitchen, hoping to scavenge some discarded food. I couldn't find any unwanted scraps, but when I saw the cook making anjeera, I begged for some.

"If you want food, you have to work for it," she declared.

"Okay, teach me, I am ready," I said eagerly. All my life I had watched the women around me cook anjeera, so the work came naturally. When I was done, she rewarded me with two anjeera to eat.

"Could you please soak it with tea and oil?" I asked, knowing I was probably pushing my luck.

She looked at me sternly but then sprinkled it with sugar and oil. "Go!" she said, shooing me out and pretending to be irritated.

From that night on, I frequently showed up at her kitchen door, and for my labors I was rewarded with warm anjeera and an even warmer hug.

WITHIN A YEAR of arriving, I started school at FFC. After my first day, I ran back toward the girls' dormitory, excited to share my news. The sun shimmered with heat as I hurried toward the shady trees, where I could see my friends chatting in a group. My friend Saynab, who had polio, was leaning on her crutch, while tall, dark Shamhad and a few other girls stood around. Everyone was talking about their day, but I knew my news would shock them all.

"I am the only girl in my class!" I blurted out.

They were shocked at my misfortune and bombarded me with more questions. "No other girls? Truthfully?" they asked. The rest of the grades had at least a few girls in each class.

"Yes. It will be the end of me. I am the smallest and youngest, too." I replied.

At that time, girls and boys throughout Somalia attended regular and Quran school together. Today, as a result of the more conservative religious tone the country has taken, not only schools but even restaurants are segregated by gender.

As we washed up and headed to lunch, we continued commiserating about our school day, although I felt nobody could top my problem. We took our after-lunch siesta and went to Quran school with the boys, but then the girls had our own after-school activities, such as sewing, typing, or helping in the daycare. Only the older girls could go to typing class, because it was held outside the orphanage walls. I sometimes chose the daycare, mostly because it was the first time I had seen children's toys and liked to play with them myself. I sometimes forgot I was supposed to be watching the younger children. When karate lessons were added to our choices, I was enthralled. I took my karate lessons seriously—I needed them to survive this place, to defend myself against the boys as well as the constant bullying and testing of position that took place among the girls. Even after the first few lessons, I felt my self-confidence and power surge. When a girl named Falestine deliberately spilled hot tea on me, I was ready.

"Why did you spill that on me?" I demanded.

"What are you going to do about it?" she taunted.

I bolted from the rock I was sitting on and flew at her. Everybody gathered around to watch the fight, eager to see who would be the winner. I would not back down and slip in rank. In the end, it was she who backed down, and I was relieved our power struggle had come to an end.

I learned more in that class than simple self-defense. I was completely surprised and captivated by our karate teacher, a young Somali woman named Layla. She had beautiful, smooth, dark skin and thick, soft, black hair, and she had traveled to other countries. She wore stretch pants and leg warmers. Layla was the ultimate "It Girl" in our eyes. Not only was she cool, but she had an air about her that said "I am enough. I don't need a man to guide me through life." She was unorthodox: she was independent and self-confident—and talked about kicking boy's butts. She told us that some street boys in Mogadishu tried to pick a fight with her just because she was a girl and looked like an easy target. Mogadishu street boys were notoriously violent, feared by everyone, but Layla beat them all up single-handedly. Layla taught me that girls could be as strong and important as boys. No one had ever told me that before. Layla taught me how to become the kind of woman I wanted to be: strong and resilient.

One of my favorite caregivers at FFC was a twenty-something white man from New York named Nicholas. He was fond of my little sister Hubi and often carried her around on his shoulders. He was always with us—telling us stories, teaching us discipline, and being the father figure we longed for. Unlike other white workers, he was involved in our daily care and took his job seriously. Nicholas made sure we had soap, baby powder, creams, toothpaste, and any other items we needed for daily hygiene.

Although he was always caring, Nicholas was also a tough father who did not let bad behavior go unpunished. He set a routine for us and made sure we all followed his schedule. Sometimes he would get angry and insult us in Somali, yelling *"Habartaa was!"* ("Fuck your mother!") I know it sounds harsh when I translate it, but his accent was funny to us, and we didn't take it personally because we knew he cared for us. Even so, if we disobeyed him, we were disciplined accordingly.

One day, Arafo and her friend Fowsiya were taking a shower when it wasn't their turn. Nicholas (who never missed a trick), marched in and pulled them out by their ears. They got dragged out of the shower room so fast they could only grab a small towel to try to cover them both. Fowsiya was a lighter-skinned Somali girl who turned red when she got angry, so it was easy to see her emotions from a distance. He made them stand outside, not caring if they were embarrassed, and lectured them about breaking the rules and showing a lack of discipline. When he felt he had gotten his point across, he let them go. Not only did they learn their lesson, but all of us watching learned it, too, and we never disobeyed Nicholas after that. In fact, I think we all respected him more.

Nicholas later converted to Islam, praying and learning the Quran just like us, which made us feel even more connected to him. At first, his conversion created confusion and dismay among his fellow roommates, who were American and Canadian, but they came to terms with it soon enough. I certainly never saw anyone giving him a hard time about it.

I was told Nicholas went back to New York after he left FFC, and Arafo and I are still trying to find him. When I think back on all of the "parents" I had growing up, he stands out. I would like to thank him for the love and care he showed me, and I would like to introduce him to my own children and watch his expression to see if he recognizes little me in their faces. I would like to hear stories about my childhood from an adult who watched me grow up, and I would like to see if he still has any of the pictures he took of us. Even though the various white workers took many pictures, I don't have any photos from my early childhood.

My friends and I sat in a circle every evening at twilight. Saynab, a no-nonsense northerner with a beautiful voice, started to chant, and we joined in one by one, until we were singing in unison. Our chanting sessions gave me a sense of belonging and contentment during this tumultuous time. The routine grew to include jokes, riddles, storytelling, and just sharing our journeys.

Saynab, Bisharo, Amina, and I bonded over chanting and riddles, although we had other friends in the group. Saynab was a master at riddles, spitting words at me while I attempted to decipher them as quickly as possible. I screamed with delight each time she signaled I got the answer.

One evening, after chanting and storytelling were over, we lingered, chatting about anything that caught our imaginations. It was nearly dark, and one of my friends proclaimed, "If a monster came through those bushes right now, I would not leave Bisharo behind."

Bisharo and Saynab were both crippled by polio, a common affliction in Somalia at that time. Saynab walked with crutches, but Bisharo was unable to go far on her own. She scooted around by walking with her hands, her strong arms supporting her body, her useless legs crossed beneath her. Her hands, knees, and ankles were calloused from constantly scraping the ground. Because of Bisharo's slow-moving shuffle, she would have no means of escaping the monster my friend had forecast. A few other girls and I all claimed to be the kind of hero who would never leave a friend behind.

Bisharo was one of the most beautiful girls I have ever known, with smooth, dark-chocolate skin, striking features, and long, thick hair that dragged the ground as she moved around. We all clamored to be the one to brush and braid her hair. I often got the job, not only because I was an expert braider but because I was the best at spotting and killing lice. I spent hours on my friends' hair when they had lice and got quite good at getting out the little buggers. This skill was to come in handy thirty years later, when I worked as a school nurse in California.

As we sat there in the gathering darkness bragging about our bravery, a large, unrecognizable figure suddenly emerged from the bushes. Despite our lofty promises of salvation, we all screamed and took off running. I stopped quickly when I heard Bisharo pleading for help. A nomad would never leave a friend in danger. I grabbed her and dragged her all the way to our building, even though she was a lot heavier than my featherweight self. As we stepped into the light cast by our house, we looked to see if the monster was bearing down on us as we feared. It was then we noticed the figure was nothing more than our kind cook, a short, fat woman who had a dark shawl wrapped around her that evening.

Bisharo, who by this time had bleeding knees, scolded the rest of the group loudly. "Shugri is my only true friend! The rest of you all left me there to die!"

As I write this, I feel a stab of guilt. After FFC closed abruptly several years later and we all scrambled to find new places to live, I lost track of Bisharo. It was not until years later, when I had emigrated to Canada and finally felt safe, that I had the presence of mind to wonder what had become of her. I asked everyone I knew, but no one knew. As of today I have found most of my core friends from FFC, but Bisharo seems to have disappeared without a trace, leaving a lingering vacancy in my heart.

As the years passed, I developed additional nightly rituals, carried out during the hours usually reserved for vampires. For my nocturnal mischief, I enlisted my favorite helper, my friend

Maryan. We nicknamed her "Miriam Makeba," after the famous South African singer and apartheid activist. Maryan and I were the Somali odd couple: she was the tall, chubby kid, and I was the short, skinny kid. Every plan or scheme I carried out included Maryan. Nobody else would have gotten up in the middle of the night with me just to play a trick.

For one of our favorite pranks, Maryan and I secretly collected ashes during the day. Once the other girls had fallen asleep we got up, tiptoed to the sinks and made a paste with the ashes and water, which we smeared on our faces. After we put on this homemade makeup, we donned black capes. "Tonight there is no mercy!" we whispered as we set our plan in motion.

We all believed our stinky bathroom was haunted by a jin, and Maryan and I knew that eventually one or more of the girls would stagger into the bathroom half asleep. We hid behind the dysfunctional door, wedged so close that we were breathing down each other's necks with nervous excitement. We stood patiently, keeping one eye on the entrance and another on the cockroaches and noisy geckos. Finally, our first victim, Shamhad, came to the bathroom to pee. As she was leaving, we leapt in front of her and growled *"Qul!"* a word used only by jin.

Shamhad, believing she had come face to face with the evil spirit haunting our bathroom, begged for mercy, "Please, Uncle, don't eat me!"

We stifled our giggles and demanded in unison in deep, dark voices, "Do you pray? When was the last time you prayed to Allah?"

"I pray every day! Please don't hurt me, Uncle," Shamhad stammered, as if she had no control over what was coming out of her mouth.

"I am jin! You can't lie to me, I will always know the truth! You don't pray!" I scolded.

Shamhad stood staring at us, her legs and feet moving as though she were running away but failing to go anywhere.

"Run!" we commanded, and her feet finally got her going as she ran back to her bed and huddled under the covers. We waited for the sounds coming from her bed to settle down as we fought to smother our laughter. When no other victims came soon enough, we crept through the dimly lit room to each bed and scared the girls where they lay. We pulled the covers from their heads, stuck our ashen faces in front of their eyes, and repeated our growl of "Qul!" They begged for their lives or spat out any prayer or curse that came to their lips. Then they would invariably pull the covers back over their heads, and utter, *"A'udi bilah,"* words known to ward off jin, and we would move on to the next girl. After hours of nocturnal entertainment, I went into my room to grab a cloth so I could wash off my makeup. One of my roommates, a very young girl I had no intention of scaring, saw me and let out a scream so loud that I ran out of the room in terror. When I made it to the sink I laughed at myself, realizing that I had fallen victim to my own joke. The next day the girls all shared their stories of the jin, and vowed to never use the bathroom at night again.

One constant source of entertainment was the old blind woman who lived on our patio. We never knew her name; we just always called her the "old blind lady." She liked to make up stories about us, to find our weaknesses and poke at them until she had us in tears, and to play us like pawns against each other. She was so astute that we were sure she either had an informant or some sort of magical powers. Often we would try to tiptoe around her to get something nearby, and she would swat out blindly with her stick, only to hit us square on the head with disturbing precision. We couldn't figure out how she knew where we were and what we were doing all the time, so we would justify her behavior by declaring that she actually could see and was faking her blindness. Deep down, we knew this wasn't true, but it made us feel a little less afraid of her.

Every day she was on someone's case, and one particular day she was picking on my friend Shamhad. The old woman claimed she had heard Shamhad peeing the night before, and by the loudness of her pee, she could tell that Shamhad was not circumcised. Since girls in Somalia were sewn up and left with only a small hole, our pee trickled down in a lady-like manner, slowly and quietly. Shamhad protested and said it was not her, accusing a different girl instead. Shamhad was a year my senior, but she was not circumcised and she carried deep shame about that. The old woman could tell by the way Shamhad reacted that she had hit a vulnerable spot, so of course she kept it up. Shamhad was eventually circumcised in the orphanage clinic, but they didn't do it the traditional way; they just cut off the tip of the clitoris. Shamhad was not happy about the way she had been circumcised, and I felt pity that no female relative cared enough to make sure she was circumcised properly. I worried for years that no man would want to marry her, and still wonder if she had to apologize to her husband for the incomplete job.

I was usually on the old woman's good list, but one day, I temporarily lost that status when she accused me of having diarrhea on the floor right behind her bed. I giggled with my friends as she described the sound my alleged loose stool made the night before.

"*Bararaq, bararaq,*" she said, and added, "I don't know what they are feeding this child, but she has no control over her butthole."

I laughed and asked her, "If I did that, then where is the diarrhea now?" looking at the clean floor where she was pointing.

She replied, "Well, you are lucky because someone cleaned up last night."

I laughed it off, the way we did most of her stories. We were probably as entertaining to her as she was to us.

One peculiar thing about the old woman was that she never went to the bathroom or showered inside. She always did her business in the bushes along the left side of the girls' house. If she wanted to shower, she took a bucket of water and soap to that area and proceeded to wash herself in the open. We got embarrassed when she faced the boys' houses by accident, creating a ripple of laughter among the young pupils. Sometimes she would miss the bushes by a few feet, and we would see her squatting in the open space. When we got a little older, we would take her to the bushes ourselves so she could have more privacy under our care. Preserving her privacy meant preserving our dignity as well; we didn't want the boys looking at a naked female body and then making comments about our bodies.

A bolted-down bench among the trees in front of the girls' area was our hangout space where we socialized, formed deep friendships, and created alliances. In this institution, it was important to have strong ties with a group of girls who would do anything for you. I trusted that they would keep me alive if needed, and I would do the same for them.

These alliances were tested when a new bully came to the orphanage. Sabad was a tyrant of a girl who quickly became our self-appointed leader, and she reigned as if she were born for the role. She was so mean that some of my friends from FFC have nightmares about her to this day. She controlled us with an iron grip and did not have pity for anyone, even the sick and disabled. I was still pretty young when she first established her unrestrained power over us. Sabad was a master manipulator and knew our strength was in numbers, so she chipped away at each girl individually. She insulted and belittled us, exposed our weaknesses, and pitted us against each other until we were fully under her control. She was also the second oldest girl at FFC, the oldest being her sister Amina, who, although she did not share Sabad's viciousness, did nothing to stop her.

Eventually, when her power grew strong enough that she knew she could get away with it, Sabad announced, "Today is hitting day."

She made all of us line up and hold out our hands. She went down the line and hit us one at a time, a process she repeated three

times or more. She hit other parts of our bodies, too. She continued with "hitting day" every Friday for years, causing me to hate
Fridays for decades to come.

On Thursdays, when Sabad would announce, "Tomorrow is
hitting day!" my stomach would instantly turn into knots and my
appetite would vanish. Even worse was the fact that my younger
sister Hamdi was getting hit, too. Arafo and Hubi were spared the
agony of hitting day by a lucky coincidence. They both happened
to be the same age as two of Sabad's younger sisters, and since
Sabad didn't want to hit her sisters, she spared anyone who was
their ages. Some kind of twisted bully logic, but it saved Arafo and
Hubi. When Sabad hit Hamdi, my little sister shook her hands
and screamed, "Ala, ala ala la la." Her cries cut me deeply and her
pleas echoed through my brain all night.

I knew I was too small at that time, but I began to plot a way
to overthrow Sabad when I was old enough. It may seem strange
that no one reported Sabad to our caregivers, but she had so thoroughly and masterfully infiltrated our structure and taken control that by the time anyone thought to report her, we were too
terrified of her retaliation to do so. Plus, she spoke English better
than anyone else and could communicate much more effectively
with our white caregivers.

WITHOUT WARNING, MY father appeared at FFC one day and
announced he would be teaching us Arabic. I was so confused!
How was my father able to suddenly invade my otherwise predictable life? What did he say to the white workers to get in here?

Apparently, my father had been keeping an eye on our educational progress, and when he found out that Guleed was struggling with long division, he hired an older boy to tutor him. When he found out we were not learning Arabic, he decided that he needed to come himself and teach us.

Since arriving at FFC no teacher had ever struck me, and as a result, I loved learning. Now I suddenly found myself sitting in a schoolroom with my friends, being taught once again by my father. Although I knew what he was capable of, my poor friends did not. Always trying to outmaneuver him, I scanned the room when I walked into his class that first day and chose the seat I deemed would be the hardest for him to smack me in. I did not warn any of my friends about him because, frankly, I thought he would only hit his own children.

The first lesson was uneventful, but the next day, he began asking us questions to see what we had retained. Poor Shamhad sat beside me, eager, excited, and full of promise as my father began. When he got to me, words flew out of my mouth without hesitation. Long-ingrained fear of him still made me excellent at retaining every bit of his lessons. But Shamhad was caught off guard. When she didn't immediately answer his question, I jumped in to help her and whispered in Arabic, *"Alshamsu gamila"* ("The sun is beautiful").

But it was too late. *Wham!* My father knuckle-knocked her on the head; he had perfected this punishment over the years to inflict the most pain in a single blow. Tears trickled down her face.

"Tell your father to stop hitting me!" she cried. "How come he's not hitting you?"

She had no idea what I had been through with my father and how I had vowed long ago to never get hit by him again. My best advice to her was, "Just pay attention and remember *everything* he says, then you won't get hit." Then one day, just like that, he was gone as abruptly as he had appeared. But he continued to pop up periodically at FFC to teach us Arabic, which kept me slightly on edge.

6 The Outside World

Hangaraarac lug uma dhutiyo.
A centipede does not limp for losing a single leg.
—Somali proverb

As I GOT older, I became more curious about the world outside our Families for Children walls. The moment I had stepped within those walls and could no longer wander freely, my nomadic soul had begun eroding. Occasionally, we were allowed to go out with our sisters when they visited, but that time was limited and controlled; if we were late, we were punished. I had been tending my own flock of sheep since I was six, and now I couldn't go out by myself? It didn't make sense to me.

I had a strong urge to explore and to make friends with some of the city kids. Walking right out of the gate was next to impossible, but I finally became bold enough to jump the wall. A couple sections of the wall were a little lower, but a spot behind the Quran school was the safest place to escape. Our Quran school, which must have been an afterthought, was made from corrugated metal and petroleum barrels split in half. It sat at an angle, so between the bushes and the building this lower section was screened from view of the guards. I spied on the boys and watched them jump over, taking careful note of the large rock the smaller boys brought from a hiding place to stand on. I kept an eye on the guards, and one day, when they were occupied with a group of boys who had gotten into trouble, I moved into action. With a couple of trusted friends standing watch, I grabbed the big rock, jumped up on it, and scaled the wall without being seen.

When I dropped to the ground outside FFC, the city of Mogadishu opened in front of me like a new world. But my sudden appearance, as if girls were falling from the sky, startled the crowd of people walking along the sidewalk. I didn't want to draw attention to myself, so I pretended I was just one of the herd. Feeling dazed, out of sync, guilty, but also exhilarated, I began walking, stretching tall, feeling like the world was mine. Cars and cargo lorries whizzed by, stray goats wandered around, and groups of children in different school uniforms chatted and laughed while they ate gelato, a gift left by the Italians after the colonization era.

I headed straight for a bakery that I had once visited with my sisters; I'd dreamed about its sweets ever since, especially the *halwa* a sticky, sweet confection spiced with cardamom and nutmeg. I sat there, eating my halwa and sipping chai, engrossed in people-watching. My daydreaming was interrupted when a Land Rover pulled up and a chauffeur stepped out, quickly ushering in a group of rich children. In Somalia, rich kids were easy to spot. They were usually overweight and a little lighter-skinned because they spent so much time inside their huge, gated houses. We imagined them drinking cold sodas and eating ice cream all day. They were always escorted on outings, rarely mingling with other kids. I could tell by the way this group spoke and acted that they had no respect for adults, and I was appalled when they began demanding certain foods and complaining when they didn't get what they wanted immediately. The chauffeur was trying his best to please everyone, but all I could think was, *What are they complaining about? They look like they have everything.* I had never seen Somali children act this way before. It never occurred to me or my siblings to demand choices. We didn't even recognize the concept of choice. In my world, you ate what you were given or went hungry.

When I was done eating I explored some more, trying to blend in with the other kids walking the streets. I eventually turned down an alley and came face to face with a girl about my own age. She was light-skinned, with big, beautiful eyes that immediately clouded with fear when she saw me. We would have to get very close to pass each other in this narrow alley, so I smiled to let her know I wasn't a threat.

She smiled in return, put down her grocery basket, and started talking to me. Her name was Hilaal, and she seemed as thrilled to meet a new girl as I was, but she was taken aback when I told her where I lived. Her family was obviously well off, and people had some strange notions about the kids who lived at FFC. Her large, expressive, almond-shaped eyes seemed to say, *Wow, it would be cool to be friends with this tough-looking girl from the orphanage.* I didn't view myself as tough looking, but I'm sure I seemed a little intimidating to her. She was surprised that I was just roaming around without a purpose. I wasn't shopping or running errands, just wandering, something no Somali mother would ever let her daughter do. Here, I was feral and untamed.

"Come visit me tomorrow after *duhur* [midday prayer]. I will tell my mother," Hilaal suggested, pointing out which house was hers. I agreed, and we concocted some sort of story to explain who I was and why I was coming over.

This first foray into the outside world left me longing for more. I was eager to meet Hilaal again and act like a regular girl with a normal life, so the next day, despite the risk of getting caught, I jumped the wall again. The minute I got to her house, the deep spicy smell of her mother's cooking made my mouth water. We went into my new friend's room and started chatting. She was curious to hear about my life and the white people who cared for us. Too soon, her mother called her to help prepare the food, so I examined their house, curious about her world, too.

We feasted on pasta with tomato sauce served with freshly squeezed papaya and mango juice. I was in heaven. I didn't even look for worms in my food. We ladies ate and chatted together in the kitchen while her father sat alone in the dining room, eating his lunch in complete silence. He wore a high-level military uniform with several stars on his shoulder. I stayed clear of him; I did not want him to ask me any questions. Neither Hilaal nor her mother uttered a word while near him either.

Being in this nice house and having this delicious meal actually made me feel smaller and more destitute than I had ever felt. For the first time, I began to wonder how society saw the FFC children. I started noticing the pitying looks they gave us. Did they really think we were bastards, or just poor, unwanted children? Why did my sisters put us in the orphanage instead of taking us in? How come this city was full of our relatives, yet no one cared about us? My mother's own sister was rich, but she never once came to the gates of our orphanage. Although I was young, I knew I did not want to live this way for long. A small realization ignited in me: Perhaps someday I could have control of my own life and choose a better path for myself.

Despite my careful planning, the guards sometimes caught me. Once, I forgot that I had jumped the wall to get out and marched back in through the main gate. It wasn't until I saw the look on the guard's face that I realized, *Oh, I am dead!* I don't remember my punishment that day, but the guards had various standard punishments, such as hitting the palm of our hands with a stick, sentencing us to time in the punishment room, or making us hold the *dhagaha qabso* position. This involved squatting down, then threading our arms behind our knees and up to grab our ears. It was uncomfortable and humiliating enough, but worse, we had to hold this position in public under the blistering hot sun for an extended time.

I recall seeing my friend Mowlid undergoing dhagaha qabso punishment one day. Rivers of sweat poured down his face, but they did nothing to help his parched, cracked lips. His eyes raised to mine at the sound of my voice, and he looked so exhausted that I felt a visceral pain for him. He was the sweetest boy I knew and treated me like a little sister. What could he have done to deserve this? I risked the wrath of the guards and ran to get him water,

determined to ease his suffering in some way. I found myself wondering *Which is worse? Dhagaha qabso or the punishment room?*
The punishment room was a small cement cell near the guard's
station by the front gate, about two feet wide and four feet long. At
least you were sheltered from the sun in there. But some guards
ignored their prisoner's pleas to go to the bathroom and as a result
it reeked so badly of urine and, at times, feces that it made me
want to vomit. But once I discovered that world outside our walls,
none of these potential punishments stopped me from exploring
it every chance I got.

IN EIGHTH GRADE I started having conflicts with some of the
boys in my class. Since I was the only girl, my teachers often protected me. My math teacher was a young Somali man in his twen-
ties, and I absolutely adored him. This teacher openly and proudly
said how smart and beautiful I was, showed me respect, and told
the boys they needed to respect me, too. "Shugri is like an egg, so
you must be gentle with her," he informed them. When he wanted
to let the class out early or do any fun activity, he would ask my
opinion and do as I said, which only made the boys more hostile
toward me.

One day I came to school and found that one of the boys had
scribbled a nasty message on my desk. "Who did this?" I demanded,
but was answered only by laughter. An older boy, Afwayne ("Big
Mouth," like the president of Somalia), said it was Ga'al, whose
nickname meant "Loved One." Most Somali children are given
nicknames; some are nice, like Ga'al's, but most are demeaning.

You have to own your imperfections in Somalia because they are pointed out to you forever via your nickname. Kids missing an eye were literally called "One-Eye." One of the boys in my class was nicknamed "Lizard" because his skin resembled a reptile's.

"Did you write that on my desk?" I asked him, hoping he would deny it. Ga'al used crutches as a result of polio, and I really had no interest in fighting him.

"What can you do about it?" he taunted.

Afwayne joined in. "Don't look at his disability and think he is weak. Ga'al has a deadly grip that will have you begging for mercy." I must not have looked sufficiently scared because Afwayne added, "He once grabbed a kid and did not let him go until he urinated and defecated."

This scared me a little, but backing down from a fight was more dangerous in the long run. I surely did not want to urinate in front of them either.

News of impending fights spread faster than lice in that place. We headed outside and were quickly encircled by almost every kid in school. Most of the boys supported Ga'al, but some supported me. Ga'al lowered himself to the ground, threw his crutches to the side, and leaned forward on his fists like an aggressive male gorilla ready to attack. I quickly made sure that none of his friends were going to try to trip me or throw sand in my eyes to give him an advantage. Ga'al watched my feet with intensity, looking for his opportunity to grab me. Adrenaline rushed through me and I kicked him as hard as I could on the left side of his head. He fell over backward like a sack of corn. Shocked and encouraged, I moved closer to hit him some more. But when I looked at him carefully and saw his body lying there, I felt bad and stopped my attack. His friends picked him up and I stood staring at him, feeling for the first time the consequences of my actions. I realized Afwayne had misled me about Ga'al's fighting prowess in order to scare me. I left feeling disappointed in my actions that day, the shame of fighting a physically challenged boy engulfing me. I had never liked physical violence, even when defending myself, and this encounter made that fact more clear to me. I vowed to protect myself, my siblings, and my friends without violence whenever possible.

As soon as I entered my teen years, I knew it was time to overthrow Sabad and her tyrannical reign. I was not afraid of her by this time; I was fed up. When I informed my friends, I could instantly see fear looming in their eyes. I imagined myself as a warrior chief trying to inspire an emotionally defeated tribe. Little by little they joined me, but I could not share my plans within the listening walls of the orphanage. Luckily, my friends and I took typing lessons together outside the orphanage, so we could scheme as we walked to and from class.

The first step was to band together and rebel against hitting day. I questioned everyone to make sure the whole group would act together, but when I got to Shamhad, I got a little worried.

She proudly explained, "When Sabad comes to hit me, I won't put the palm of my hand out in front of me like usual. I will put my hand out for her, but behind my back instead!" To Shamhad, this seemed like a refusal, but I was shocked by her answer.

"What!?" I cried in dismay. "You are still letting her hit you!"

Shamhad lowered her gaze, knowing that I was disappointed.

I needed to show the girls that we were all in this together, and unless we resisted as a group, we would forever be slaves to Sabad's power.

Saynab spoke up courageously in her cute Northern drawl, "Shugri, I will not only resist, but I will help create a riot if I have to." When Saynab spoke, especially when she was upset, she slanted her lips to the side, giving her a look of confidence.

Physically attacking her was not the answer, but we needed to send a strong message, something Sabad couldn't overlook, that her bullying had to stop. The most insulting, drastic retaliation to her abuse we could think of was to smear feces in Sabad's bed. I smiled, feeling excited about the idea. For some reason, it felt wrong to use waste from us older girls. Instead, I asked a sweet little six-year-old girl named Little Sa'diya to defecate in a can. She stared at me with a confused *What do you need my shit for?* look on her face. She repeated my request back to me, as if she had misunderstood. I did not want to give her too many details since she was young and could be made to talk, but my close friends and I took her into the bathroom and convinced her to do what we asked.

Just before dinner, I went to Sabad's bed, my friends standing guard. Her covers were gone, perhaps on the drying line, leaving just a mattress with a sheet on it. It wasn't enough to just dump the contents of the can. I wanted to really rub it in, so I used one of Sabad's shoes to smear the shit all over her bed. I knew I'd be in

serious trouble if she discovered who did this, but I was charged
up, determined to end the suffering of my little sister and all the
others Sabad had abused for years.

Luckily for us, when Sabad returned to her room and the smell
hit her nostrils, she made one tactical mistake. Instead of gathering us together and torturing us one by one as usual, she called the
guards, who in turn called the main captain in charge of security,
Captain Indhadeero. The captain interrogated all of the girls one
by one, but no one revealed me as the culprit. Just when I thought
I had gotten away with it, the last girl interviewed revealed my
identity.

Finally, Captain Indhadeero, a tall, nice-looking middle-aged
man called me in. I liked him as a person and he had never been
unkind to me in any way, but I was still mistrustful of him. Somali
clan systems run deep, and Indhadeero shared a direct clan line
with Sabad, so I assumed he would automatically take her side and
be unfair to me. He sat me down and asked me what happened.

All the emotions I carried about Sabad's bullying for years hit
me at once and I flew into a rage. I jumped out of my chair and
started flipping chairs and tables, screaming all the while. My
reaction shocked him; I had never acted like this before. I saw
no way out of this situation—either he would punish me now or
Sabad would get me later. Alternately yelling and crying, I told
Indhadeero everything Sabad had done to us over the years.

He looked shocked, but instead of handing down a punishment, he talked to me calmly. His kindness surprised me and I
eventually let down my guard and began to trust him. I looked

him squarely in the eye and said, "If you send me back, Sabad will kill me while I sleep."

He studied me intently but finally decided I spoke the truth, because he assigned an older military woman to stand guard over us at night. I felt elated that my friends and I would finally be safe from Sabad. But he and I both knew there was no way I could escape punishment entirely. So, despite the fact that I had committed the "crime of the century" at FFC, I got off pretty easily: no beating, just time in the punishment room.

LIFE FOR THE girls of FFC changed for the better after that incident, especially with the presence of the guard in our quarters. As we soon learned, however, life outside our walls was deteriorating. A combination of political, social, religious, and economic unrest made the country unstable, and Siad Barre had waged open war against the Somalis in the north. The effects of the war eventually brought enough unrest that the foreigners who owned and worked at FFC were no longer safe in Somalia.

Early in 1988, we were told that the orphanage would need to close. The owners scrambled to find homes for all of the children, which was especially difficult for those who were severely disabled, like Bisharo. So deep was their concern for our well-being that at the end, the owners handed out large sums of money to all of us as they left. I never saw our money again; we gave it to our sisters, who in turn gave it to our father.

By this time, I was fourteen and about to start high school, and Arafo, Guleed, Hubi, and I were the only members of my family still living at FFC. A couple of years earlier, Saada had married a man from a wealthy family and moved to Italy, and a year after her marriage she took Hamdi and Liban to live with them. At that time, my sisters and father agreed that those two were the most in need out of all of us: Liban because he was still so young and Hamdi because she would benefit from good medical care for the hand she nearly lost as a baby. Now that it was impossible to keep us all together, safety became the primary concern. Arafo was placed with Sofiya, who was now married to her second husband and living in Mogadishu. Guleed, Hubi, and I went to live in Mogadishu with Abshiro, who was married and expecting her first child.

7 Beautiful Mogadishu

Ama buur ahow ama buur ku tiirsanow.
Be a mountain yourself; or lean on something like it.
—Somali proverb

I FELT LOST. Even though I was living with a sister who loved me, and had some of the freedom I had been craving, my daily life unsettled me. For the past five years, everything had been prescribed for me: when I got up, had meals, went to classes, and had free time. Now I was in charge of getting myself up for school, going to market every day for food, hanging around with neighborhood teens, and walking myself to school. It was like being released after years of imprisonment.

To make sense of my new world and recapture the stability I craved, I decided to find and visit all my old FFC friends. I traveled to remote places in Mogadishu to see them. I even sought out Sabad. Our tension had eased, and she and I forgave each other. War was looming, our futures were uncertain, and petty arguments were not important. I had been with these girls twenty-four hours a day for more than four years, and that shared experience bonded us forever. My friend Sofiya, who had a heart condition, seemed to have ended up in the worst circumstances. She was living in a rundown house with visible holes in the roof, taking care of a younger brother, and her mother appeared to treat her like an unwanted burden. Seeing my old friends in difficult circumstances was a turning point for me. It opened my eyes to the fact that I was living a very good life, in the comfortable middle-class neighborhood of Boondheere, with my sister Abshiro, who loved me unconditionally. This realization propelled me forward to accept and start living this new chapter of my life.

Abshiro's house had six bedrooms arranged in a circular fashion around a large, roofed, space where we dragged mats or low stools for gatherings. We had an indoor bathroom. I didn't have to battle flies or cockroaches to do my business! My sister and her husband, Ahmed-Nur, had the room next to the kitchen; beside them was the TV room, which doubled as my bedroom, and Guleed had the room next to mine. On the other side of Guleed's room was the living/dining room, and then a room occupied by Ahmed-Nur's brother, Mahamud. The last room was shared by Hubi and my young niece, Abshiro Yarey.

Guleed almost didn't come to live with us at Abshiro's; my father wanted to take him instead. Abshiro vehemently insisted on keeping our brother, and later she told me why. When my father visited us at FFC a few months before it closed, he and Guleed had a heated argument. My father's anger flared, and he choked Guleed until he fell limp. When Abshiro heard the story, she panicked because she, too, had been choked by our father. As a teenager, she had returned home late one night and he immediately accused her of being with boys, when in fact she had gone to the hospital to retrieve something our mother, who had recently given birth, had left there. When she got there, she heard so many women in labor calling for help that she stayed to assist. After she returned home, our father was furious and refused to listen to her explanation. He came after her and squeezed his hands around her neck until she passed out.

The next day, Abshiro gathered stones and threw them at him in quick succession, defending her actions and insulting him the whole time. Abshiro maintained her innocence so fiercely that our father began to doubt his original conclusion and eventually apologized. He confessed that he had choked all of his girls at one time or another to scare them away from boys, but vowed to never strangle one of his daughters again after that. I am lucky to be one of the few who escaped that punishment. Unfortunately for Guleed, he left the boys out of the deal.

Abshiro was not going to let Guleed live with our father. Guleed was a volatile, out of control boy whose behavior became more unpredictable as he entered his teen years. He frequently threatened Abshiro, by this time pregnant with her first child.

"I will disembowel you if you come after me!" he yelled once as he ran away.

Guleed was always running away, and my sister was so worried that the street gangs would hurt him that she searched for him for days on end every time. If that didn't test her love enough, he found a new way to torment her. He once sent her a message that said, "Your brother Guleed is dead." Can you imagine the horror she felt when her gaze fell upon those words? And yet she went looking for him again, relieved when she found him unharmed. Her relief was short lived, however.

"If you come any closer, I will gut you and pull your baby from its womb!" he screamed.

She pleaded with him to come home and assured him that she loved him. I know she meant every word, because I saw how much she cried every time she could not find him.

Guleed had seen a lot, and had often been the recipient of our father's temper. Abshiro's persistent and unwavering love eventually made its way through the layers of defense mechanisms he laid over the course of that first year, and I saw him soften and become part of the family. He would tenderly play with our little niece, the very baby he had threatened to cut from the womb.

Ahmed-Nur became a father to all of us. He worked two jobs to support us, made sure we were fed and clothed well, and most important, was kind and gentle. He even found time to play with us. He knew marrying my sister would mean taking in her four orphaned siblings and her niece, but he never once made us feel as if we were a burden.

Although we lived a comfortable life and even had a maid to help with housework, all of the girls had chores. Mine was washing laundry by hand, a responsibility I often shared with Arafo when she visited us on weekends. Arafo and I had it down to a science: we alternated washing and rinsing clothes just like a washing machine, except we were the washing machine. Large items like sheets and heavy clothing required all the strength two rather small teenagers could muster, and we were always exhausted by the end of the day. Eventually, I got out of being the washerwoman because I developed oozing blisters all over my hands and feet from an allergic reaction to Omo, the laundry detergent we used at the time.

Abshiro Yarey, "Little Abshiro," had the chore of starting the morning fire. Abshiro Yarey's nomadic mother, Aanood ("Milky"), had too many daughters. Each time her mother-in-law heard that Aanood had yet another daughter, instead of "Congratulations!" she would remark, *"Yaa kuu dirsaday?"* Literally translated it means "Who asked you?" but the hidden meaning was, "Tell me when you are giving birth to a son. Don't bother me with your girl news because I'm not interested." Extra daughters were often sent to relatives in the city as domestic help, but Aanood brought her daughter to Abshiro hoping the child could get an education, as well as to protect her from one of her husband's other wives. This stepmother had beaten Abshiro Yarey so relentlessly that when she arrived she had laccrations all over her scalp.

Abshiro Yarey was eight or nine when she moved in with us, and I adored her. She wore her hair short like a boy's and her protruding, round belly made her resemble a rich Somali man. She was quiet, always addressed adults with respect, and did what she was told. Having Hubi as a roommate might not have been the best idea for a timid girl like Abshiro Yarey. Hubi was outspoken, a know-it-all kind of kid with an overdeveloped sense of righteousness, and she bossed Abshiro Yarey around for years.

Once, in the middle of the night, I woke up to find Abshiro

Yarey starting a fire in the kitchen brazier. "What are you doing, Abshiro Yarey?" I asked.

"I'm starting the morning fire, Aunt," she replied.

As soon as she turned to answer me, I realized she wasn't awake. I was familiar with sleepwalkers; I had once chased Hubi in the blackness of night as she led me on a sleep-*run* through FFC, zig-zagging through the trees with eerie precision.

"It's too early for a fire," I told Abshiro Yarey. "You should go back to bed."

Even when asleep, she was an obedient child, so she did what I asked. She was found starting fires in the middle of the night at various times by other family members, and each one would calmly send her back to bed. Despite her nocturnal ramblings, Abshiro Yarey couldn't be replaced as the fire-starter; Arafo and I already had a heavy load of chores on top of our schoolwork. At least she always started her fires in the right place.

FOR THE FIRST time in years, I was living a carefree existence. The sense of contentment I had as a nomadic child returned. Though this new place was filled with cars, people, and permanent stone houses, I did not have to jump any walls or worry about being punished if I just wanted to wander around or go to the market on my own. In place of my nomadic ayeeyo, my sister became the keeper of my world. Food was plentiful, I felt safe, and my material comfort was far beyond what I had experienced at FFC. I soon came to realize that it was beyond that of most people in my neighborhood.

We had a car, maids, and a TV, which was synonymous with "well-off" in Mogadishu. In the evenings we sat and talked, told stories, or watched TV together. Gathering in the evening had always been part of my life: as nomad, in the orphanage, and now here with my sister. That ritual anchored me, and gave me a sense of belonging.

As if a TV wasn't a big enough luxury, we also had a videocassette player, and Friday movie night was an event at our house. Friends and neighbors came over and we indulged in a favorite Somali entertainment: watching movies from India. But the activity I most enjoyed was listening to music, especially when doing chores. I never could memorize all those forefathers of mine like I was supposed to, but I knew all the words to my favorite songs and sang along while I danced enthusiastically. My favorite singer was Omar Dhuule—his songs spoke to me deeply, especially when I was getting over crushes. Sometimes my sister Abshiro would join in, and we would sing and dance together. Life was nourishing and predictable in my sister's house in Mogadishu, and I grew to love it. The little things—like dancing in the house, going to the market, getting gelato with my friends, and simply being part of a family—made me feel happy and content in those days.

One drawback of living in an old, densely populated neighborhood in the middle of the city was that I developed asthma. After each attack, I lost weight and my sunken eyes reflected the difficulty breathing and loss of sleep. Sometimes my pregnant sister joined me, both of us sitting upright with our arms held away from our bodies in an attempt to get a full breath. Her belly pushed on her lungs, and I watched helplessly as she struggled to breathe. I could practically see death hovering around her, and for the first time in my life, I was terrified that she would die. She was my world—my mother, father, and sister all at the same time.

My asthma kept getting worse, and finally I went to see a doctor, a middle-aged man whose office was a few blocks away. When I was finally called in, he asked me to lie on the exam table and then he pushed my shirt all the way up. I felt embarrassed about revealing my body to a strange man, but he was the doctor and I trusted him. He placed electrodes all over my chest, touching me everywhere, including my nipples. Still it didn't occur to me that he was doing anything more than a medical examination. He hooked a machine to the electrodes, and when he was done, he removed them and told me to stand on a stool. He faced me, lifted my chin, and abruptly shoved his mouth onto mine.

I was completely stunned, and for a moment, I didn't know what to do. Shame and fear overwhelmed me, and I pulled my chin down. "I want to go home," I stammered, and rushed out of the room while he was still insisting that he was not done examining me. *What a sick man*, I thought. I may have been naïve, but I knew kissing was something adults did.

I hurried back to my sister in the waiting room. "All went well, *abaayo*. I am okay. Let's go home."

I decided I'd rather die of asthma than be sexually violated. I was so ashamed of what happened that I did not utter a word to anyone. Looking back now, through the eyes of a nurse, I know all of what he did was for his own sick enjoyment. I was having asthma, not a heart attack or breast issues, yet the only thing he did was perform something that may have been an EKG, as an excuse to see my breasts. He never even listened to me breathe.

Arafo got a bad case of bronchitis a few months later and had to go to the same doctor. She came back scared. When I saw the shame in her eyes, I said, "He is sick, abaayo," and with that, she started talking. From what I understood, the exam never left Arafo's breasts. We decided that we would not see this doctor again, even if we were dying. It was healing for both of us to talk about our experiences, and I felt the veil of shame lift from me.

I am sure this man preyed on many young Somali girls, but sadly, none of them would have reported him for fear of being blamed and enduring the stigma that comes with reporting sexual abuse. To be honest, I don't think I would have been so forthcoming in writing this if I still lived in my country. It's just the way Somali social structure is: you keep these things hidden for fear of bringing dishonor and shame to your family. In the Western world, the reason for talking about sexual abuse is to gain justice and emotional closure. In Somalia, if you talk, rumors spread quickly that you are not a virgin anymore and no man will want to marry you. And to a Somali woman, that is too much to lose.

I THOUGHT I would be a picky eater all my life, but my sister's cooking greatly improved my relationship with food. In the orphanage, I had found the institutional food repulsive. But in most Somali households, including my sister's, meals had a ritual all their own. It started with a trip to market each morning, and by midday, the smell of well-seasoned food sizzling away filled not only our house but the whole neighborhood. Just before sitting down to our lunch, the largest meal of the day, we squeezed fresh papaya, mango, and grapefruit for juice. Our family gathered and ate together, and after lunch, when the sun was at its hottest, the whole country took a siesta, resting and digesting contentedly. Some days I didn't feel like resting and would wander outside, but the harsh, white-hot sun and the sight of streets empty of all but a few stragglers would usher me back in.

My favorite part of the ritual was walking to our neighborhood market each day. It was more than buying groceries; it was a chance to dress up, socialize, and slyly check out the handsome boys in the neighborhood. I often went to market with Laja'el ("Loved One"), a friend and neighbor about a year younger than I. She was a giggly girl who saw humor in everything. We wanted to be mischievous together, but I swear Laja'el's mother knew this and kept a vigilant eye on us. She was a sweet woman but kept my friend busy with endless chores; going to the market together was our only chance to briefly be free. As we walked, more women and girls would join us, all carrying their baskets on their arms like we did. I knew we were getting close when the alluring aroma of spices and fresh herbs hit my nostrils. It instantly gave me a craving for *sambusa*, fried pastries filled with potatoes or meat, which was sold along the way. The open-air market reached its bustling peak around midmorning, and we excitedly wove through the crowds of women wearing colorful tunics and babies strapped to their bodies, the scent of frankincense lingering behind them.

Laja'el and I hurried to get our groceries purchased first, so we would have some time to enjoy ourselves before we were expected back home. We bought sambusa and roasted peanuts from the street vendors, and on hot days, we stopped for cold gelato. We giggled our way back home, baskets laden with food, still keeping our eyes open for boys.

Some days, my family made brunch, so we went to the market early to get goat liver or goat meat, which we chopped finely, seasoned, sautéed, and served with anjeera. Our family frequented the same vendors, buying from whoever gave us the best price that day. It was very important to get the best cuts of meat because it showed your ability as a woman to shop and negotiate properly. If you came home with leftovers and scraps, your family looked at you as if you were a child just learning how to shop. Laja'el and I made sure we quickly became as skilled at hustling the butcher as her mother and my sister, so we could continue going to market for our families.

As we walked through the center of the market, we examined the freshly butchered goats hanging from hooks, looking for one that would provide the best cuts. Sometimes I chose *dhaylo*, baby goat meat, which was particularly soft and delicious. Dhaylo was more expensive and I was lucky my family could afford it. The last thing I grabbed before my shopping was done was *sambab* (lung, something Somalis never consumed) for our cat. She was not really our pet; she forced her way into our lives and demanded food. She took up residence (along with occasional litters of kittens) in the rafters of our house and meowed incessantly if we didn't feed her. That cat was so smart that she came down from the rafters at the precise moment I returned from market. I immediately threw down her sambab, then quickly unloaded my groceries while she was busy consuming her prize.

One afternoon, I walked into my house after shopping, my eyes down on the cement floor in front of me. Suddenly, my gaze fell upon my ayeeyo, sitting on our floor with her legs extended, her face turned away from me. The minute I saw her gray eyes glance sideways at me, I jumped into her arms and smothered her with so many hugs that she had to grab my shoulders and push me back to study my face. She always had a way of looking at me so deeply that I felt she was looking into my soul. I moved and sat on the floor beside her while she stroked my hair and back. I could feel her arthritic fingers cupping over my spine as she caressed me. I looked at her exposed shins, covered in long, thin scars, attesting to a lifetime of walking past the desert's unforgiving bushes. I scooted down toward her legs and began massaging them.

My ayeeyo told us that she was staying with our Aunt Maryan, our mother's rich older sister, the very one who never visited us at the orphanage. Aunt Maryan did not want Ayeeyo to visit us. "There is no way I'm going back without seeing Ruqiya's children," she had told our aunt defiantly. Aunt Maryan despised us, which I didn't understand at the time. To add to my confusion, she was loving toward our Uncle Qoodaar's children who shared the same clan as her. But to my ayeeyo, we were all her grandchildren regardless of our clans, and she made us all feel important.

My ayeeyo made this rare journey into the city because she

needed a new male camel to carry her huts and water. Abshiro gave her money to buy the camel and our ayeeyo blessed her. My only regret about that day when my dear ayeeyo came to see us was that, like many situations in life, I took it for granted. Had I known that would be the last time I would ever see my poetic, witty, intuitive grandmother, I would have paid closer attention, letting every moment sink into my soul.

AT MY FATHER'S insistence, after we moved in with Abshiro, I started ninth grade at an Arabic school called Sakhawadin Secondary School. I hated that school. My teacher was a small, old Egyptian man whose education style consisted of screaming his lessons to his students, getting louder and louder with every confused look we gave him. I guess he thought he could imprint his lessons directly into our brain cells if he yelled loudly enough. Worse, his discipline methods were reminiscent of my father's; they must have learned the "knuckle rap to the head" from the same master. I turned right back into that scared little girl who was so terrified of not learning her lessons that she peed on the floor.

I endured that school for a whole year, but I finally broke down and begged my sister and brother-in-law to let me change schools. They eventually relented and took me out, and I started my sophomore year at Sheikh Hassan Barsame, a public school within walking distance of our home. The school's beautiful downtown location made it a magnet for rich teenagers whose parents held high government positions. It was an aristocracy in which money was the gateway to popularity, and the school courtyard and the street in front of it became the place for those teens to show off their wealth. These kids lived in huge gated houses with their maids and chauffeurs. Many were brought to school by drivers in expensive cars. Not only were these students rich, but they had high social status because of their fathers' wealth. I started to see that perhaps I was not as well off as I thought. I felt small and invisible there.

As a newcomer to this world and its great divide between rich and poor, I watched how the students interacted from the sidelines. I heard whispers swirl around me.

"That is the highest minister's daughter! Look at her Italian-made sandals!"

"Do you see him? He's so handsome! His father is a colonel, and they just came back from vacation in Germany."

Constant chatter surrounded these students, as if royalty or movie stars were walking in our midst. Outside of school, clothes and hairstyles mirrored those of American youth in the late 1980s. Everyone, from poor street kids to the rich clique, wanted a Lionel Richie afro or Michael Jackson–inspired clothes or hair. How successful you were with the look depended on your wallet, and no one could compete with the affluent teens, who went shopping in America and Europe during summer vacation.

Yet when I walked home from school with the whispers of *Did you see her new clothes?* or *Did you see that big car that picked him up?* echoing in my brain, a voice would often break through, pleading, "We are hungry. Can you give us money for food?" I would look up, into the haunted eyes of a ragged mother with runny-nosed children or a crippled old man leaning on a stick, and hand over what little change I had. The economic injustice that I witnessed all around me was helping to lay the foundation for the civil war that was soon to consume our country.

I was awkward and uncomfortable around these rich kids. I did not know how to relate or connect. But in my junior year, I made a few friends among them. One was Sagal, who was much wealthier than most kids in that school, but she never flaunted it like they did; she was a sweet-natured girl who treated everyone with respect. Her mixture of innocence and compassion drew me to her.

One day I came to school and heard anxious chatter spreading throughout the schoolyard. I immediately knew something bad had happened. Then I heard it: Sagal had been shot in the head while she slept. Some said it was a robbery gone wrong, and others said her jealous stepmother tried to kill her. Her family tried to fly her out of the country immediately for treatment, but couldn't get her out. Instead, Sagal had been taken into the local hospital, and my chemistry teacher offered to take me to see her.

I had already learned that my teacher had a crush on me, although I had no interest in him. But in this desperate moment I needed his help, and took advantage of his affection for me. In return, he took advantage of my desperation and stopped us off at a sweet shop for chai and pastry as if this were a date. We eventually arrived at the hospital, which was bustling with activity, despite the fact that it was siesta time.

I spotted Sagal's bed in the center of a spacious room. She lay there motionless, covered with a white sheet. I could see only half of her swollen face; the rest was wrapped with white gauze. Stressed relatives moved in and out of the room, as if their urgency could breathe life into her. My teacher went to speak with the grieving family while I tried to make myself small and unnoticeable in a corner. It didn't work—a woman who was fanning Sagal headed straight toward me with an irritated look. I explained that I was Sagal's friend from school, but she still demanded that I leave. I looked at my friend's still body one more time and left with tears in my eyes. Sagal died a few days later. She was so lively at school that I could not fathom that she could die just like that. But violence was creeping into our lives.

THAT SAME YEAR, I developed a crush on a cute baby-faced boy in my class. Our flirtatious looks across the room morphed into frequent conversations in the courtyard. Somalis never display affection in public so we never held hands or anything. We never even got to the point of declaring we were girlfriend and boyfriend. Our budding romance died in its infancy, as soon as I realized he had joined a growing movement of ultra-conservative Islam stemming from Saudi Arabia: Wahhabism.

Wahhabism insisted on a rigid interpretation of the Quran. It was seen as extremist by most Somalis at that time and conflicted with the Sufism that Somalis had practiced for centuries. In Wahhabism, there was no chanting, praying, or appeasing of the saints like in Sufism. Sufism was a moderate and mystical form of

Islam, and no Sufi sheikh told us to abandon our traditional way of living or dressing. In the Sufism I knew, culture and religion complemented rather than opposed each other, and I loved that.

A competing version of conservative Islam, called Ikhwanu al-muslimeen ("Muslim Brotherhood"), had made its way into Somalia years earlier. I didn't really understand the difference between them. They both wanted women to abandon our traditional clothing and wear all-concealing burkas. I did notice that Wahhabi men were required to have a beard and wear pants that did not touch their ankles. They also had a particular obsession with separating men and women, particularly in their Quran schools, which were popping up throughout the city. The Muslim Brotherhood movement lost momentum as Wahhabism rose. Wahhabis covertly spread their message, which they truly believed was the only way to practice Islam, and the new Wahhabi leaders were careful not to attract government attention. Religious leaders had been killed by Siad Barre in the past for spreading extremist ideologies.

I believe Wahhabism might have been making its way into our culture longer than most Somalis suspected. In retrospect, I can recall a change in my cousin Sandoon over the course of the years that he visited us in the orphanage. One day I came running toward him, expecting him to bury me as usual in his loving hug, but instead he stopped. I gave him a confused look. He could see that I was hurt, so he leaned forward and explained, "Abaayo, you are a big girl now, so you can greet me but don't touch me."

I was stunned, but my cousin acted as if nothing had happened.

In my mind, I was thinking, *You're my cousin, so why does it matter if I am a young woman or small girl?* I felt ashamed, as if my own changing body caused this problem. I was relieved that his older brother Abdullahi continued to hug me, and the minute he saw me would excitedly announce, "My beautiful cousin is here!" He made me feel like the most important person in his life every time he saw me. In time, I found out that Sandoon had begun practicing Wahhabism. As the boy I had a crush on got more and more involved with this new version of Islam, he, too, began to avoid girls, and our little crush came to end.

About this time, I met a sullen girl from the Isaaq clan from Northern Somalia. She had this aura about her, the kind that said, *Mess with me and I'll beat the life out of you.* I let her borrow my newspaper one time at school, and when I came back to get it, she had found a picture of the president and cut out his eyes and the area where his testicles were.

"Why did you do this?" I asked, confused.

She gave me a terrifying look, and I wanted to say, "Never mind!"

Yet she talked. "That man is slaughtering my people!"

The dialect of the Isaaq clan is so different from those in Mogadishu that we were on the verge of needing a translator, so at first I thought I had misunderstood her. I had never heard anyone openly criticize the president and had no idea the Isaaq clan was being targeted. Her hate was palpable, and I could see that her pain was deep and dark. I could not imagine the world she spoke about and was astonished that such a thing had happened. I had no understanding of what was happening beyond the cocoon of Mogadishu.

I soon started to notice that same hatred for the government springing up from many different directions. Along with the new religious conflict, the clan tensions that Siad Barre had long suppressed were rising up. The disparity between the poor and the rich was reaching dangerous levels as well, as corrupt government officials went unchecked. In retrospect, clues that my country was heading into mayhem were everywhere. I was just too caught up being a teenager to recognize them.

As my hormones came to life, I started to care about how I looked. I spent hours on my long, curly hair and welcomed the flirtatious looks I got from boys. I went to the tailor and showed him designs of exactly how I wanted my clothes to look. One of my favorites was a form-fitting dress with a red skirt and white top. I wore the dress with brown sandals and my long curls down and hit the streets of Mogadishu, convinced I looked beautiful. Even though I liked attention and was curious about boys and sex, I was always acutely aware of my responsibility as a young woman to protect my reputation. It had been ingrained in me since childhood that I had to guard my virginity with my life. But the problem was, I didn't know exactly what that entailed.

I began a quest to learn more about the taboo subject of sex. But who could I ask? I could not ask any adults, even my married sisters, about this subject without having a random object hurled at me. The sense of shame that comes with becoming a woman in Somalia is blindly inherited and prohibits curiosity about our bodies. Most Somali girls were as curious as I, but we were praised for acting ignorant on the subject; sexual knowledge suggested we might not be virgins or, worse, were *dhilo*—sluts. However, I refused to play that game and let my quest for knowledge go unanswered, so I turned to my peers, which proved to be a disastrous decision.

My friend Arwa, whom I knew from FFC, had an older sister who had recently married. I knew they were very close. A few of my friends and I approached Arwa; she promised to ask her sister about sex. The next time we saw her, we whispered, "Did you ask your sister what men and women do to each other?"

"Yes!" she answered. We made sure to find a place where we would not be disturbed by an adult or overprotective brother. We closed in, eager to hear the truth at last.

Arwa leaned forward to impart her wisdom. "My sister said that once a vagina and penis see each other, you have no control over them."

What!? I thought. I'm sure the shocked look on my face gave my thoughts away.

"Yes," she went on, "but this can only happen when your privates are naked."

"Yes," we all murmured, leaning in even more.

"My sister and her husband were sitting across the room from each other when they undressed. All of a sudden they were overtaken by a strong force and then SLAM! Before either of them could register what was going on, their two private parts had hit

each other with great impact!" It sounded like something I had
heard in my physics class, not sex.

Frankly, I was a bit disappointed with this news. I thought I had
power and control over my body, but it seemed the opposite was
true. In the back of my mind, though, I was beginning to question
whether my friend was telling us the truth or just some nonsense
she had heard in the street. I left that day feeling dissatisfied—and
still curious.

A FEW MONTHS later, a young married couple moved into our
neighborhood. The woman, Sofiya, was eighteen, and she and I
soon became fast friends. We hung out a lot, drinking tea and
going to market together. It occurred to me that I could ask her
about sex, but I didn't want to bring up the topic so early in our
friendship.

One day I saw Sofiya walking gingerly, as if she had pain in her
lower abdomen. "Abaayo, what is hurting you?" I inquired.

We sat in her kitchen on low stools, and she leaned close to me,
wary of eavesdroppers. "Sleeping with my husband is causing me
pain," she confided.

Her answer was certainly not what I expected to hear. I asked
some questions, trying to clarify this all in my mind. It didn't even
occur to me that the small opening we were left with after circumcision would figure into this picture, let alone cause major
problems.

"Every night since we married, my husband has tried to open

my closed-up privates with his. I cannot even skip a night, or it will close up again and become even more painful."

She told me how she screamed and moaned with pain as her husband tried to penetrate her. I was shocked by how matter-of-factly she described the agony. After every attempt, she went into the bathroom and cleaned herself with betadine to prevent infection. She did this night after night until her hole was big enough.

I was mortified to hear her explanation and felt sympathy as she spoke; I finally began to fit together all my little scraps of knowledge about sex. *How would a baby ever come out of this hole?* I wondered.

As we spent time together in the coming weeks, I watched as her pain intensified. She lost weight and her face was drawn in agony. It must have been comforting for her to have someone to talk to, because she continued to educate me.

"Some women have themselves sewn back up after every child," she announced.

I added this information to the list of things I now knew about sex, though I still didn't really understand why a woman would do that. It wasn't until I was an adult and had traveled to Switzerland to visit my sister Sofiya that I understood what she had been trying to tell me. I was talking with one of Sofiya's friends when the subject turned to circumcision.

"I know a woman from northern Somalia who bragged to me about having herself sewn back up after she divorced her husband," she said. "She wanted to give the next man the sense that she was a virgin again."

"You women from the south don't know how to get a man!" this northerner had told her. "We get ourselves sewn back up just like when we were little girls." The northern woman was so proud that she told her new husband, "Abdiyow, isn't my hole so tiny? You can barely get in it!"

I laughed in disbelief that a woman would do that to her body on purpose, enduring not only the pain of the sewing up but of the opening again. But this description triggered memories from my own youth. I heard little girls playing in the courtyard bragging things like, "My hole is so small even a little twig can't fit in there!" If another girl insulted you by calling you *kintirleey*, "the one with a clitoris," you immediately went into a corner with her and flashed your private parts to defend your purity. This behavior was so common among school-aged girls that we took it as part of life. No girl wanted to be accused of having a clitoris. It was not surprising that women wanted to be closed up again; it made them feel more normal and worthy.

Any lingering questions I had about sex were answered in a most unanticipated way. Late one evening, I had just finished watching a black-and-white French movie in the TV room at home. The tape was still running, but I was too tired to get up and turn off the VCR, so I just let it play out. All of a sudden, the forbidden land appeared right there in front of me. I snapped to attention. After the credits rolled, a half-naked woman with a big bosom ran across the screen with a completely naked man chasing her, his penis swinging from side to side. They ran around, fast and comical, like an old Charlie Chaplin movie. There was nothing attractive or alluring about the scene, but I needed these naked people to educate me. I closed the door but remained vigilant in case anyone walked in; I would be in serious trouble if I were discovered. With my heart beating with deafening sound, I continued to watch.

Soon enough the man was on top of the woman, and I felt an odd mixture of shame, guilt, and excitement. When I heard noises coming from behind the TV room door, I jumped up in a blind panic and fumbled with every button and switch, trying to make it stop. When the horrible noises didn't stop, I yanked the plug from the wall. I stood frozen in the middle of the room, trying to process the information I had inadvertently received.

For weeks, any time someone wanted to talk to me, I was certain they had found me out. I was so jumpy that I often dropped anything that was in my hands. I never watched French movies again while living in that house, and I was sure I was the only Somali girl who had seen any kind of pornography.

As if my father instinctively knew of my growing curiosity about sex and boys, out of nowhere he came and announced that he wanted to take us all to his hometown of Galkayo. I was settled happily into life in Mogadishu and was attached to my sister and her family, especially my baby niece. Arafo was happy living with Sofiya. Life was good again, and here was my father, who had not been involved in our daily lives for the past five years or more, wanting to take us away. In all honesty, I had no attachment to him and when I thought of him, the only thing that came to mind was his brutality.

My father had decided that he really did not know us, and he was upset that Hamdi and Liban had been taken from the country and he had lost connection with them. Odd that he decided to get to know us in the middle of political unrest. Abshiro was against my father taking us to a place that was already experiencing violence. But my father was determined. We were told to pack all of our belongings, right down to our beds. He meant to keep us for good.

In the end, Arafo, Guleed, Hubi, and I were forced to go with him. The only concession our father made to our worried sisters was that if the fighting escalated, he would bring us back to Mogadishu.

8 Journey

God hadimo ha qodin, hadaad qodana ha dheerayn—
ku dhici doontaa ma ogide.
Don't ever dig a treacherous hole in the ground; and if you
do, do not make it a bottomless pit, for you might just end
up in it.
—Somali proverb

THE JOURNEY TO my father's hometown, a place I hadn't seen since I was a little girl, started early in the morning. We boarded the bus, our possessions strapped to the roof along with all the other travelers' bundles. The bus was filled with people and their belongings. The only thing missing were goats in the aisles. Even though the safety of the roads had become unpredictable as political unrest had grown, and people had been attacked on this very road, life continued as usual, out of necessity. I settled into the seat next to Arafo, by the window in case my famous motion sickness overtook me. We still felt apprehensive, but at the same time we were excited to see my father's other family.

I watched the sun rise and set in its never-ending dance with the sky during our two-day journey to Galkayo. My favorite moment was when the sky turned red behind the dark silhouettes of the acacia trees, in that instant before the sun headed to its hole and night swallowed the evening. It left me feeling nostalgic, longing to hear the sound of the camels' wooden bells and the bleating of baby goats. The beauty of nature enchanted me, and I felt happy to be on the move once again. Not only was I swept away by the passing landscapes, but as we bumped along that road, my siblings and I talked together in a way we had not for a long time.

The bus abruptly slowed as we came to an unusually rough patch in the road. Before we had time to think about what was happening, tough-looking men with guns swarmed out and surrounded us. We knew bandits preyed on unsuspecting travelers, but never thought it would happen to us. One man, with deep black, haunted eyes, boarded the bus and demanded that people give him their belongings.

My father told the man to leave us alone. "We have nothing of value," he said. "You are frightening children and women."

The man grew agitated and ordered everyone to get off of the bus or else he would hurt us. Bandits were notorious for raping young women, and our fear escalated.

"Leave us be," my father pleaded. "If you do so, Allah will reward you for your good deeds."

By now, more men had come on board. My father's words seemed to enrage them, and they started shuffling passengers off. In the midst of this confusion, out of nowhere, the loudest voice we had ever heard in our lives filled the bus. It brought everything to an instant halt. People glanced around with bewildered faces.

Who was speaking in such a voice? It was my father. He stood, and his prayer call echoed throughout the whole bus.

My siblings and I sat frozen with shock and confusion.

"It is not a prayer time, so why is father calling for prayer?" Arafo whispered.

Our father continued to call *"Hayi alla fallah, hayi alla salah"* at the top of his lungs.

Oddly, the men, dazed and confused by the forceful prayer, ran off of the bus. They were no match for my father, who was an expert at fending off jin. In no time, the whole group of bandits disappeared from view. My father's tactic had worked, and we were safe for now. The people on the bus all got up and thanked him for his courage and told stories of being robbed by bandits before.

My siblings and I felt relieved—and proud of our father as well. He had proved he could keep us safe after all. At that moment, we all felt our father's love for us. It was a rare feeling.

We finally arrived at his house in Galkayo, which was now occupied by his wife, Sureer, the girl he had married in Luuqjeelow almost ten years ago. The house was filled with her children and two children from one of my father's other wives, to whom he was no longer married. Sureer was a tall, lean, dark-skinned woman with well-defined features. Although she was only in her midtwenties, she looked much older.

The house was dirty, smelled terrible, and was in desperate need of repair. Paint peeled off the walls, both inside and out. The cement floor had cracks here and there, and random holes everywhere. My father was nearly seventy by this time, and I just figured that he didn't care to quarrel with his young wife about how to keep a home. I did not like seeing another woman in the space my mother once inhabited so lovingly, and the house felt distant and strange to me. The last time I was here, my mother was alive, the house was clean and welcoming, and there was a feeling of warmth and comfort. That feeling was gone now.

The pigeon coops my father had built so many years ago still clung to the eaves of our house, although they also looked dilapidated and held fewer birds. When I was little, I felt like my father gave more attention to his pigeons than to us. Once, a huge *uri*, a feral tomcat with a big head and strong jaws, cleverly figured out a way to climb our tall, straight cement wall and get to the pigeons. My father tried everything to scare that uri away short of reading the Quran over him, but once the cat got a taste of pigeon, he wasn't easily deterred. Suddenly, the cat disappeared. Although he never said anything, we all knew our father had eliminated the threat to his pigeons.

We had barely settled back into Galkayo again when our father heard a cat yowling loudly in distress. I believed my father and cats were sworn enemies after that incident with the uri back when I was little, but he appeared unsettled by the cries and went to investigate. He discovered that the cat was stuck in our septic tank with no way to escape. My father tied a reluctant Guleed, who was small for a fourteen-year-old, to the end of a rope and lowered him into that excrement-filled hole. Our brother picked up the filthy creature and held him while our father pulled them out. After Guleed and the cat were both doused with buckets of water, that ungrateful cat took off running.

I was really perplexed by my father's actions. No one I knew in Somalia owned a cat or a dog as a pet. Any person who dared to mention the idea of a pet hospital would have had found themselves tied up and having the Quran read over him so fast that whatever jin was determined to possess him would have fled in terror. Sometimes I felt that my father valued animals over his children. His behavior was certainly contradictory. One minute, he could be making sure we got the best education possible, but the next minute, we could be lowered into a sewer. To me it seemed like his actions said, "I have so many kids, I can really spare you." Deep down, I know my father cared about all of us, but sometimes now I wish I could ask him, "What on earth were you thinking, Father?"

ONE MORNING, WHEN we hadn't lived in Galkayo more than six months, we woke as usual, ate breakfast, and began preparing for school. But as we got ready, we noticed our father was very quiet and pensive. He was sitting on his prayer mat, and my eyes fixed on his thick fingers as they rapidly flicked over the prayer beads in his hand.

As we were about to leave the house, he stopped us. "Just sit for a minute. There is no school today." At this point, he had to tell us the truth. "The Habargidir and Macherten subclans went to war last night and the whole city is deserted."

This went far beyond the usual intermittent fighting among

clans; this was full-blown war, a greater reflection of the turmoil that was making its way into the whole country. As we slept peacefully in our house, people were slaughtered just outside our door. Abshiro had feared this would happen, and now my father knew that he had made an error by bringing us to Galkayo. We were filled with apprehension, but not yet panic. We listened carefully as our father instructed us to prepare for traveling. We packed a few belongings, but it never occurred to me this could be the last time we saw our house in Galkayo.

The reality of our situation hit us as we walked through the empty town. Stray dogs wandered, bewildered, and the only sound came from the wind, which blew flocks of abandoned papers around. Together we moved as quickly as possible through the abandoned city. My eyes were drawn once again to my father's fingers, which urgently worked over the prayer beads in his right hand as he silently prayed. When I recall our flight out of Galkayo, the worn brown prayer beads in my father's hand stand out most in my memory. He seemed calm, but we could still feel his unease as he guided two-thirds of his offspring through a dangerous killing zone.

We walked toward Halibokhad, a town ten kilometers away that my father had established himself, where he had another home as well as a farm. Several cars stopped to offer us a ride, but my father waved them on when they didn't have enough room to take our whole family. We must have walked close to eight kilometers before an open cargo truck came by, and we all gratefully climbed in the back.

My father was well respected in Halibokhad, and most of my siblings had spent time there as kids. It was a kind of summer-house for my father's families. When school was out or on week-ends, they headed to Halibokhad. It was a smaller community where most people were transitioning from nomadic life to town life. My father was known for something in every town he lived in, whether it was the big military tent he erected in my mother's yard in Luuqjeelow or the pigeons in Galkayo. In Halibokhad, he was known for the deep well he once dug. The town had fertile soil, but the inconsistent water supply depended heavily on the unreliable seasonal rains. He believed a well was the answer to the droughts the town experienced. My father, workers, and machines dug for years, and the hole was so deep that I imagined it was inch-ing toward the core of the earth. But it never produced a drop of water. It was a colossal waste of manpower and money and in the end became the most feared hole in town. The uncovered well was very close to our house, and all the dirt that had been excavated from the well created a hill around it—very enticing for children to climb.

When Hubi was just a baby, she crawled up the hill, but kept sliding back down before she got to the top. My mother spied her just when she finally made it to the top and ran toward her child without a word, fearing Hubi would get distracted and fall. Hubi was saved, and to my knowledge, nobody ever died in that hole, which is miraculous. It was such a long, narrow well there would be no way to retrieve a body to give it a proper Muslim burial if someone fell in. You'd just have to rest in peace there. My father continued to dig this hole for most of his life. A share of this house and the bottomless, waterless pit that goes along with it is part of my inheritance. I think I'll stick with my ayeeyo's goats.

My siblings and I had been working on our father's farm in Halibokhad every weekend since we came to Galkayo, and now that we had moved there, we worked every day. Arafo, Guleed, and I built a wire fence all around the farm and tended the watermelon and beans my father planted. Other people from my father's clan thought eating beans was beneath them, but my father told us beans were nutritious. Even as an older man, he was health conscious and fit; he even ran for exercise. Normally, people in Somalia run only if an animal is chasing them.

I worked so hard on my father's farm that Arafo became worried.

She nudged me as I was immersed in my work one day. "Don't give our father a reason to keep us here longer, Shugri. Do you want this life for yourself?" she asked.

I did not want our father to keep us as laborers, but I knew what he was capable of when angry. I didn't want to get in trouble with him, but Arafo thought if we acted useless or inept, he would send us back to Abshiro, which was what we both wanted.

It didn't matter—we weren't long in Halibokhad before it, too, began to feel unsafe. A feeling of lawlessness thickened the air, and we watched a constant parade of men with guns passing through this once-quiet town. My father was particularly worried that we older girls would be raped under his watch, so Arafo, Guleed, Hubi, and I were packed up and dropped off at the safest place he could think of: the nomadic land of his brother, my *adeer* (uncle) Shafi'i. Father figured we could stay there for a short time until the war subsided and then could return to Galkayo. We got a ride to a place called Ba'ad Wayne, and from there we walked. We walked . . . and walked . . . and walked . . . until we came across a young girl looking after her goats.

We asked her how far we were from our destination, and she said, "It is behind those trees. Keep walking and you will see it soon."

When a nomadic person tells you something is near, assume you will have to walk at least another twenty kilometers. We finally got there, exhausted and hungry. To other nomadic people, we had not done any walking at all. *"Ba, aa,"* they ridiculed, "are you complaining of this little walk?" They looked at us as if we were weak or sick, which we were by then.

I was a nomad again, this time as a teenager. My obsession with my hair and tailored clothes faded into the background and the profound groundedness and connection to the land that rooted me as a child flooded back in. The longing and sense of nostalgia I had buried deep inside when I arrived at the orphanage surged up, and my soul was finally at ease. I was home. After all, I had once roamed this terrain under the protection of my ayeeyo. Here, she imbued me with a love of poetry, storytelling, and above all, the beauty of our culture. Seeing vast open land again triggered a need for ritual: for daily duties and the responsibility of nomadic life. I was ready to herd. But I soon learned you face more dangers as a teenager than as a young, curious, but blissfully ignorant child still under your grandmother's watchful eye.

As the night lifted on our first morning, my adeer's close-knit family rose and began their daily work. This rhythm felt both familiar and comforting. I knew what to do, but my body had grown soft after living in the city. I was also unfamiliar with this particular area; these were not my ayeeyo's nomadic lands. Still, I was excited to get back in the routine, herding animals to grazing land and bringing them back home in the evening. My city-raised siblings did not appreciate my self-righteous air of "Let me show you how this is done."

On my first morning, I went with my cousin to herd the goats, while my brother and sisters stayed close to the hut. My cousin was happy for the company, and we chatted about life along the way. As usual, I was full of questions, especially about the kinds of dangers on their land. I used her knowledge to verify my own memory and to make sure my intuitions were right. We made sure to watch for predators. Nomads don't usually send two young women out to herd together for fear they will get distracted by socializing while foxes or wild dogs eat away at their precious livestock. However, they made an exception in this case because they considered me a city girl, incapable of herding alone. It was like a training period. But no one needed to worry; we took our job very seriously.

At midday, as the heat of the desert sun peaked, we brought the animals close to the hut and left them resting in the shade while we went in to get what I hoped would be a full lunch. But all they gave us was a steaming cup of hot chai with milk. The inside of that hut, with its fire burning, felt even hotter than the sunbaked land outside. We had walked for hours, and a little meat would have helped, but we were only offered hot tea. My cousin was quite satisfied with this lunch, but I was still hungry. The irony was, the meal was similar to what I ate for lunch as a child, although ayeeyo always added a little oodkah, but I had become accustomed to a full meal in the middle of the day. Worse, there sat Arafo, happily chatting with an older woman, acting like she belonged there. Sweat ran down my back, mixing with the layer of dirt covering me, triggering an itchy rash. I knew there was not enough water to rinse myself off, and I longed for the good showers and baby powder we had in the orphanage. But nomads do not complain, so I followed my cousin back to resume our herding.

I spent several days working happily with my cousin. And yet I realized that some things that never bothered me as a child were uncomfortable now. Not only could I not wash regularly, but even when we did get a little water to wash with, privacy was nonexistent. Everything took place in the open desert where anyone could walk by. When I was little, going to the bathroom outside was normal. I even used to like watching dung beetles roll my waste along the desert floor, leaving fine tracks behind. Now I felt like a wild animal myself, and burying my feces was a job I did not want to deal with. I had to laugh at myself. I had been teasing my siblings about being city kids, but I had grown soft myself.

One day while my cousin and I were out, I saw oxen grazing in the distance. The whole area seemed covered with them, although I did not see their herder.

As we got closer, I asked my cousin, "Why are there only bulls? Where are the females?"

"They keep the females separate. They export the bulls to other countries when they are fattened up."

I saw that the oxen were not branded, which seemed odd to me. "You don't know who the bull herders are then?" I asked.

"No. Everyone knows our clan and so there is no trouble," she answered with pride.

I was unsatisfied with her answer, but I told myself I should trust her because she knew the rules here better than I did. But a feeling deep in my gut told me, *You should be worried.* Within minutes, I saw a figure hiding in the trees, slowly coming toward us.

I turned to my cousin and asked, "Is that normal? Look, a man is hiding in the bushes. He is getting closer. Look, he's hiding behind a different tree now. Abaayo, is that okay?"

My anxiety grew even deeper as I saw the man pick up his pace while still hiding in the bushes. He was running toward us faster than I could communicate with my cousin. I was now convinced that he had a plan to hurt us. In the very instant that I grabbed my cousin to warn her, he broke toward us at full speed. We turned and ran toward home, but heard his heavy breathing a few steps behind us. It was clear that he did not care about our clan or fore- fathers; he wanted to attack us. As we ran, we scanned the land for anyone who could help. Ahead, I saw a group of nomads talking among themselves. Luckily, we made it to them before our feet gave out. Gasping and out of breath, I blurted out, "That man is chasing us for no reason."

In that instant, he stopped behind us, panting as hard as we were. I could see that he was a thin, tall, dark-skinned young man of about twenty with an ominous gaze.

He stared directly at us and insisted, "That is not the truth. I wanted to talk to them, but they just started running."

One of the women started scolding him, evoking both my uncle's name and our family tree. "Why did you chase them then? If you want to die, then go ahead and bother these girls." The man looked startled, apologized, and left.

Our forefathers are our security officers; the more respected your lineage, the more protection you have. But this only works if the person who wants to hurt you knows your clan lines and is afraid of the consequences. This stranger would have raped us regardless of our clan if he could have gotten away with it. I had never been so scared—we feared rape so much that we thought it was better to be killed than to be raped.

That bull herder knew from the way I was dressed that I was not a nomadic girl, which may be one of the reasons he came after us. I was still wearing tailored clothes, an eighties hairstyle, and sandals. He assumed he could get away with attacking us. Also, because his bulls were not branded, he knew there was no way for us to find out who he was. I realized then how widespread the political unrest was. The sense of lawlessness that it brought was even infiltrating the nomadic way of life. The whole country was heading into mayhem, and there would be no escaping it.

ALTHOUGH THE INCIDENT with the bull herder had me scared, I needed to be busy and out in nature with the animals. So the next day, I went to herd the camels with another one of my other relatives, a teenager a little older than I. Like my other cousins, she had a strong body; she was not skinny for someone living in this environment of scarcity and hardship. My uncle did not want us to take the camels as far as usual because one of the females was about to give birth.

The camels were grazing peacefully when suddenly I saw a male camel break into a trot, heading straight at me. His huge eyes were fixed on me, his mouth was covered in white frothy spit, and he was grunting loudly. I bolted out of his way and hid behind a tree hardly big enough to hide a baby goat. He picked up speed and then stopped right in front of my tree, his eyes darting around as if he was trying to find me. Suddenly, he produced a huge red sack of skin, which dangled out the side of his mouth like a giant bubble, and let out the scariest grunt yet. His disgusting display was intended to persuade females to mate with him, and for some reason he was fixated on me. I moved from one tree to another to try to trick him, but this massive male camel in full heat was not fooled. My cousin laughed as I pathetically hid behind the scrawny trees and he continued to display his big red sack and court me with loud, disturbing noises.

I answered her with nervous laughter, "If this camel spends

any more time chasing me, he's not going to get any female camels to mate with him."

My cousin thought it had something to do with the bright red dress I was wearing, but I wasn't convinced at the time. When I told this story to a friend in California recently, however, I guessed, "Perhaps male camels are like bulls and don't like the color red."

But my friend had a different theory. "Some female animal's butts turn big and red when they are in heat, so he must have thought you were a female camel. He was probably thinking, *Oh, she's ready!*" We laughed hard, thinking about the camel who was aroused by my red dress.

WHEN THE NEXT dhaan day arrived, my siblings and I accompanied my uncle and my cousin Faduma to the well. Faduma and I were spending more and more time together, and I was becoming quite fond of her. She never minded my endless silly questions like other nomads did. We started our day early so we could get back before nightfall, leading just one camel to fetch the water. It was not normal for this many people to lead one camel, but they were patient with us city kids. My siblings and I went along partly for the experience, but more important, to wash ourselves and our clothes at the well.

On the way, my uncle warned us about the camel that would be carrying the water. "He was once bitten by a hyena, so when night comes, if he hears the hyena, even from a distance, he destroys all that he is carrying and takes off running."

This is good to know, I thought, *but it does not matter to me because I will never be leading this camel anyway.*

My cousin took the camel's reins as I continued to pepper her with questions about the land we were crossing. "What lives there? How about there?" If I heard something in the distance, I asked, "What was that?" not from fear but curiosity.

Soon she pointed to a rocky, covered area far away from us and said, "That area is where the lions reside."

I felt uneasy. I feared lions more than any other wild animal. The stories I heard as a child of lions eating my people had still haunted me. I comforted myself by thinking, *No one in my nomadic family seems to be scared of the lions, so why should I be afraid?* To be honest, I was still brave, but not as brave as that little girl back in Ayeeyo's nomadic lands.

When we reached a large, dry, grassy area, my cousin said, "This is home to hyenas."

Knowing we had left the lion's territory, I began to feel more comfortable.

After a long walk, we finally reached the well, which was surrounded by herds of people and animals. A kind of organized chaos with a sense of excitement buzzing through it filled both the crowd and the herds of animals. Each family waited their turn while young camel herders with beautiful, smooth, black skin and breathtaking smiles pulled up the water with fluid grace and speed. They used a pouch made from the flexible inner tube of a tire to draw up the water, filled their own vessels, and then helped a few families, before turning the job over to the next group of young men. The air was rich with the sound of the men singing in unison as they went about their task, the bleating of goats, mooing of cows, the soft bellow of the baby camels, and the sound of the water filling the long wooden trough the animals drank from. The soil turned a deeper shade of red near the well, where it was always damp and you could see the footprints of animals and humans alike.

The men lingered, eager for a chance to spot a beautiful girl. Flirtations were exchanged, but almost imperceptibly. The well provided a place and time for youngsters to mingle and socialize. Since our help wasn't needed, my siblings and I washed ourselves by a tree that provided a slight shelter and tried to forget we were taking a shower in front of everyone with our clothes on. Then we just stood and watched the festive gathering around us while the sun quickly dried our clothes.

This water hole is life, I thought as I watched streams of livestock and humans approaching the well and leaving with bellies so distended they looked like they might pop. I was so mesmerized by the scene that I wanted to linger longer before we headed home. A woman leading multiple camels laden with huts approached from the left side, and in that instant, I thought of my ayeeyo. It felt bittersweet to be in the nomadic lands where I felt so close to her, but the distance and danger was too great for me to travel to see her. I watched as the woman moved closer, hoping she would turn out to be my ayeeyo, but she was much too young to fool even my hopeful heart.

When it was time to start the journey back home, my uncle

suddenly announced that he needed to go to the city to get some essentials, and that he was taking our cousin with him. *Well,* I thought, *we are all heading to town then.* But my uncle said he wanted someone to take the camel back home.

Confused, I thought, *Does our uncle want three city teens to take this camel home?* I was sure he had some other plan. But before I had a chance to ask, my siblings announced they were heading to town with him. I wanted to go with them, too, but I respectfully waited for my uncle to tell me his plan. I was sure that since my siblings were excused from leading the camel back, then I was, too. But luck was not with me.

My uncle announced, "The family has been without water for days; this dhaan must head back home tonight. Who needs a blessing and will take this dhaan back to the family?"

Blessings like that are funny things: if you don't obey them, they turn into curses. I also didn't want to disappoint my uncle, so I agreed to take the camel back. I pleaded with my siblings to come with me, but they had made up their minds. They were not heading back to that predator-filled desert without my uncle and cousin. They went so far as to physically separate from me, standing with my uncle and cousin. I felt that taking this dhaan by myself was a death sentence, but clearly my uncle had confidence in me. I quickly prodded my cousin for more details on how to lead a camel and asked my uncle what to do if the camel ran for his life and deserted me.

His only answer was, *"Insha Allah* ["God willing"], all will go well."

Gripping the reins as if my life depended on it, I became acutely aware of my fate. I pictured the wild animals that might be lying in wait for me, including hyenas or worse, lions. Regret sank in immediately, and I turned to call them but it was too late. They were gone.

Frightened and alone, I started my long journey home. I took off in the direction my uncle pointed out, hoping the night would have mercy. I thought, *If I am going to die tonight, at least it will be because I was being brave, and that is an honorable way to die.* I looked up at my camel. His big eye with its elegant eyelashes regarded me with an "I hope you know what you are doing" look. To show the camel I was in charge, I moved with authority, hiding my terror. I started to sing the old nomadic songs my ayeeyo had taught me, to dispel the eerie quietness. When I ran out of songs, I talked to the camel like a friend, sharing my fears. I figured the sound of a human voice would keep the animals away and might trick them into thinking I was not alone.

As the sun set on the unfolding terrain and night approached, I became more and more terrified. *What should I do if I am attacked?* I had no clue. I just had to deal with problems as they were thrown at me. There was no other choice but to be brave. I forced myself to focus on the camel's behavior; it would be catastrophic if he decided to destroy the water vessels.

Finally, the fullness of the night was upon us and I could hear birds, what sounded like a distant lion, and a hyena whining close by. With every step I took, it seemed like something moved or jumped out of my way, but I refused to investigate. My only guide toward home was my uncle's last instruction, "As you travel farther in that direction, you will see a fire. That is where you need to head." My camel, having keener hearing than I, wanted to pull the reins out of my hands to show me who was in control as he got more frightened. I knew he heard the hyenas laughing in the distance, and I remembered my uncle's warning about his fear of them. I tightened my grip and pulled the rope closer to me. I was now making loud, random, incoherent noises to look more intimidating, which would have been funny to anyone who heard me. It took my whole ninety pounds to control this oversized, increasingly agitated beast who wanted to run wild. At one point, I was so frightened that I thought about climbing on top of the camel so that if we were attacked, I could jump down, leap over our attackers, and run while the animals fed on the camel. But then I decided that if I were to get wounded in the process, my blood would bring all of the wild animals to me. I decided to keep walking and meet my fate. I didn't have long to wait.

We heard the sharp cackle of another hyena, and without warning, my camel sat on the ground, threatening to destroy our water vessels. I would not be the one to leave families without life-sustaining water, so I tried to pull my thoughts together and figure out how to make this camel do the impossible: get up. I stood in front of him, screaming and pulling the reins in all directions. The camel complained and whined with every tug. He was now leaning from side to side, trying to unload himself. Out of desperation, I picked up two sticks and tickled the inside of his ears. It looked like he wanted to get up, but he sat back down whenever I softened the tickle. Encouraged, I found two stronger sticks and swirled hard inside his ears. My camel whined loudly—and at last launched into an upright position. I took the lead, cursing at him as we headed toward the fire twinkling far in the distance.

In the utter blackness of night, I finally made it to the village. My uncle's family helped me unload the water while I told them of my adventures with the camel. They laughed but were impressed with my solution.

The next evening, when my uncle arrived, another relative told him my story. He praised me, saying I was one of a kind. He pointed out that this was the first time anyone had managed to stop this camel from sitting down and destroying the water vessels. My uncle laughed hard when he learned what I had to do to get the camel to cooperate. "You did what to his ear?" he asked in between laughs. Even now, I feel proud when I recall that journey and how I conquered my fears.

ALTHOUGH I WAS enjoying myself, happy to be back in the desert, Arafo was miserable. "This is not our life," she told me, frustrated because I wasn't eager to leave like she was. I liked being with the animals, but even a placid cow made Arafo feel uneasy.

My uncle was milking his cows one evening when he asked Arafo to bring him the hadhuub, the milking bowl.

"I can't, adeer."

"Why not?" he asked in confusion.

"Because the cow is looking at me, adeer," she replied.

"So, the cow is looking at you. What does that have to do with you bringing me the hadhuub?"

"I am afraid of her!"

My uncle broke into laughter at such a ridiculous statement and asked his little boy to fetch it for him. Our cousin ran right over and brought it to him, crossing right in front of the scary cow without a thought.

Shortly after that incident, my father came to visit and my uncle had a serious talk with him. My uncle was concerned for our safety. Besides my close encounter with the bull herder, more stories of young women getting attacked had reached our uncle. My father had brought us here because he thought it would be safer, but my uncle could see that his nomadic lands were no better. He could see we stuck out from the nomadic way of life, bringing ourselves unwanted attention.

"This one is afraid of cows and hides in fear when she sees any man she doesn't know," he said, pointing to Arafo. "You need to take these girls back home," my uncle pleaded.

My father had to stop and think about where to take us. The fighting had intensified in Galkayo and the surrounding area, so that wasn't an option. He decided to take all of us back to Halibokhad and, from there, to find transport to Mogadishu. When Abshiro learned we were trying to get back, she arranged for our nephew Abdirashid, who was a long-distance truck driver, to bring all of us girls back to her house. My father insisted on keeping Guleed with him in Halibokhad, however.

We were indeed lucky; soon after we made it to Mogadishu, the road we had taken became impossible to cross. Abdirashid was attacked on his next trip to Mogadishu. Bullets hit his back, paralyzing him. He was rushed abroad for treatment, but he never regained the function of his legs. Today he lives in Canada, wheelchair bound. I am forever in his debt for saving our lives. His wounds are a reminder of how close we all came to getting killed that day.

9 Goodbye, Mogadishu

*Maroodigu takarta isaga saran ma arkee, takarta kan kale
saaran ayuu arkaa.*
*As each elephant can easily spot the flea on another
elephant's back, so some men can only find fault with
others but not with themselves.*
—Somali proverb

I STILL HAVE an image of Mogadishu as it was when Somalia was
at peace, which contrasts with the reality of Mogadishu today:
war-torn, ravaged, and seemingly sent back to the Stone Age. In
my Mogadishu, the sky is blue, the streets are white, the ocean is a
beautiful turquoise color and is edged by soft white sand; flowers
bloom with unnatural beauty in all seasons. Peace, prior to the
late 1980s, was taken for granted, as it should be, and everyone was
busy living life. Neighbors loved and checked on each other; even
our clan differences did not stop us from caring for one another.
Religion was practiced with kindness, and cultures were valued. I
loved that Somalia, and I still long for it.

When I was in my early teens, Mogadishu was at the peak of
its progress. For Somali women, cracks of change appeared everywhere, thanks to Siad Barre's policies. He treated women as equals,

which angered conservative religious men. I am not overlooking the fact that we were living under a dictatorship. Siad Barre forced anyone who disagreed with him, even highly educated people, into exile or had them executed. He committed many more atrocities, but I wasn't aware of them at the time. In my teenage world, free from adult responsibility, I only saw the positive changes.

In the early 1970s, Siad Barre had insisted on literacy for all Somalis, regardless of age, social class, or gender. His investment in education, especially for girls, narrowed the gender gap that was prevalent throughout Africa. By the time I was a teenager, before Wahhabism took hold, I was benefiting from the fruits of his labor. Somali women had more opportunities and enjoyed greater freedom and inclusivity. Women could attend universities alongside men and enter the workforce in any field they chose. In the city, they started talking about the negative impact female circumcision was having on women's health, which was a big step forward for women's rights. I saw two of my sisters attend university, and another work for Somali Airlines. Their success showed me that I, too, could aspire to be anything I wanted—my gender would no longer limit my future.

WHEN WE RETURNED to Mogadishu in mid-1990, I settled back into my normal routine with my sister and her family. But a strange energy permeated the city, and for the first time, I could feel fear in the air. At my school, there were a lot of new students who were clearly not from Mogadishu. Some came to the city from as far away as North Somalia, looking for one last place of refuge. One look in their eyes and I could tell they had already seen the horrors of war. They expressed their hatred of President Barre openly.

For the first time ever, I was mugged. My friends and I had gone out for afternoon tea and were walking back from the sweet store, lost in conversation. We passed the statue commemorating Sayyid Muhammed Abdullah Hasan, a fierce resistance fighter from the Colonial Era, whom the British called Mad Mullah after they could not beat him. When two teenage boys walked toward us we didn't think much about it, but the next thing I knew, one of the boys had grabbed my gold necklace and torn it from my neck with such force that he spun me halfway around. I was caught so off-guard by the attack that all I could do was watch him flee with my jewelry.

Despite this low-grade violence, Mogadishu was still a little island of peace in the midst of chaos. My father even had Guleed flown to Mogadishu when fighting in Galkayo escalated. We had no idea that we would all soon be engulfed in a war that would eventually kill half a million people.

It started with random gunshots at night. During the day, when the shots abated, we went to the market for our daily groceries. In the evening, neighbors gathered in front of their homes and speculated about what was happening. In those early days, most people thought that clan forces had joined together to overthrow Barre, who had openly declared war on the north. Reports on the government-controlled radio and in newspapers indicated that everything was under control, but what people saw and heard outside their own doors contradicted the government's assurances.

"They must be holding a gun to the announcer's head to get

him to say nothing is wrong," one man said. As weeks passed, the reports from the streets became even more ominous.

"I saw a dead body in an alley on my way to market this morning," one neighbor reported.

"The market was practically empty today," another added, "and they didn't even have everything I needed."

Despite these reports, the violence still seemed disconnected from our daily life. But that all changed when gunshots were suddenly fired in broad daylight. People were randomly hit by flying bullets on their way to and from places that were supposed to be safe. Women reported bullets just missing them on their way to market. Our daily shopping became a suicide mission, yet we needed food. Sometimes I was pulled out of school early because violence had erupted nearby without warning.

It was clear something had shifted; tension between clans was smoldering. Neighbors who did not share the same clan started to mistrust each other. I heard whispers that my friend Laje'el's clan would wipe us out. Under the influence of fear, rumors started that our kind neighbors were collecting guns and machetes to kill our clan members. This was the worst thing that could happen in Somalia because, in reality, no family is purely of one clan. You could be from the Darod clan on your father's side, but your mother could be from the Hawiye clan, and then what? Do you stay under the protection of your father's clan, or run because your mother's clan might kill you?

I was frightened and confused by what was going on, but I didn't fully register the danger we were facing until something happened that I couldn't ignore. I was sitting in front of my sister's house, watching the happenings of my neighborhood as usual, when something flew past me and hit the wall behind me with a whizzing sound. I turned and touched a hole left in the cement. A bullet had missed my head by just a few inches. *I don't believe it. Am I hallucinating?* I thought. I buried my panic and never told my family, convinced that talking about it would make it more real. Like most teenagers, I thought I was invincible. But now I understood why my sister insisted we stay inside the house. She had even made the girls matching pajama dresses to wear as we stayed home, as if to say, "We are all in this together." At that point, we still had hope and thought if we stayed safe for now, things would get better.

One morning, I was sitting on Hubi's bed when I heard a noise coming from outside the window. I crept closer and saw a wild-eyed man with a gun crouching beside our house. His eyes were bloodshot, and he looked like he had not slept for nights. I looked over him to scan the open street beyond our house. The street was eerie and empty, with the exception of a few other men crouching by the windows of other houses. I gazed back at him and saw that he was chewing *qaad* leaves, an amphetamine-like stimulant common throughout the Horn of Africa and Arabian Peninsula that is also known as *khat*. The qaad protruded under his cheek and green stains covered his gum line. One look at his eyes told me he was under its influence. He whispered something—his accent was distinctly that of a northerner. The only clear message I got from him was when he put his finger over his lips. I did not make a sound after that.

I didn't know how to think about this strange Somali man. On one hand, he looked like my uncle, brother, or any other man in my life whom I loved. On the other hand, he had a look about him that scared me to the core. I comforted myself, *He is Somali. He will not hurt me.* But in reality, nothing about my country or my people was normal anymore. I knew that if I did not obey this man, things would go terribly wrong, so I closed the window and pretended that all was well. He did not bother my family. He was after a bigger fish: the government.

ON DECEMBER 31, 1990, Mogadishu entered into full-blown war.

Our lives changed in the weeks following December 31. We had been living on rice and pasta with butter and sugar, but even that was becoming scarce. There was no sautéed liver for brunch, or yellow rice topped with seasoned goat meat for lunch with fresh papaya juice to drink. It had been a long time since we had been able to go to market, and really, I didn't even think there was a market anymore; it was too dangerous. Neighbors shared whatever they had. We ate sitting in a circle in the center of my sister's house, away from the windows and stray bullets, always afraid that every meal would be our last.

One sound in particular filled me with panic and dread: the sound of a bazooka firing. It made a strange siren sound when it was launched, and the terror I felt in the time it took to hit its target was so raw that I can still feel its echo in my body all these years later. I never knew where it would hit. Would it be our house? Our neighbor's house? Somewhere far away? It was impossible to judge its destination. All I could do was run frantically around the house, waiting for the bazooka's warhead to hit its target. Once the sound ceased, I knew my life was spared and my family was safe, for the time being. While eating lunch one day, a loud bazooka hit near us unexpectedly, and I jumped and found myself sitting on top of the big plate we ate from communally. I felt bad for wasting our precious, meager meal, but during bouts of heavy gunfire, my body became spastic, reacting with every shot as if the bullets had struck me. At times, I literally had to search for bullets in my body, sure I had been hit.

For Abshiro, the scariest day was when she heard Siad Barre's warplane take off. She was convinced he would do what he had done in northern Somalia: bomb without regard to civilian casualties. She found herself on her knees, with her face on the floor, praying as the warplane hovered over our neighborhood, prepared to strike. Barre didn't drop a bomb that day; no one knows why he changed his mind. We lived in the center of the city in a densely populated neighborhood; the casualties would have been devastating.

As the fighting escalated, neighbors divided themselves along clan lines. It was no longer just military men or rebels fighting; ordinary men joined the fight to help their clan gain an edge. My Quran teacher was now teaching the Quran by day and concocting plans to attack my family's clan by night. The strange thing was that I had never thought of who my teacher's clan was before; he was just my Quran teacher. Suddenly we were his enemy.

Pickup trucks full of men high on qaad roamed our once-safe streets, agitated and ready to fire on anyone who wasn't of their clan. It was more important than ever to know your lineage; in times of uncertainty and chaos, people automatically reverted to their long-held clan ties. Siad Barre had promoted being Somali, and his regime forbade use of the clan system, but ironically, every man who protected him belonged to his own subclan. I never thought that one day I would need my dead forefathers' bloodlines to save my life. I only knew my full name, my main clan, and one subclan on my father's side. And in this climate, I not only needed to know my father's bloodline but my mother's and all the other clans in my genes.

We needed to leave. People were dying in Mogadishu's streets daily, and it was only a matter of time before my family joined the legions of dead bodies littering our streets. But how we would escape the city would prove more difficult than we anticipated.

For months, my sister had been telling her husband not to empty their savings into the huge new house he was building for the family. He didn't share her concern about the situation and continued to pour cash into the new construction. In fact, even after December 31, he was more relaxed than Abshiro was. But Abshiro was the mother of a toddler and a newborn and had the welfare of her siblings to worry about. Even if the children avoided being shot, lack of food and clean water was a threat to their little bodies. Abshiro gathered all her gold jewelry and the little cash she had and told Aadan to get all the men in my father's family together to get us out of Mogadishu. My father had remained in

Galkayo with his other family, so it was up to the other men of his family to help us.

When three days passed without hearing from Aadan, Abshiro grew even more worried. She sent Guleed to get Aadan, but he failed to come back as well. Desperate, she went to look for them herself. When she finally reached the Madina district of Mogadishu, she found Aadan and Guleed casually gathered with our other male relatives and their families. It looked to Abshiro like he had completely forgotten the dangerous state he had left us in, for Madina was a safe zone at this point. "How could you do this to us?" she wailed, sinking in despair to the floor.

Our relatives helped her to her feet and promised to help. They provided Aadan and Abshiro with an open cargo truck to collect the rest of us with and sent two male cousins to help. On their way back to our house, men wearing military uniforms and strapped with AK-47s stopped them and demanded they give up the truck they were driving. Everyone was fleeing Mogadishu, but there were not enough cars; people were mugging and robbing others in order to get their own families out of Mogadishu.

At gunpoint, my sister, brother, and cousins were ordered out of the truck. Abshiro felt her stomach sink with terror, but in her mind, there was no way she was returning empty-handed to her family.

When the commander put his gun to my cousin Hassan's head, Abshiro went into full protective-mother mode. She grabbed the commander and all his ammunition in a smothering hug and wailed, "*Abti, Abti* [Uncle, Uncle], don't you remember me!?"

The commander, dismayed and confused by my sister's outburst, took a step back from her grip and gave her a questioning look. She kept repeating, "Abti, abti," until his eyes softened. She had vaguely remembered seeing this man visiting our aunt, our mother's rich sister. Desperation had fueled her memory's quick recollection of a one-time encounter. It turns out this commander was related to my aunt's husband. The word *abti*, uncle, and seeing this mother's determination softened his heart. He not only gave her back the truck but ordered two of his men to go with them to secure safe passage.

While my sister was away getting help, the rest of the family and I were gathering our belongings. It was hard to think clearly enough to decide what I needed to take. My thoughts fired incoherently; I was in a state of shock and incredulity over what our life had become. I finally gained enough clarity to put the few clothes I had into a pillowcase. I scanned the house and saw pictures on the walls, cabinets full of unused dishes, and lines of clean clothes hanging in the center of the house. I wondered if I would ever see any of it again. It was all so surreal. I was being forced out of my nest. But at that point, the only thing I could think was, *Just don't get killed.*

Abshiro came home and told us we needed to walk to where they had parked the truck, behind an old Italian cathedral about two or three miles away. The truck could not fit through the narrow streets of our neighborhood, so she left it there, with the boys and the two military men guarding it. She told us we would head to the Madina district to stay with the rest of our family, and when the fighting subsided, we would come back home.

ON JANUARY 15, 1991, we set out on foot, leaving our Boondheere neighborhood and descending onto the paved streets of Mogadishu Center. It happened to be the deadline of the ultimatum that the UN Security Council had given Saddam Hussein: to either exit Kuwait or suffer the consequences. My family and I trudged through the streets, our backs laden with our large loads of possessions and children, our souls saturated with sadness and shock. We were not the only people fleeing the city; war had forced our fellow travelers out of their houses, too. Everywhere I looked, I saw people on foot, carrying baskets and babies. It was eerie and strange to see my people in this state.

As we got to the main street, I looked to the right, toward my high school. Only a few weeks ago, I had sat at my desk, studying chemistry. Now the building stood empty. I wondered what the rich kids were doing. It was no secret that the minute the situation got bad, those who had money or high governmental status took their families abroad. Some rich folks, though, did not believe this doomsday would come, and they found themselves in the same sinking boat as us.

As we walked along, we encountered groups of soldiers stopping civilian men. Some rebels had posed as civilians and attacked the soldiers, so they were searching everyone. At this point, Arafo was at the end of our group, behind Abshiro's epileptic brother-in-law, Mahamud. As she came over a rise, she saw a soldier holding a gun to Mahamud's head. The soldier was yelling orders at him, but years of seizures had altered his judgment, and he often escalated situations without meaning to. Arafo noticed that the soldier had lost his patience and was ready to fire, but he had a wounded arm and was fumbling with the trigger.

She ran up behind the soldier and called out, "Abti, I know this guy from my neighborhood; he is crazy."

Crazy was the only acceptable word to get him out of trouble, and luckily the soldier studied Mahamud's face and saw that he was drooling slightly. He lowered his gun and uttered nasty words at Mahamud as he ushered him along. Arafo may have saved him that day, but unfortunately, a year later, a bullet struck Mahamud and his school-age niece, killing two family members at once.

When we reached the old Italian cathedral, we were confronted by a scene of utter chaos and hell. The beautiful church and the trees around it were ablaze, flames dancing toward the sky. Smoke and sparks flew everywhere, and I suddenly became aware of the dead bodies scattered all around us.

My sister's voice broke through my thoughts, "Don't look down. You don't want to have nightmares."

I drew my eyes upward instead, to the steeple of the church. To my dismay, I saw the cross burning, hanging by a thin string. That cross had been a symbol of our coexistence with Christians. It signified that if one wanted to get respect for their religion, then they should do the same for others. Now that was all lost in a nightmarish haze.

We continued on, and to my relief, I finally spotted the truck waiting for us. Aadan helped me climb up, and it struck me that my brother looked more hardened and manly than he had just a week ago. *When did that happen?* He not only looked rougher and tougher in his cargo pants and boots but also walked and talked with a confidence and maturity that made me feel safe. We drove off, on edge, wondering who would attack us next.

Within minutes we were stopped by gunmen demanding to know our clan. I remember looking up at the men and thinking, *We are done.* Miraculously, we shared a clan with those men, so they let us go. We finally made it to the Madina district, where we planned to stay overnight. But Abshiro and Arafo returned to Boondheere, because Abshiro had quickly realized Madina wouldn't be a safe place to stay for long and her children did not have enough supplies for a longer journey. At this point, Abshiro was fearless; if she thought she needed to go back for something, no one could stop her. I watched with trepidation as my two sisters left, making their way on foot back into the war zone we had just fled.

While Abshiro was gone, more and more of my father's relatives began gathering in Madina, including many I had never met before. The only person missing was my father; he still refused to leave Galkayo. "I am *waadad*—a man of God. No one will bother me," he claimed. And it seems he was right. No serious harm came to him or his family. But the rest of my male relatives were arming themselves, preparing to protect and defend us by any means necessary. Aadan took a Land Rover from the cathedral, something he still feels guilty about, and Hassan took a large cargo truck. When Abshiro found out, she was upset with them. "Who is fool enough to steal only cars and leave a church full of gold and money behind?" she mocked.

My two sisters made it to our house and were relieved that it had not been looted yet. Arafo knew this might be the last time she saw the house, so she took some important personal items with her as well: pictures, letters, and her journal. On their return trip, Arafo encountered her beloved chemistry teacher, laden with all his personal belongings, a look of despair on his face. She loved this teacher very much and it broke her to see him this way. He was a cool, young teacher and all the girls in her class had crushes on him. She hid from him when she passed.

"What happened? Why are you hiding from him?" Abshiro asked.

"I don't want him to know I saw him in that state," Arafo replied.

On January 16, our whole family, numbering 250 and including screaming children, moaning elders, and young men and women alike, left Mogadishu in a caravan of cars, pickups, and open cargo trucks. That day, America, led by President George H. W. Bush, began bombing Iraq, an assault known as Operation Desert Storm. That event meant most of the world never knew of our suffering. Abshiro listened to BBC Somalia, hoping to hear news about our country, but our full-blown civil war received only a passing mention. Even a war was not enough to bring attention to our tiny, poverty-stricken country with so few resources.

We headed to Kismaayo, about 500 kilometers down the coast

from Mogadishu, closer to the border of Kenya. It was the safest place for members of our clan to live, and we still hoped that after the fighting subsided we could return home. We passed by Afgoye, a lush, green farm town where wealthy Somalis went for weekend getaways, before detouring to Shalambood, a city where one of my first cousins lived. She welcomed us by slaughtering goats for us, and all of our 250 family members slept wherever they could. Somalis have a saying, *"Ga'al isma ariiriyo,"* or "Loved ones never crowd each other." We slept well there, with our bellies full of seasoned goat meat and in the company of family.

When we arrived in Kismaayo, each part of the family arranged for their own lodgings. We stayed with relatives of my brother-in-law Ahmed-Nur. One afternoon I awoke dazed from an afternoon nap, with tears streaming down my cheeks. Abshiro was in the room with me, breastfeeding little Ruqiya. She had been watching me as I cried and sang in my sleep. She told me that I had been singing *"Maba doonayaane in aynu dowlad ahaano"* ("Don't they want us to be a unified country?"). Now that we had stopped moving, the atrocities my people were committing against each other finally hit me, weighing heavily on my heart. I couldn't understand how people could speak of their clan so highly while killing another clan. *Couldn't they see we were killing our sons, uncles, and aunts, raping our sisters and cousins?* My Somalia, I thought, was better than that.

Even in Kismaayo, we stayed in the house or yard most of the time, for safety. Rumors flew about which clan had the upper hand and where they were moving next. One late afternoon, as I looked through the cracks of the wall that surrounded our house, I saw a small, thin man leading a donkey laden with a water tank, plodding along without complaint. I assumed he was getting water for his family who lived a great distance away. He walked with a tired, haggard look on his face, his shoes covered in dust from a long journey, a mere piece of cloth wrapped around his waist to cover him. He was not dressed like other Somali men; clearly he was extremely poor. His features identified him as a Bantu man. I suddenly realized, *This is what happens to people who are always discriminated against. They are always poor.* Today, when I hear Somalis complain about being discriminated against in Western society, I find myself thinking, *Well, actually we are being treated with more hospitality and in a more humane way than we treated our own Somali people.* I hope we are learning through our current experience not to be bigots like we were when we had the upper hand.

I studied the poor man more closely as he passed my fence. He was middle-aged, light-skinned, with an innocent manner about him. Suddenly, a tall, haughty young man appeared out of nowhere, approached the Bantu man with the donkey, and began asking about his clan. The young man moved with arrogance, but I could tell by the way he carried his gun that he lacked experience. I was sure that once he discovered that the older man was Bantu, he would release him, since they were not involved in this war. I found myself silently pleading with the younger man, *Please let him go. He is a poor man who has come far to get water for his family. He has no clan, but he is Somali, just like us. Please don't hurt him.*

Faster than I could blink, the young man backed up, pulled the gun from his shoulder, and just like that, shot the Bantu man from head to toe. He instantly became a rag doll, his lifeless body falling in slow motion to the ground. I gasped and heard my own voice cry out. Grief and horror clasped my heart tightly, and I went cold. Before my eyes, a Somali had killed another Somali. *My people are horrible,* I thought.

That pompous young clan man killed the innocent Bantu man that day because he knew he could get away with it. Under Siad Barre's regime, he would have faced immediate consequences. He was taking advantage of the political unrest—there was no longer a government in place to enforce justice. Killing, looting, destruction, and chaos was now our norm.

Something in me died that day. It took me many years to get over seeing this murder, and sometimes I'm not sure I ever fully recovered. After that incident, I joined the sleepwalking ranks of my family. Sometimes now, after a particularly stressful time, I find myself experiencing night terrors. I wake up screaming, sweat soaking my sheets, with a sensation of being helpless, as if I couldn't save somebody from dying. I still find myself taking the blame for what happened that day, though I know rationally it was not my fault. For years after leaving Africa, the death of that man continued to haunt me. I finally found myself face to face with a therapist, sobbing because of what I witnessed that day. I still feel sad when I think of him. He is a reminder of all that went wrong in my country.

Kismaayo was a beautiful coastal city, with sparkling blue water and white sand. When it felt safe, I headed to the beach like a tourist, to lose myself in my own thoughts and ruminate about my current situation and past times. I walked along the shore as waves moved gently over my feet, water tickling my toes. I began to feel like a child who was free to play again. I was not the only person who was there to cleanse herself of the nightmares of war. Teen boys swam in the blue sea, their smooth, beautiful faces shining in the blazing sun as they moved in and out of the water like dolphins. I sat on a little white hill of sand dotted with plants and watched people from a safe distance. *How can my people spill blood in this beautiful land?* I asked myself. As the afternoon waned into dusk, I headed home and learned that our president had also fled to Kismaayo.

January 27, 1991, the day Siad Barre fled Mogadishu, marked the end of my hope of ever returning home. Arafo became obsessed with seeing the president; she figured this would be her only opportunity. Like an old nomadic woman in search of rain, Arafo searched Kismaayo for President Barre. She finally found him one day, standing outside his hotel, dressed well, wearing his black sunglasses, carrying a cane, surrounded by his defeated army. He looked to be in great distress, pacing from one tree to another in disbelief. He had ruled Somalia for twenty-one years in an absolute dictatorship. There is no question that Siad Barre did a lot for his people, but it was all overshadowed by the destruction he caused toward the end of his regime. Like a true dictator, he became obsessed with power, a disease that has no remedy.

Once Siad Barre fled to Kismaayo, our tenuous situation became desperate. He was the ultimate target, and Kismaayo would soon become the epicenter of the fighting. We needed to get to Kenya. It became a battle of choosing between two equally dangerous paths: fleeing via water or via land. We had heard horror stories of people drowning or becoming forever lost at sea. Desperate people crammed into overcrowded boats that were extremely unsafe and many capsized, but the practice continued as long as the smugglers got paid. My current best friend, Halima, whom I would later meet in Canada, had tried to leave Somalia herself aboard such a boat. She was a young mother of an eighteen-month-old toddler when the war broke out. Her husband was abroad, so she fled with her relatives to Kismaayo, but as the situation escalated, she decided to take a boat to Kenya. On the way to Kenya, the boat capsized. Because of its great size, it took two hours to sink. Like most Somalis, Halima did not know how to swim. She found herself on the part of the boat that sank last. In the shuddering, cold blanket of night, people screamed around her, dying in the black water, moonlight falling on their faces as they cried out for help. A young man who said he was an excellent swimmer called up to her to drop her baby down to him. But when Halima looked over the side, all she could see was black water and she was too frightened to release her baby from the safety of her arms into the unknown.

She clung to her child as the water closed in. As the last part of the boat sank, the force of the water pulled her baby from her arms and they both went under. Halima finally resurfaced, gasping for air, but her baby was gone. She couldn't even process the terror of losing her child; she was fighting for her own life. Flailing around in the water desperately, her hand suddenly caught a piece of wood. Her relief was short-lived when she realized that her lifeline was in use by others who would not share. A father with eight children was saving his family with that one piece of wood. The father tried to push Halima's fingers off the makeshift raft, but she stubbornly refused to let go.

"I don't know how to swim!" she yelled.

He tried hitting her hands, afraid she would capsize his whole family back into the water. When he realized she wasn't going to let go no matter how hard he hit her, he finally said, "Lady, move your legs back and forth in the water or you're going to sink us all."

Fortunately, the boat sank close to a coastal Kenyan tourist town full of vacationing Italians. The desperate cries for help, which carried across the water through the darkness of the night, were heard. Help arrived just in time, saving Halima from drowning, but her baby was one of the hundreds who died that night.

It would have been easy for Halima to be a victim of her circumstances for the rest of her life, or to blanket her grief with alcohol or drugs. But the woman I know has grit, resilience, and a kind soul. She healed herself with long hikes in the tall mountains of Canada, the comfort of books, and the support of caring people. The image of Halima that lives forever in my memory is of her atop a Canadian mountain. We had hiked all day, leaving the summer-like weather at the base of the mountain and reaching the snowy summit, which felt like the dead of winter. Halima stood triumphantly, walking stick grasped in her hand, and said, "Don't we feel like real nomads? I must say a few lines from *The Lord of the Rings*." She proceeded to recite lines about mountains and the beauty of nature, while I looked around nervously at the handful of people who were also at the peak. We were the only two black people up there, and my friend was joyously freeing her soul by reciting J. R. R. Tolkien. *They must think we are crazy*, I thought, but soon her magnetic energy drew me in and I started laughing. I joined in her expression of joy, reciting the few lines I knew from *The Lord of the Rings*, then switching to Somali poetry. We were two women who had been through hell, but who found solace on the peak of that wintery mountain.

My family had heard stories like Halima's, however, so when it came time for us to decide which route to travel, we ultimately chose land. It was equally dangerous, but at least we didn't have to fear drowning. Plus, it was cheaper.

Abshiro and her husband had already decided not to travel to Kenya with us. Ahmed-Nur's father was too old to make the journey and his sister was dying of liver failure, so he wanted to stay with them. After we left, their infant daughter, Ruqiya, fell gravely ill, so Abshiro actually traveled alone with the baby back to Mogadishu to get her medical attention, getting rides from whomever passed by. Even in the midst of the war, members of the clan that chased us out of Mogadishu were trying to create some semblance of government, so it was still the best place to obtain medical care. They had antibiotics in Mogadishu, and enough government structure to give my sister six months of her husband's back pay. Abshiro was stopped and questioned at each checkpoint along the way, but she was so well versed in our family's various clans that she confidently recited whichever lineage would get her through.

Once, when she claimed to be from our father's mother's clan, the rebel who stopped her didn't believe her. "You are not from our clan," he insisted. "Why are you pretending? Did they tell you we rape pregnant women or nursing mothers? We do not do that!" The man was insulted but let her go.

Abshiro made it to Mogadishu and stayed with Ahmed-Nur's Yemeni aunt, Faduma, a loving woman who used to visit us every Friday. She was there for three weeks while her baby recovered, and then she returned to Kismaayo. Sadly, one week after Abshiro left Faduma's house, it was obliterated by a bomb. Nobody was able to recover that sweet woman's body to give it a proper burial.

ON FEBRUARY 24, roughly one month after we had arrived in Kismaayo, we embarked on our next journey, tightly packed into our transport trucks, Land Rovers, and pickup trucks. The land we had to cross was unforgiving. It was covered with dense forest, rarely driven through, and home to lions, poisonous snakes, and aggressive baboons. They called it *habaar waalid*, "parent's curse," meaning you only found yourself on this road if your parent had put a curse on you. My cousins Abdi Salam and Hassan, along with Aadan, spearheaded this huge undertaking. They made sure we had enough fuel for our cars, food to last us a few days, and ammunition to protect us from other clans and the dangers of the forest.

As the trip began, I found myself seated in the low bed of a pickup truck along with my cousin Salad's family. Our pickup was somewhere in the middle of the caravan. Several cars behind us was the huge two-segment cargo truck full of our belongings, with most of the men and teenagers riding high atop the pile. One of my first cousin's sons, Heese ("Singer"), drove the big truck, intending to go back to Kismaayo to get his father's side of the family once he got us across the border. Along the way, we stopped for a break, and the girls and I went to relieve ourselves in the bushes away from the boys.

Without warning, one of the girls who was squatting near me let out a bone-chilling scream. "There is a lion sleeping here!"

The other girls and I did not even wait to pull our clothes back on, we just ran. All of the bravery and boldness I'd once held so deeply dissolved immediately when that girl shouted "lion!" I jumped two feet, leaping over bushes and anything else that stood in my path. Only when we caught sight of the men did we halt to put our garments back on. We returned quickly to our various vehicles and resumed the journey as planned, driving well into the evening. Years later, my teenage son bragged to his friends that I had once peed on a lion. Well, not quite.

One of the young men riding on top of the big cargo truck was

Bashir, the driver's brother. He got either restless or bored and started sticking his foot up into the air, letting the overhanging branches brush against his leg as the truck passed through the dense forest. Suddenly, one of the branches caught him firmly by the foot and dropped him squarely between the two segments of the cargo vehicle. Bashir was run over and killed almost instantly. Blood splattered everywhere, shouts went up, the caravan stopped, and urgently the whole family descended from the surrounding cars.

I did not witness the accident because I couldn't see the cargo truck behind us in the gathering darkness, but our driver abruptly abandoned us with our pickup parked halfway into a ditch. From the screaming that erupted, I understood that something terrible had occurred. I was in the far corner of the truck bed, closest to the ditch, and was tilted almost to ground level by the way he had parked. All I could see was the dark outline of the dense forest. Suddenly, a cacophony of roars emanated from the jungle beside me. *Lions!* my thoughts screamed in recognition, and I knew we were in danger. Lions don't arbitrarily attack people. We didn't have livestock, just cars filled with people, so something must have triggered the attack. *Someone must be bleeding,* I thought, *and the lions have come in for the kill.*

My heart beat with an audible rhythm as another roar erupted close to me. I was certain I was going to die that night. In a panic, I lifted the garments of the older woman I was sitting next to and disappeared beneath her.

Appalled, she demanded, "What are you doing?"

I was small, I was at the edge of the truck, and I was convinced that it wouldn't be hard for lions to drag me off the vehicle. But in the end, I didn't have to give her a response; the look of terror on my face was answer enough. I was not going to be a meal for this lion.

The lions' terrifying, vibrating roars continued all around us, but this time they were answered by gunfire. Apparently, the lions had approached the men, open mouthed, ready to drag Bashir's body away. While some of the men fought off the lions with guns and loud noises, others recovered his body. Aadan was the one who had the courage to pick up the young man's brain matter that had spilled onto the earth. They loaded the body into Aadan's Land Rover and we swiftly left. When the men washed his body for Muslim burial the next day, they found an unexploded hand grenade in his pocket. The tires had missed it by mere inches.

Bashir's brother Heese had to continue driving the cargo truck, despite the shock and grief he felt at having accidentally run over his younger brother. Heese was one of the few drivers who was skilled enough to drive a large transport truck. That family was destined for more tragedy. Not only did Bashir die on the journey, but Heese himself was killed when he returned to Kismaayo.

Exhausted, we finally arrived in Kulbiyow, a town close to the border of Kenya. Kulbiyow was a dead town, with only a small population of desperate people and donkeys roaming about. A sense of foreboding greeted us, and I was reminded of the town where my mother died. We remained there, resting and recovering, for a few days or maybe a week before heading to the town of Haluuqo, on the border of Kenya, hoping to enter the country there.

All our hopes vanished, however, when we saw Kenyan military guards in green uniforms pacing back and forth in front of the fence that kept us from entering their country. In my naïveté, I thought we would be able to enter without a problem, and then leave when we wanted to. I couldn't have been more mistaken. I became hopelessly aware that I was now a refugee who had not only fled my home to survive, but whose fellow Africans wouldn't accept me into their country either. I was about sixteen, but prior to that day, I'd never seen or met a Kenyan. I didn't know that borders existed between African countries. It was so strange to me that we had been in this great hurry to get to Kenya, only to encounter resistance at the border. But my family and I had nowhere to return to without being raped or killed, so it was either enter or die here.

We stayed in Haluuqo because we had no choice. The town essentially became a refugee camp, as more and more Somalis fled the war. Somalis did not trust the young men guarding the border, and my female relatives and I were told to stay together and avoid the guards. From a safe distance, I watched their daily ritual and thought, *Those well-fed young men in their freshly ironed uniforms have no idea what my family and I have been through to arrive at their fences.*

We settled in, like true nomads, between two water reservoirs: one for washing up, and the other for drinking. The people who lived there waited for the rain, just like nomads. We made our house from bushes covered with long shawls to protect us from the blazing sun. The villagers warned us that we had built our temporary shelter in a flood zone, but we were weary from traveling and just wanted to root ourselves; the possibility of a flood didn't concern us. It rained while we were there but it didn't flood, and the villagers proclaimed that we were a blessed family.

During the day, when the sun got very hot, we sat in the shade of our makeshift house, but at night, we slept outside. The evening was spent socializing and staying up late, since we had nowhere to go the next day. I liked getting to know all of the family members I had never met before. We reminisced about good times and the life we had before the war. We listened to the lions in the distance, and older family members shared their wisdom with us. "That is the sound of a lone male lion," they would say, or, "That is a group of lions fighting over a kill." We reverted to being a nation of poets and storytellers now that we were not under attack by lions or guns. We did what we had always done: we simply gathered under the moon, drinking our tea with milk, and told stories from long ago.

SOME OF THE men made a plan to return to Kismaayo to help Ahmed-Nur and his wealthy family save their cars and a huge bus they owned. As a token of appreciation, he promised to give them a Toyota pickup. Aadan and his friend Abdirashid Yare, who had real battle experience and practical counterinsurgency skills as a member of the elite infantry brigade of the Somali National Army (SNA), made the trip, along with my cousins Abdi Salam, Hassan, and Abdirashid Yasin and several more male relatives. They were reentering the battle zone, so they carried AK-47s and ammunition. Along the way, they met another transport truck and they made a pact with the other driver to protect each other if they were attacked.

As my brother recounted later, their truck had just stopped for an old man who needed a ride for his wife when they suddenly heard shots being fired at the other vehicle, which was just ahead. Aadan, Abdirashid Yare, and Abdirashid Yasin all ran to help, while Hassan and Abdi Salam stayed to guard their truck. Shots were fired at them in quick succession from every direction.

Hassan felt bullets hitting his truck, so he jumped in and drove back in the direction they came from. Abdi Salam and a few other men took off on foot to the old man's village, where he hid them from his clan, who would have killed them. Most of the men from the other truck ran off into the jungle. Meanwhile, Aadan's group remained locked in battle with the bandits, exchanging bullets until they were finally able to defeat them and get the truck back.

Hassan had reached Haluuqo by then, and our Uncle Yasin told him of another route to Kismaayo, so he turned around and reached Kismaayo before anyone else. When he got there, he mistakenly told the rest of the family that all the others were dead. My cousin Dahabo went into labor upon hearing the news.

After winning their battle, Aadan and his group drove to Kismaayo as well. When they reached safety, they realized they had a dead body in the truck: the young man they had given a ride to had been hit by a bullet during the intense exchange. Hassan,

Abshiro, and the rest of our relatives were overcome with joy to see the rest of them alive. The cousin who had gone into labor named her new baby Abshir ("Good News").

After comparing stories, Aadan recognized that Abdi Salam and the rest of the men were probably alive and needing rescue. The men gathered more clan power and guns and stormed into the old man's village looking for them. But there was no need to fight. They thanked the old man for keeping their men safe and quickly returned to Kismaayo.

Unfortunately, Ahmed-Nur's rich brother, Ahmed Fiyad (nicknamed after the Italian car, Fiat), refused to allow them to take any of the vehicles, so all of the men returned to Haluuqo empty-handed. Within days of their departure, Kismaayo was taken over by Mohamed Farrah Aidid, the leader of the USC (United Somali Congress), who promptly stole the cars Aadan intended to rescue.

Aidid was one of the most divisive leaders I've ever heard of. He was a skilled warrior who could have ended the war, but his obsession with power and his hatred of Siad Barre and anyone who shared Barre's lineage overshadowed the love for his country. Aidid was the madman depicted by journalist Mark Bowden in his 1999 book *Black Hawk Down: A Story of Modern War*, which was made into a film by the same name in the United States in 2001.

In October 1993, nearly two years after Aidid took Kismaayo, UN and US peacekeeping forces were sent to Somalia to protect humanitarian aid workers under attack by Aidid and other factions. The US-led mission to capture Aidid backfired when two

Black Hawk helicopters were shot down in Mogadishu. Aidid's men proclaimed victory by dragging the body of an American soldier through the streets of the city. Seventeen hours of continuous fighting followed before the surviving US troops were rescued.

Several months after I immigrated to Canada, I watched in confusion as this footage played out on TV. My confusion turned to horror when I realized that the same man who killed and displaced thousands of Somalis and chased me from my homeland was responsible for yet another atrocity. This image flooded me with warnings from the past: *Run! Aidid's men are coming! They are raping women! They are looting again! They just took another city! They leave nothing but death and destruction in their wake!* Aidid destroyed my last bit of innocence about Somali men and my notion of protection and safety. I was out of his physical reach, but the menacing look in his eyes could still trigger fear in me. Aidid was not responsible for all the atrocities of that war—somewhere along the way, all the clans became power hungry and it disintegrated into nothing but a vicious hyena attack. Somewhere in Somalia was a young girl deathly afraid of my own clan. Everyone had blood on their hands.

AT THE HALUUQO refugee camp in Abshiro's absence, Arafo and I had to act more grown-up than we were, but we lived with so many extended family members that we were never alone. Life at the camp was miserable, and we soon found ourselves eating the kind of food we had fed to our goats and cows back in the city, such as boiled corn. I had been a picky eater all my life, but now that food was scarce, ironically my appetite was fully back. I daydreamed about all the foods I loved to eat in Mogadishu. I was ready to hunt if I had to in order to satisfy my craving for meat.

Abshiro Yarey's protruding tummy was now all gone, and with her shaved hair she looked more like a little boy. In fact, when I looked around, it became apparent to me that my whole family was becoming thinner. We all began showing early signs of malnourishment and dehydration. I did not know if we had the energy to continue with this journey, but I didn't think we had any choice.

Our drinking pond was home to some of the ugliest fish I have ever seen in my life. But since meat was scarce, Guleed and our nephew Jama quickly became amateur fishermen. They were both great swimmers, so they hunted fish and brought them to our camp. Arafo and I cooked the scary-looking fish with their long whiskers and they tasted so delicious we left nothing but the eyes and bones. Even without salt and seasoning, any food tastes good when starvation is the alternative.

Since we were stuck in place until we could get across the border, we developed some routine in our daily lives. The men provided protection and worked on the problem of getting into Kenya, while the women either collected water, cleaned clothes, or visited friends. There wasn't much to do in this town. Some of the girls and I created a ritual of going to the pond to bathe and relax around the water. A new rumor began to circulate; maybe it was invented to keep the girls close to camp, but we took it seriously. Being a society with an oral tradition, we believed 100 percent of what we were told. They warned us not only to beware of the border guards, but said the monkeys in this town raped young women, too. I believe they were talking about baboons, which are quite large and fearsome, but the Somali word *daanyeer*, which translates as "monkey," is used for all primates. I see clearly how ridiculous this sounds now, but at that time, I was too hungry, too afraid, and too lost to think rationally.

One day, Abshiro Yarey and the other girls were washing up in the pond when someone screamed, "The daanyeer are here!" Overwhelmed with fear, every single girl ran to safety as quickly as she could.

Another day, I was at the pond bathing with some girls and glimpsed the baboons hanging around in the trees by the water. After a few moments, they quickly headed our way. I leapt out of the water and took off running, barely clothed. In hindsight, I am sure now they came to drink the water, not to attack us, but that is not how it looked to me at the time. It was one thing to say, "I have been raped by a man," but it was a completely different thing to say, "I have been raped by a baboon."

Baboons were a danger in the daytime, but the night belonged to the lions and hyenas. Arafo bathed in the pond at night with some of the adult women who were more modest about their bodies and did not want to risk men seeing them. One night they were all in the midst of washing up when they heard a loud hyena laugh coming from the far side of the small pond. Arafo, who was well known for her fear of wild animals, sprang out of the water and ran naked toward the men.

The woman closest to her called, "Arafo Ma'lin Said [out of shock adding my father's name and title], why are you running without your clothes on!?"

Arafo looked down and noticed she was naked, but her fear of being eaten by a hyena kept her frozen with fear. She eventually managed to run back for her clothes, but I don't think she took any more night baths after that.

We were one of the lucky families in the refugee camp, which was quickly filled by a huge influx of people displaced by the growing war. As it turned out, our paternal grandfather was originally from Garissa, a town in eastern Kenya, and some of our family members still lived there. What's more, my grandfather had lived in Kenya while it was a British colony, so they had documented his presence. The British had registered his full name, enabling us, his descendants, to enter the country. My grandfather had never gone back to Kenya after returning to Somalia, but here we were, benefiting from his legacy long after he was gone. There was no better time for our forefathers to come to our rescue. We were blessed; many people paid thousands in bribe money and still lost their lives while waiting to enter Kenya. Paperwork was filed on our behalf, and to our astonishment, in early April of 1991, just a few months after arriving in the miserable camp, our whole family was approved to enter Kenya as "returnees." We were lucky to escape before we ran out of food or succumbed to the diseases rampant along the overcrowded border.

10 Garissa

Allahayow dhib badanaa qof ka tagay dhulkiisii.
Oh lord! How sad is the soul that leaves its native land.
—Somali proverb

WE ARRIVED IN Garissa on April 11, 1991. Although it was in Kenya, most of the people who lived there were Somali-Kenyans, known as Suji. Most Suji spoke Somali, Swahili, and English, but their Somali dialect was so different from ours that it was both confusing and entertaining. At first, I thought they were making jokes, but I quickly discovered they were serious. For instance, Somalis say *abaayo* ("sister"), which is a term of endearment for girls, never boys. Brothers, or those you regard as brothers, are called *aboowe*. The Suji people switched these words around, so they called the boys "sister," and the girls "brother." This was a minor confusion, compared with what I would run into later.

In Garissa, we rented two rooms from a family related to some high government officials in Kenya. They were Suji, but if we dug deep enough, we shared some forefathers. Their family compound held several cinder block buildings and a main house. An older woman lived in the main house, which had its own fence, and her daughter lived in one of the other houses with her husband. Arafo,

Hubi, Guleed, our niece Abshiro Yarey, and I rented two rooms that faced the main house. Our aunt, Eedo Maryan, rented a room from the old woman's daughter in the house next to us, and various other family members rented rooms in the same compound. We were instructed to call Eedo Maryan if the Kenyan police or anyone else bothered us, but most of the time we just took care of ourselves.

Since we had entered the country legally, we thought all was fine. But none of us had individual IDs yet, and the Kenyan police were apprehending anyone without documentation. The most feared Kenyan words for Somali refugees were "*Leta kipande*" ("Show me your ID"). These words were basically a money-making machine for the Kenyan police, and Somali refugees were crammed into overcrowded jail cells until we paid the price or were deported. I feel like we walked around Kenya with dollar signs on our heads, but if we were sent back, that dollar sign would be replaced by a target.

One ordinary afternoon, I was in the kitchen outside our rooms preparing to cook dinner. I was covered with smoke and soot from fanning the charcoal, which refused to light. I was usually good at keeping one eye open for the Kenyan police, but the stubborn fire had my attention and I was caught off guard. When I finally saw the two policemen within feet of me, I ran toward Eedo Maryan. Before I got to her, the younger policeman grabbed my sooty dress and pulled me back.

Despite his firm hold on me, I twisted and squirmed until I escaped, all the while screaming and calling my aunt's name. I ran and came to a full stop in front of my eedo, who was just getting ready for her daily prayers. She was what Somalis called a *labo lafood*, a big-boned woman. She was tall, strong, and proud, commanding a certain respect with her presence. The police caught up with me and grabbed me again while I informed her that they wanted to take me to jail.

With authority, she immediately pulled me free from their grip, leaving them stunned. She went about her business as usual and they were left standing there like two little boys who had been reprimanded by a parent for poor behavior. When they complained, she scolded them as if they were her servants. She continued to prepare for her prayers and went to the bathroom.

The two men used that time to strengthen their posture. They took out police sticks, looking like roosters ready to fight. When my eedo came out of the toilet, one of the men grabbed her hands as if to arrest her.

She screamed at him, calling him all kinds of mean names in Somali, adding, "You filthy dog, don't touch me!" She was glaring into his face, making fun of his features, and forgetting for several moments that these men had power over her. I was embarrassed to the core as people gathered to see what was causing the commotion.

Finally, the two policemen tired of her insults and took us both off to jail. On the street outside our house, we joined a growing line of Somali detainees they had gathered along the way. My eedo must have hatched some kind of plan; without any warning, she broke loose and ran toward another kitchen to hide. She gestured to me to follow her at the last minute, but I was quickly caught.

"My mother is in there!" I blurted out.

My eedo came out and scolded me for being slower than an old woman. She said, "Ma'alin Said's daughter, you need to move faster next time," but we never got the chance.

When we finally arrived at the jail, I was surprised to see a few other relatives of mine in there already, including my Uncle Yasin. He was a tall, hunched-over old man who looked like he struggled to carry his own long bones. Seeing my uncle in this state made me very sad. Thankfully, we didn't have to sleep in the jail. I don't know if my family paid off the guards or if someone showed them our temporary documents, but we were released by evening.

After that, I decided I was not going to jail again and I contrived a plan. I had a Somali-Kenyan friend named Deeqa, who was fluent in Somali, Swahili, and English. She taught me how to say some Swahili words just like the natives so when the Kenyan police talked to me, I could quickly answer them in their own language. To look more convincing, I braided my long hair just like most Kenyans did and I took to hanging around with Suji girls. I became a chameleon, blending into my environment as best I could, which kept me out of jail for the rest of my stay in Garissa.

FOR SEVERAL WEEKS, I had noticed a black Land Rover parking behind our rooms every night, but I didn't think much about it. In hindsight, I wish I had paid attention. I also wish I had been more suspicious of the short, round woman we rented rooms from. Maybe I would have noticed that her easy smile masked a devious plan. But I was young, trusting, and inexperienced.

One evening, the old woman called me in for a cup of tea. Her invitation was paired with a warm, inviting smile. When we met, she informed me that Idiris, the man who owned the Land Rover, wanted to take me out for tea in town and get to know me. It turned out that the old woman was his father's step-mother, so even though they weren't related by blood, he called her Grandmother. In the Somali culture, we place great emphasis on respecting our elders, so I assumed I'd be safe since she had vouched for him.

As promised, he took me to the most expensive sweet store in Garissa. I was about seventeen, and he was slightly older, maybe twenty. I felt awkward as he sat across from me, staring at me. I tried my best to carry on meaningful conversation, but he seemed distracted. My efforts at small talk never really worked. I felt that spot in my gut, that place where we hold our intuition, nudging me, trying to tell me there was danger ahead. But my mind was giving me the opposite message, telling me I was safe with him because the old woman had vouched for him. I didn't know which to believe.

He talked about his mother and siblings, so after the sweets, when he suggested we see his house, I naïvely believed he just wanted to introduce me to his family. Each step of the way, I trudged through warnings, red flags, and signals coming from within me saying, "He's lying to you; don't go with him." And yet,

I hate to say it: I quelled those warnings, and continued forward anyway.

The large entrance gate to his home was a bold declaration of wealth right up front. I was startled to see a uniformed guard with a gun standing stoically at the gate. I later learned that his father and uncle both held high positions in the Kenyan government. These were not just any positions of power. His uncle was the number two man in Kenya, a general who commanded the army and worked closely with President Daniel Arap Moi. His father held an equally important position. A blinding light emanated from behind the gate as the guard greeted Idiris with a submissive smile and nod, and opened it to let us drive through.

Idiris parked the car and we both approached the large, beautiful house to our left. I had not seen a house that could compare to its size or grandeur in all of Garissa. I was surprised to find it empty when we stepped through the doors of the living area. "Where's your family?" I asked.

As if rehearsed, he replied coolly, "They all flew to Mombasa a couple of hours ago." I froze with absolute terror as he sat down beside me, grabbed me, and forcefully tried to kiss me on the lips as if he had a God-given right to my body. I yanked myself backward as hard as I could to avoid his lips so he kissed my neck instead and began pulling at my clothes with the intent to rip them off. I pushed him away, every cell in my body revolting against him, but he overpowered me. I fought back, and we hit the floor with all our limbs entangled. I was lucky he was a skinny man. Though I was small, when provoked and with adrenaline pumping through my body, I could fight with the strength of a lion. I was not going to return to my brothers and cousins and tell them I had been raped. I was fully aware I would be blamed. I could hear the men in my family accusing me, saying, "You did this to yourself! Who asked you to go with this man?" Girls who found themselves pregnant as result of rape or sexual intercourse outside the confines of marriage were beaten, kicked out of the house, and ostracized for life. I did not want that to be my fate or reputation to live with.

Surprised by my strength, he intensified his attack. He tried to pin me down using his body weight, but I pushed him off. Within seconds, it became a wrestling match, both opponents giving everything we had and neither of us winning outright. I was moving too quickly for him to be able to pin me down and hold me there.

In the middle of our fight, we had to take a break. Beads of sweat were forming on his forehead, and he looked exhausted. I think I looked worse. My small body was buzzing and my heartbeat raced as fast as a hummingbird's. When he'd had enough time to catch his breath, he flew at me with an arrogant *I can't believe you think you can actually fight me* look plastered on his face. As before, I fought back and was lucky that he never pulled out a weapon. Even if he had, I wouldn't have surrendered. Finally, he gave up his attempt at rape and uttered his last words to me: "You girls from Somalia like to play games. You want to have sex, but you act like you are too important. I want you out of here; I'm going to take you home now."

It was over. Relief washed over me, which was soon replaced by anger. *What an animal! What made him think I wanted to have sex with him?* This was one of the biggest shocks of my life. *How did a simple tea turn into this?* Idiris was one of the ugliest men I had seen in my life, made even uglier by his ego and by what he tried to do to me. His mouth was full of saliva when he spoke and his lips were so wet that it looked like he needed to spit. Much to my surprise and to my great relief, he didn't utter another word while he drove me home.

Once I was safe, my mind drifted to the old witch who had arranged this hell for me. *Why? What did I do to make her hate me like this?* I contemplated whether to confront her or let it go. If I confronted her, she would definitely deny any knowledge of it, and my family might find out that I had gone out with a strange man without telling them. But the old woman and Idiris had deceived me, and I burned with anger and shame. I was not used to letting go of injustices but felt I had no choice. After all, this was not my country and my legal status was not solidified. Although I knew the incident was not my fault, I tortured myself most of the night with guilty thoughts. *The old lady picked you because you're an easy girl. A man who wants to have sex with you on your first date despite your customs must have seen a weakness in you.*

When I woke the next morning, I was in that innocent, heavenly state, the place between sleep and being fully awake. The previous day's events had not flooded back in yet. I didn't put two and two together about the severe aching in my muscles and bones, but as I gained clarity, memories from the previous night began to drown me. My heart began racing once again as I recalled the violation of my body and my rights.

Not long afterward, the old woman called me in again for another meeting. I tried to speculate what she could possibly want from me now. "Idiris's Kenyan ID is missing, and he asked me to find out if you took it," she said, eyeing me suspiciously.

As if attempting to rape me wasn't enough, he is now accusing me of stealing his ID!? I could feel every part of my body screaming with rage. I knew he'd probably lost his ID while we were wrestling on the floor. I wanted to yell at her, *When he told you he suspected I took his ID, did he also tell you how he tried to rape me?* I was angry and felt my face burn. "I didn't take his ID," I said to her in all honesty, and with the most confidence I could muster in spite of my anger. Then I walked away, letting her stew in the wake of my silent spite.

Arafo saw my look of distress and came to me. "What was she asking you about, abaayo?"

I felt my shoulders sag. I wanted to tell her everything but knew I couldn't. Instead, I replied, "Nothing, Abaayo," trying to downplay the situation. Today I have enough life experience to fully understand the significance of what Idiris did to me. It bothers me that he probably holds a high governmental position like his father and uncle, and saddens me that he was never held accountable for his actions. He likely perpetrated the same offense on other women.

Soon after this, Guleed came to me, exuding an elation I hadn't witnessed in him before. He didn't hesitate to tell me that he'd had sex with my friend Deeqa. I was mortified by his statement, and for several moments, I thought he was boasting. My friend didn't look like the kind of girl who would freely give her body, and I found myself wondering if this kind of behavior was considered normal and acceptable for Somali-Kenyan teens.

Despite my attempts to reassure myself, all the fears that had run through my mind as I'd fought Idiris resurfaced. *Oh my god, this girl is going to get pregnant. Then she'll be disowned by her family.* I found myself struggling with whom to believe and whom to support. Deeqa was my friend, and Guleed was my brother. I knew men liked to boast about sex they never had just so they'd look good, so part of me failed to believe Guleed. It crossed my mind that Idiris could be marching around boasting to people about intercourse that never occurred between us. The irony of the situation was depressing. I was terrified of people finding out I was almost raped, and my brother was proudly boasting about having sex with my friend. That is how it feels to live in a culture where women are shamed, overburdened with guilt and blame, and men are empowered, guilt-free, and valued above women.

IT TOOK TIME to recognize the figure that approached me as I prepared food in our outdoor kitchen. I blinked at the woman who stood before me, a shadowy reflection of a woman who once was. This couldn't be Abshiro. I hadn't seen my sister since she decided to stay behind in Kismaayo four months ago. With every new wave of refugees entering Kenya, news of increased fighting and destruction reached us. I was not even sure my sister was alive.

The woman in front of me was underweight, her head shaven, a hollow look in her eyes. Who was this? Two children clung to her side, and I felt tears burning my eyes as recognition of my own flesh and blood took place. Sobs escaped my mouth, horrifying, unladylike wails that were quickly echoed by Arafo. It was indeed Abshiro who stood before us. *Oh my God,* I thought. *What happened to my sister? Who has done this to her? How could someone change so much in just a few months?*

We took her inside, fed, washed, and clothed her and her children, and let them rest a bit before turning to ask my sister more questions. "Why did you shave your head?" was the first thing we asked.

"When I passed through the refugee camp in Liboya, people were infested with lice and scabies," she said. She told us about a wealthy real estate agent she saw, a man who used to sell expensive homes in Somalia. As she approached to greet him, she saw that he appeared dazed and sickly, picking a louse off the nape of his neck. Abshiro quickly turned away from the man, fearing that his seeing someone who knew him as a rich man would only increase his suffering. Even now, the image I carry of that man is a reminder of how every Somali was blanketed by the tragedy that befell our nation.

We continued with our questions. We were desperate for news about the state of our country and curious as to why our sister had arrived with just her daughters, not her husband. The stories Abshiro told us were so horrific that I buried some deep in my mind, willing myself to forget them. She explained that after she returned to Mogadishu, the city came apart at its seams and all hell broke loose.

My sister saw what Aidid and his men were capable of: unspeakable, heinous acts that bring a chill to my bones even now. Soon after Aidid took Kismaayo, a group of men he had captured managed to escape. Some were wounded, others unharmed. My sister met one of those men when she returned to Kismaayo and he shared his story with her. For a few, rare moments, he felt fortunate to be alive. Aidid's men, however, knew the escapees would eventually need water, so they strategically guarded all the wells in and around the city. Eventually the men, dying of thirst, decided in an act of desperation that it was worth the risk of being shot to quench their craving for water. Aidid's men began to shoot them there at the edge of the well, one by one. I hoped, for the sake of human compassion, they would at least let the men drink before killing them, but my sister said they were shot before they could taste even a drop. Having spent my early life searching for water in the desert and knowing first-hand the agony of thirst so extreme that you may not live much longer, the image of their dead bodies lying inches from water is a haunting one. Thousands of such stories played out during the course of this bloody war. The only reason this story was passed on was because the man who told Abshiro his story had refused to accompany the others to the well that day and thus managed to survive.

After we fled Kismaayo, my sister had remained in that same house, which belonged to one of Ahmed-Nur's distant relatives and seemed relatively safe. But Ahmed-Nur had to care for his sister who was dying of liver failure, his elderly father who had gone mute with shock, his mentally ill older brother, and his epileptic brother Mahamud, all of whom lived in a house on the other side of the city. Once we left, the house where Abshiro was living became a little refugee camp of its own. Most of the men had to flee for their lives, so during the day, the house became filled with women and children of all ages. They stayed inside and tried not to draw attention to themselves while they waited for their own clan to take back the city. At night, most of them found other safe places to sleep.

My sister slept in the house with a beautiful young teenage girl, a young woman with an infant and her middle-aged mother-in-law, and the mother-in-law's nephew, who guarded them at night. Trouble started when one of Aidid's men demanded to marry the beautiful young girl and her father flat-out refused. Aidid's man was furious and determined to take her, so her father removed the girl from Abshiro's house in the middle of the night and hid her. He didn't tell anyone where she was for fear that someone would reveal her location under torture.

Aidid's men seemed to become obsessed with rape. Abshiro and the remaining women could hear the screams of other women in nearby houses being attacked at night. Around this time, a story circulated about an attack on a beautiful twenty-year-old woman. As they attempted to rape her, the woman stood in defiance. "I swear, you will not rape me while I am alive!" With a single blow to the head, they killed her.

My sister worried that unwanted attention would be focused

on their house as the man who wanted to marry the young girl continued his search. Women could no longer depend on the unwritten rules of our culture, which spared the old, pregnant, and postpartum. The fact that my sister had an infant and young child would not save her from becoming a target. Abshiro and her little band hatched a plan to fool Aidid's men. At night, the women and their children hid together in the cow stable in the middle of the house's courtyard. The men would enter the house, looting and searching for women they could prey upon. The rebels didn't think anyone would hide in cow manure and stench, so my sister and the other women were spared many times using this tactic. But even surrounded by cow manure, she never felt safe.

The women knew that if they wanted to stay one step ahead of Aidid's men, they needed to devise more skillful tactics for avoiding them. They began sneaking into the abandoned house next door to sleep. This worked for quite a while, until the day my sister saw Aidid's men outside their home, deep in conversation. One man gestured to the abandoned house, and the men all nodded in agreement as if they had deciphered a code. Terrified, Abshiro gathered the women and begged, "We cannot sleep next door tonight."

"Why?" the women all asked, seeing the fear on Abshiro's face.

"I think the men figured out how we are tricking them," she replied. She felt convinced they were all in imminent danger and hoped she could make the others believe her. Her solution was simple: sleep somewhere else that night.

Hesitantly, the women collectively decided to ignore her advice and sleep in the abandoned house. More and more women had been sleeping there and it had felt safe, so they chose not to go with Abshiro. My sister knew an *Asharaf* man (a man of Arab descent) who guarded his daughters with guns at night, and asked if she and her children could sleep with them.

"Of course," the man replied, "You're welcome to sleep between my daughters. We're all in this together."

She fell asleep that night, tucked between strangers, protected, and worried for her group of friends. As soon as the sun came out, she thanked her guardian and hurried to check on the women at the abandoned house. As she approached, she knew that unspeakable atrocities had occurred there. The nephew of the older woman staggered out to meet Abshiro in the road, despair sagging his shoulders and a glazed look in his eyes. My sister recognized that expression, and with great grief, she wailed uncontrollably.

The man informed Abshiro that, just as she'd predicted, Aidid's men entered the home at night, tied him down, and beat and raped each woman, one by one. They didn't even spare his aunt or her postpartum daughter-in-law, he lamented. The young mother had fought the men fiercely during the rape, and as a result, she was gravely injured, with multiple lacerations over her thighs, inflicted by the sharp blade attached to their guns.

My sister fell silent. She was devastated by this news and wondered how she could ever step through the doors of that house again. What would she say to the women when she saw them? At that moment she decided she must leave Kismaayo. Ahmed-Nur could not yet leave his father and sister, but Abshiro knew Aidid's men would never stop, so she traveled with another woman she knew to the refugee camp at Liboya.

In addition to being infested with lice and scabies, the refugees there were emaciated, with sunken eyes peering out of skeletonlike bodies. Disease, starvation, and dehydration claimed the lives of young children and the elderly first. The people just arriving at the camps along Kenya's border had already faced greater hardships as the fighting continued to escalate. A bridge between Mogadishu and Kismaayo had been destroyed, forcing many to cross the crocodile-infested river. Others fled into the desert, where they were injured or eaten by wild animals. My family were some of the lucky ones; we got into Kenya before the situation deteriorated even more.

When Abshiro told the refugees at Liboya that she had come from Kismaayo, they quickly retorted, *"Naaya, naa ma lagu kufsaday?"* ("Hey, woman, were you raped?") It was the spiteful tone that accompanied those words that told my sister what they truly meant: "Hey, woman, we know you were raped. Just admit it." My sister knew they wouldn't believe her if she denied it, so she endured their criticism just as she'd endured the rest of her trials.

Abshiro found our cousin Dhuhaa, his wife, and four children in Liboya. In the five months since they arrived, they had not found a way to get across the border. Dhuhaa appeared beaten down by his circumstances, informing her that while he could obtain an American visa if he got to Nairobi, crossing the border into Kenya was an impossible task. Abshiro was not one to sit

around and wait. She quickly began walking around camp, finding out who to bribe and who to stay away from. Within mere
hours of her arrival in Liboya, she wove together the information
she collected and came up with a plan.

My sister, who had the equivalent of one hundred US dollars in
her possession, quickly located a Kenyan man who could be paid
to smuggle people across the border and made a deal to get them
all into Kenya, including the woman who had traveled with her.
The woman had kindly helped my sister with her children, and
Abshiro wanted to help the woman to safety.

Laden with their belongings, my sister and her companions
walked away from the crossing gate toward the meeting point,
which was out of sight of the border guards. As they were about to
get into the waiting truck, a group of Somali-Kenyan men sprang
out from the bushes at the edge of the road and threatened to
hand them over to the police. At the sight of the men, Abshiro's
ride took off into the distance, leaving them behind.

As they were being led toward the police station, my sister realized this was simply a business opportunity for these thieves. She
began to bargain with the men. "You'd take us, fellow Somalis, to
the Kenyan police?" she asked, appalled that her own would do
this to her.

One man gruffly replied, "We're not the same Somali."

My sister was undeterred. "If you're not Somali, then let us
bargain," she said.

"Now you're talking," the man answered harshly.

My sister possessed thirty-five hundred Kenyan shillings. She gave the men holding them captive six hundred shillings in exchange for their freedom and the men went on their way. She still owed fifteen hundred shillings to the runaway driver, but she supposed that would have to wait for another time. Just as they were walking back to the refugee camp, Abshiro spotted his truck hiding in the distance. The driver was smart and knew the ins and outs of border crossings. He'd merely pretended to drive off, waiting until Abshiro and her group untangled themselves from the thieves. She was impressed that the driver kept his side of the bargain; he showed more kindness to my sister than her own fellow Somali men.

After my sister made it to us in Garissa, she gave one thousand shillings to Dhuhaa and his family to get them to the capital, Nairobi. It only took her a total of three days to get out of Liboya, an impressive accomplishment, since many were stuck there for years. A few months later, Ahmed-Nur joined us in Garissa. His brother Ahmed-Fiyad was now living in Cairo and helping him to get the rest of the family out. After he flew Abshiro, their children, and his father to Cairo, he joined his family in Cairo, too.

Around that time, I began to develop pain in my breasts that was so severe I could not ignore it. My breasts felt hard and full and very painful to touch; even my clothing brushing against them caused pain. I had limited knowledge of anatomy, but I knew deep down that something was very wrong. I thought a bra might help to add extra support, but women in my culture who are unmarried and without children did not wear bras because they believe it would ruin their breasts. The pain was so intense that I used my hands to support my breasts when no one was looking.

I finally confided in Mama Amina, a kind woman who often came to visit our landlady. Mama Amina was the older wife of Idiris's uncle, the head of the military. She arranged right away to have me flown to Nairobi in a private military helicopter belonging to the president of Kenya.

11 Nairobi

Dani waa seeto.
Necessity is an inescapable knot.
—Somali proverb

I LANDED IN Nairobi and was brought to a mansion that belonged to Mama Amina's co-wife, Mama Gini. I stood staring, open-mouthed, at the biggest, most beautiful house I had ever seen. When I stepped inside, endless elaborately decorated rooms overwhelmed me. Everywhere I looked I saw servants bustling about. As soon as I saw this palace, I felt sure that Mama Gini would be hospitable and let me stay here while I got treatment. Surely one small teenager would be no burden. I could have lived in a closet and no one would have noticed.

But Mama Gini was not welcoming at all. Her demeanor was guarded, as if she wanted to say, *You'd better look for a place to live because you are not staying here.* I believed naïvely that she wanted me to be respectful and ask her directly if I could please stay. After all, she was Somali, too, and Somalis are always hospitable. When I asked politely, Mama Gini flat-out rejected me. I froze, suspended by shock, my hurt evident on my face. *You have all this space!* I thought, as my brain searched for a logical reason for her rejection. But she got up and left the room. Coldness seeped through my body, and I felt like an unwanted orphan all over again. It felt personal, as if I had done something wrong. I thought of all the suffering my family had gone through as I stared, bewildered, at the opulence around me. *She has no idea what I have been through and where I have been living. How could she dismiss me so easily?* It took me a while to realize that a single girl of seventeen would pose quite a threat to a rich woman with a polygamous husband.

Luckily, a distant cousin, Ibrahim, was a member of Parliament in Kenya and had a four-bedroom townhouse in South B, a middle-class neighborhood in Nairobi. Aadan and a first cousin, Abdi Salam, were already living in Ibrahim's house along with what felt like forty other displaced Somalis. I don't know the exact number of people sheltering there, but that house felt as if it were blooming with people in every room and corner. Nairobi, with its large number of embassies, was a gateway to Western countries, and refugees from all over Africa gathered there to obtain visas and proper paperwork.

I shared a room with six other girls; some were extended family who had journeyed from Mogadishu with us and some I had never met before. We bonded quickly by sharing our individual survival stories of the mass exodus from our homeland. We didn't even think about the fact that some of the girls came from Aidid's clan, which was currently trying to wipe my clan out of existence. Most of these girls and I shared the same blood. The distinction is that we shared the same blood on our maternal side, and the clans are patrilineal. The girls and I cared for each other as women. We endearingly addressed each other as Aunt. That is the insanity of the Somali system: we give birth to each other and later try to kill each other.

I HAD VERY little money, so I went to the cheapest doctor I could find, who turned out to be a thin, middle-aged Indian man with a little protruding belly. His office was in a rundown building in a very poor area. This doctor examined my breasts for a few minutes and then blurted out a word I had never heard in my life: cancer. I did not flinch, cry, or get sad; I did not know what cancer was. He gave me an appointment to come back so he could cut away the malignant tissue from my breasts. I felt relieved that this doctor had a solution to my problem. I knew nothing about the medical world and would have let him do whatever he thought was best, but I knew enough to do one thing right: I called Abshiro in Cairo.

"I have cancer," I told her with lightness in my tone. "The doctor just needs to cut out the bad parts of my breasts."

My sister fell from her chair and dropped the phone. When she came back on the line, her voice shook, as if I had just told her I was going to die. I did not like hearing her distressed voice. Her reaction alarmed me, and for the first time I asked, "What is cancer?"

Her answer immediately took the smile from my face. "You are not going back to that doctor! I am going to send you money to see a specialist, Abaayo," she commanded.

She sent me enough money to see a well-respected Kenyan

gynecologist. He did a more detailed examination and told me that I did not have breast cancer. He blurted out another big medical word I didn't understand, but he assured me it was an innocuous disorder and that the changes in my breasts would rise and fall with my monthly cycle.

After a few months, as my pain subsided a bit, I wanted to get out and explore Nairobi. My nomadic instinct was to first get the lay of the land. Where do I get food? What dangers exist? The first person I made friends with was our Kenyan maid, Jane, a teen about my age with a boxy build and close-cropped Afro. I followed her on her household errands and got to know our neighborhood shops very well this way. I felt the unfairness of her situation: she had been hired as a maid for one family—which quickly became a large band of refugees. Despite some of us lending a hand when we could, poor Jane was constantly in motion.

When Jane ventured farther into the city, the girls and I stuck to her like a herd of baby goats. Unlike Jane, we Somali girls had to watch out for the Nairobi police, who were notorious for harassing refugees. They seemed to have a talent for nabbing people right before they were clear to leave the country and then demanding large sums of money from them.

As I became more confident in my ability to navigate the streets of the city while keeping an eye out for the police, I began to appreciate the beauty of Nairobi. It was more developed than Mogadishu, with high-rise buildings, well-dressed citizens, and more white people than I had ever seen in one place. Everyone moved about with purpose. It looked a lot like the Western cities

I had seen in movies. The *matatu*, or minibuses, were the primary mode of transportation throughout Africa, but in Nairobi they took it to a whole new level. The matatu played loud music to attract attention. At each stop, young men yelled out their destinations over the hustle and bustle of the city, trying desperately to drown out the cries of their competitors. The first time I ventured out alone, I stopped to ask one of these young men if this was the right bus for me. "Yes, yes!" he cried, "Come in! Come in!" I looked at the full minibus dubiously, thinking there was not enough space to squeeze in even my small body. The man grabbed me by the shoulders and shoved me hard, packing me in so tight I could not move. I found myself wedged between a mother holding her child tightly against her body and an older woman holding a live chicken. When my stop came, I quickly wiggled out of the bus before more people were shoved on. As time went by, I got better at understanding the system and the language, even learning to drown out the catcalls of the matatu boys, who added a flirtatious tone whenever any young woman walked by.

"Come here girl, I want to talk to you," they crooned. I saw an older woman approach the bus station, and heard their voices change to a more respectful tone. "Mama, mama, let us help you," they gently coaxed, while their body language changed from confident rooster to humble servant. They knew exactly what to do to get customers' attention. They even repeated their cries in several languages, which helped me learn Swahili, English, and some Kikuyu.

In Nairobi, I had a little more freedom to go out alone or with my friends, and one of my favorite things to do was indulge in the local street food. Street vendors made the best food in Somalia, and it was no different in Kenya. Their sambusa was spiced a little differently but was equally delicious. I ate a lot of street food, but chips (French fries) were my favorite. I had gotten too skinny since fleeing the Civil War, but once in Kenya, my appetite returned completely. I loved every ounce of the weight I was gaining. I was becoming a woman with curves and was thrilled when Abshiro sent me some stylish clothes from Cairo. My friends and I fought over who would wear my new wardrobe whenever we were going out, but we compromised by taking turns, always taking a good sniff before wearing the outfit to town.

Kenya was a great place to be a teenager. We went to the movies, hung around downtown, and watched Kenyan and American sitcoms. I was surprised by the number of channels they could watch and the amount of regularly scheduled entertainment. After a while, it occurred to me that the power didn't fail in the middle of the movie like it did in Mogadishu! My cousin and his family liked to watch *The Fresh Prince of Bel-Air*. Because the show was in English, I did not understand much, but I did develop a small crush on Will Smith.

After living in Kenya for several months, it became perfectly clear that we would not be able to return to Somalia. Saada, who was now living in Canada with her husband, spearheaded the campaign by the oldest girls to get all the younger siblings out of Kenya. Canada was one of a handful of countries opening its doors to African refugees, but Saada could only sponsor a couple of us at a time.

To stay in communication with Abshiro and Saada, I frequently had to make long-distance phone calls, which were very expensive. The rumor from the Somali community was that some clever Somalis had figured out a way to illegally hack the Kenyan telephone system. They wired their phone lines into big government offices, leaving the government with huge, mysterious phone bills, and charged their fellow immigrants a more affordable rate to make the long-distance calls. These were prepaid phone calls, Somali style. You paid, and they told you how many minutes you could talk. A person sat right there, cutting you off when you reached your limit. Habesha people, those of Eritrean or Ethiopian descent, were also fleeing political unrest in their own countries, so we often ran into each other while making our phone calls. We Somalis are loud and talk in long words. Ethiopians are quiet and can speak many words in one minute, yet the rate was still the same for both of us. I teased my Habesha friends in broken English about how unfair this was. They would laugh and say, "Blame your language, not us," and then we would walk out together, laughing.

As I waited to make a phone call one day, I locked eyes with a Habesha boy. Warm feelings flowed in my veins, and I felt an instant connection. That boy stole my heart at first encounter. Never in my life had I experienced such an intense reaction to a boy. Fortunately, he felt the same way and made the move. But we had a problem: Somalis and Ethiopians are ancient enemies. And worse, Dereje was Christian. That was a definite no-no for Somali girls—a forbidden love. I was well aware of the expectations my culture and religion placed on me, but I was young and under a spell and did not care about the rules. A distant voice echoed the warnings of my childhood: *Don't bring shame to your family.* But I ignored it.

Our first kiss was exhilarating. Dereje consumed my thoughts, and most of my energy was spent trying to make sure we weren't discovered. The men in my family kept a close watch on me, but I became good at hiding our relationship. I always walked in the opposite direction from Dereje's house and then looped back to his street. If we spotted any Somalis, we quickly separated and pretended not to know each other. The Ethiopians didn't care if we were together, but my family would not have let this go without punishment.

My cousin Ibrahim's house had a separate unit in the front yard that was rented to a group of young Ethiopian women. Initially, I didn't interact with them, other than to say hello in passing. They may have looked similar to me, but we didn't speak the same language and their lifestyle was quite different from mine. They were independent, with no men watching over them or trying to control them. I saw them come and go at different times, well dressed in Western-style clothing, and although I was curious about them, I only watched from a distance.

I walked out my front door one day and came face to face with Dereje. Confused, I turned to run back into the house before my family could spot us together, but it was too late. It turned out Dereje was friends with the Ethiopian girls, and one of them, Zeituna, was already introducing him to some of my relatives. Running away would arouse suspicion in my vigilant family, so I lined up with the rest of them to be "introduced" to my boyfriend. I practiced my innocent "I've never met you before" look while I waited to shake his hand. When I glanced up, I saw that instead of innocence, his face sported a mischievous grin and a daring look. I held out my hand, hoping he would shake it and move on. To my horror, he grabbed my hand and pulled me closer to him. *O God!* I thought. My eyes moved rapidly from my hand to his face, my heart rate accelerated, and my eyes pleaded, *Don't do it!* I tried to wiggle my hand out before anyone noticed us, but he had a strong grip. I was not the last one in line to be introduced, so fortunately he had to release me and shake the next hand. If he held on just one second longer, I would have been in serious trouble. They would have literally disowned me if I was caught with a Somali from an inferior clan, let alone an Ethiopian whose lineage they could not trace. You don't get to marry a Somali daughter unless they know your blood lineage very well.

The next time I saw Dereje, I let him know what I thought about his little prank. "You are seriously going to get me killed!" I pleaded.

He just smiled the cute smile that always softened me, and said, "I can get away with anything. I know you love me." I don't think he truly understood how much danger he was putting me in.

Dereje was in Kenya in hopes of getting to Dallas, Texas, where his older sister lived. When he told me he had finally received approval from the American embassy and would be leaving the following month, I was utterly heartbroken. This was good news for him, but we both knew it was the end of our relationship. I cried hard, already grieving his loss. He held me closely and tenderly, but I felt like I was falling into a black hole. As the day of his departure neared, I got a sinking feeling in my stomach whenever I saw him, and I completely lost my new-found appetite. His love had soothed the trauma of war and distracted me from the chaos I had endured. Losing both Dereje's love and the comfort he gave me made my body feel more broken and weaker than when I fled the Civil War.

His departure date seemed to arrive suddenly. He was to leave at 3:00 a.m., and I knew there was no way my family would let me accompany him to the airport, but there was also no way I would miss these final moments together. I threw all caution to the wind, risking the wrath of my family and the police, and made up some excuse to get out the door in the evening. I stayed with Dereje until he left, deciding that the beating I would receive would be well worth it.

When I got to his house, the atmosphere was festive, with a hint of sadness. Dereje was happy about his prospects; he had waited a long time for this day. It was a dream come true for him, but my own dreams were shattering. I was not ready to let him go. I imagined a scenario where he would say, "I am not leaving you here. I can't live without you." But endings like that only happen in romantic movies. As he hugged his friends, I studied him one last time. He was beautiful, with smooth black skin, high cheek-bones, a neat Afro, and his trademark infectious smile. He gave me some pictures we took together on a beautiful sunny day in Kenya. We promised to keep in touch, and I was determined to do so, but to be honest, I knew this would be our final contact. My last vivid memory is of him hugging me goodbye as I sobbed. The cold night air hit me hard in the face and the wind whipped my clothing around me as we stood outside his house saying our final goodbyes. I normally get cold easily, but on this night I noticed nothing but the stabbing in my chest as I watched him climb into a car and drive away forever.

I walked home around 4 a.m., tired and sad. I did not care what my family would do to me.

Abdi Salam was waiting, burning with anger, and began questioning me as soon as I stepped inside. "Where were you all night?" he demanded.

"I was arrested by the Kenyan police," I told him. That was always a possibility, so it sounded believable.

But Abdi Salam didn't fall for it. "You were out with boys!" he fumed. "You will not bring shame to our family under my watch!" Anger raged on his face as he took off his shirt, a form of intimidation to let me know he was serious and ready to beat me up. "You need to be disciplined!" he yelled.

It suddenly occurred to me that I was about to be beaten by a grown man I hadn't even known before the war started, who wasn't my brother or my father. But this was the Somali mentality: any male relative, no matter how distantly related, had the right to control the young women in the family by any means necessary, as if we were goats that needed to be herded through life's ins and outs. I remember him taking a swing at me that night, but to be honest, I don't remember him hitting me. I do recall, however, that Abdi Salam's yelling woke other members of the family, and several of my older female cousins stepped between us. Abshiro said later that one of the women told her that Abdi Salam beat me that morning, but all I remember is sitting in my room, feeling sad, bruised, and hopeless.

Later that day, as I stood at my window thinking about the night's events, I saw Zeituna and one of the other Ethiopian girls coming back to their little house, laughing and carefree. It struck me that these young women were in charge of their own lives and were not led around by the reins like a camel. They seemed so much happier than I was.

This was a turning point for me. I felt inspired by the other girls' independence and vowed to live my life without answering to a man. I visited the girls and they were very welcoming, offering me Ethiopian coffee, which had its own serving ritual, and delicious food. My family thought girls living on their own must be loose women, but that was not the case. These young women knew how to take care of themselves and didn't care what anyone else thought of them.

Zeituna and I crossed paths again years later in Canada when my new fiancé, Selehdin, also Ethiopian, and I visited his family in Toronto. Zeituna happened to be best friends with Selehdin's sister Nejat. When I walked into the apartment, Zeituna recognized me

right away and greeted me with a squeal. "You don't have to introduce us! I knew Shugri way before the two of you!" I was equally
delighted. It really hadn't been that long since we lived next to
each other in Kenya. I left Kenya early in 1992 and I met Zeituna
again in Canada in the summer of 1995. It must be true when they
say we all have six degrees of separation. As I was falling hard for
my first love in Kenya, my husband, the *real* love of my life, was
only one degree away. I marvel at the mysterious workings of our
world and how connected we all are. I recently teased Zeituna for
not introducing me to my husband sooner. She could have helped
me to avoid the heartaches along the way.

"Shugri, you were in the Dereje boat back then."

I laughed. "You are right."

Soon after Dereje left me heartbroken, Saada came to Nairobi,
visited me briefly, and then headed to Garissa to see the rest of my
siblings. She had the paperwork to take three of us this time, and
planned on taking Aadan, Guleed, and Hubi. I was not going and
I was sure Abdi Salam had given Saada bad reports about me. But
while Saada was in Garissa, my breast issue flared up again, and as
promised, I called Abshiro to let her know. Abshiro immediately
contacted Saada and said, "It would be wise to take Shugri; she is
the one who is sick and we don't really know what is going on with
her." Saada did not want to change her plan, but Abshiro insisted
on my behalf.

The papers Saada obtained only allowed her to take one girl
and two boys, so she needed a good reason to switch me with Hubi.
Hubi was a priority for Saada because she was young and needed a

motherly figure. Saada said, "If I take Shugri instead, then she had better be good at housework and helping with children."

I really didn't care if she switched me, because despite my heartbreak and my run-in with my cousin, I was enjoying my life in Nairobi. But Abshiro was worried and wanted me to leave Kenya as soon as possible. "There is no one who takes care of kids better than Shugri. She became a second mother to my children. If you need help with the kids, then I advise you to take her."

Saada finally relented. When she came back to Nairobi with Guleed, she told Aadan and me to pack our things. She bought a lot of African artifacts and clothes to take back with us, and showed us the heavy winter clothes we would put on after we landed. I stared at the clothes thinking *What kind of climate would require clothing like that?* I could not comprehend weather that cold.

12 The Promised Land

Hadaad tagto meel laga il la' yahay, adna il baa la is tidhaa.
If you happen to find yourself in a strange land where everybody in the country has somehow lost the use of a single eye, then it's likewise prudent to lose one of your eyes.
—Somali proverb

ON THE DAY of our departure for Canada, Guleed appeared wearing an outfit that made him look like an African tourist: khaki shorts and a shirt with black drawings of African people printed on them. He looked so comical that I laughed, but the outfit served its purpose, which was to make him look younger than his age to match the papers Saada had obtained. He looked more like a Somali stand-up comic than someone ready to travel abroad, but I could see he was excited about going. I wasn't as excited as he was; I was still in a state of disbelief about my sudden exchange with Hubi, as well as mourning the loss of the first man I truly loved. I had to remind myself that I was living the dream of all those desperate refugees stuck in Kenya. I was going to the land of opportunity.

To get myself in the right mind, I tried to imagine what life would be like in Canada. I pictured North America as some kind of magical land where white people lived with their fancy machines and easy lives. Western countries were so technologically advanced compared to Africa that it became a national joke in our country. Supposedly, President Siad Barre was once traveling and didn't know he had to push a button to make his bed pop out from the wall so he just slept on the floor. I couldn't wait to push a button and watch some amazing event occur, but at the same time, I was terrified. I wasn't afraid of taking my first airplane ride, I was more worried about doing something to embarrass myself. What if I pressed the wrong button on the plane and ejected myself? Perhaps my biggest misconception was that poverty did not exist in North America.

We arrived in Ottawa in the thick of winter. I looked down in shock as the airplane descended. The mountains were completely white.

"What is that?" I asked my sister.

"*Baraf*," Saada replied. Baraf is the Somali word for ice. We don't have a word for snow.

Wow, these people live inside ice?! How is that possible? I leaned back in my seat and tried to wrap my head around this concept. I searched my brain for any memory similar to what I was seeing. I recalled watching a Somali music video while living in Mogadishu with Abshiro. I thought it was filmed abroad because the landscape was all white and white flakes fell around the woman as she sang and danced. But since she was wearing her regular clothing and the flakes looked like they were being poured on her, I didn't connect it with the idea of coldness. Seeing entire mountains covered with ice was concerning. *How are you going to survive, living in ice?* I worried. In Somalia, I never even owned a sweater. I played outside in the warm rain. I could not begin to imagine how many layers of clothes I would need just to step outdoors. As the plane began its final descent, my stomach twisted and turned with a combination of motion sickness, excitement, and fear. I panicked when it was time to get off, glancing around at how the other people were feeling about our predicament. Nobody else seemed worried about freezing to death.

I was relieved when I found it was warm inside the airport, which seemed like a city itself. But I was quickly overwhelmed by the sight of elevators, revolving doors, strange toothed stairs that moved, information signs, not to mention the cacophony of sound that accompanied them. People buzzed around me with great urgency and purpose, even little children. I huddled close to my sister, afraid to make any mistake that could send me back to Africa. I became so overstimulated that I couldn't process anything more; I withdrew and let my sister herd us around. When she approached an elevator, I grew terrified. I had seen an elevator once in Kenya, but had never stepped foot on it because I wasn't sure where it would take me and what would happen to me along the way. I numbly followed Saada inside, relieved when it didn't swallow us. I thought I had conquered my biggest fear, then I saw the escalator. *Those people are riding death itself!* Luckily, Saada knew it would be disastrous to force us on to that moving beast that day. I breathed with relief when she passed it by. I focused so much of my energy on every move my sister made that I was exhausted by the time we made it out of the airport.

I put on the snow jacket my sister had bought me and stepped outside. It was so cold that the breath left my body and I was instantly covered with goosebumps, literally from head to toe. I had no idea you could get goosebumps on your face! My first impression was how organized and pristine everything looked, from the clean roads and sidewalks to the buildings, which all looked brand new to me. In Africa, life was raw. You might see a high-rise building, but next door would be a corrugated hut with goats in the yard.

I looked out the window as we drove to my sister's house, trying to take it all in. *Is this really happening?* In Somalia, when traffic got hectic, a policeman stood in the center of the road directing everyone. I was often entertained by his funny gestures. Here the well-coordinated traffic signals moved everyone along in an orderly fashion. And so much light! I didn't even realize how dark the streets were in Somalia until I saw the streetlights of Ottawa illuminating everything around. The electricity was on everywhere I looked, as if having reliable electricity was never an issue. Before we were halfway to my sister's house, I was accepting this as my new normal.

When we arrived at Saada's, my reunion with Liban and Hamdi wasn't a laughing, hugging moment. Instead, we stared cautiously at each other for a few minutes. I hadn't seen them in about five years, and they seemed more like strangers than siblings at that moment. I immediately noticed how pale they looked. *Does the sun never rise from its hole here?* To add to the strangeness of the situation, they spoke to me in English!

Of all the strange English words that were thrown at me that night, the one that stuck in my head was *burned*. It rolled off Hamdi's tongue so easily (she had burned the dinner) that I thought I could say the word back to her with similar fluency.

"Bun," I said.

Hamdi laughed and tried to help me say the word again, without much success.

"Burd," I tried, not willing to give up. Pronouncing one consonant next to another was a tongue twister for me. I tried over and over, until Hamdi threw up her hands and gave me a *You're going to need some serious help* kind of look. As she walked away, I realized that our physical distance had been replaced by a looming cultural distance. Alone by the door, I continued to try to pronounce that little word over and over. *Why am I so determined to get this word right?* I wondered. This word represented a bigger obstacle in my life, and conquering it felt like maybe I could gain some control over this crazy new world.

The next day I wandered around the house, curious about my environment. It was a typical three-bedroom, one-bath house with a family room and a kitchen. *This isn't any different from my cousin's house in Nairobi*, I thought. It was decorated Somali style and full of Somali relatives, so from the inside, I did not feel like I was in a foreign country. Only the heavy, dark curtains in the living room gave me pause. They felt depressing and unwelcoming. I was surprised that I didn't find machines everywhere, performing magic at the touch of a button. They did have a microwave, which I had never seen before. *Is that all?* I thought. *Only one magic machine?* When a blast of sound suddenly hit my ears, I followed it downstairs to the basement. Liban was watching Batman cartoons on TV, his favorite activity at the time. The light was dim, making the enclosed, cluttered space feel sad and lonely. Clothes hung all around, and my brother sat on the only couch. A thumping noise emanated from a big white machine, which was vibrating as if it were alive.

"What is that thing doing?" I asked Liban.

"Washing the clothes," he answered. "The other machine dries them."

I had washed clothes by hand my entire life, so this machine was truly magical to me. Over the next few months I found that it was much more complicated than my idea of simply pushing one button. That machine and I had our share of battles.

The following morning, my eagerness to see this world in which I had landed overtook my fear of the ice and I opened the front door. I was greeted by a cold blast of wind that took my breath away. A rough-looking middle-aged white man walked down the street toward me, an aggressive dog on a chain at his side. As he got closer, I could see tattoos crawling up his neck, drawing my gaze to his sunken cheeks and missing teeth. His dog lunged at me as they approached, and I recoiled. Before the cold forced me to retreat back inside, I caught a glimpse of a young black man about my age disappearing into a nearby house. Still curious, I climbed the stairs and parked myself at an upstairs window. I spent much time there over the next few days in an attempt to get a better picture of the place where I had arrived. My new neighborhood turned out to be a mix of Somalis, Palestinians, Eritreans, Jamaicans, Lebanese, and whites, but they seemed to have one thing in common: everyone was struggling. It was one of the poorest ghettos in Ottawa.

The Somalis in my neighborhood were afraid of the white people who lived there, who used drugs, were always smoking, yelling, and swearing at each other and their children, and all seemed to have vicious dogs. Somalis are terrified of dogs, so we leapt out of their way whenever they approached. Most Somalis had converted to ultra-conservative Wahhabism after the Somali Civil War, and consequently the women covered themselves with solid-colored, thick, clothing from head to toe, no matter the weather. Their long garments dragged on the ground behind them, enticing the dogs to chase them.

I cooked, cleaned, and looked after Saada's toddler and infant, eager to earn my keep, but Saada's demands were greater than I could meet, and I was soon overwhelmed with chores. I was raised to have respect for anyone older than me, so I did what Saada asked the first time, without complaining. Hamdi, however, often refused to help, which was shocking to me. She yelled, complained, muttered insults, and banged the dishes so hard that Saada and I were sorry we had even asked for her help. *Ingenious*, I thought at times, but for the most part, I hated when she acted like that.

For the first time in my life, I felt like a maid, not a sister.

Saada's husband had a *This is your problem ladies. I'm not getting involved* kind of attitude. The fact that she had brought us to Canada before he could bring his own family over was a constant source of conflict in their marriage, as well as fuel for gossip in the neighborhood about who was the head of the household. To placate him, I had agreed to falsely marry his brother after I got my papers so he could come over from Somalia as well.

More than anything, I wanted to dive into this new culture, learn the language, and make friends, but being stuck at home was frustrating. I began resenting Saada. Since arriving, the only places I had been were the immigration, welfare, and health care offices. And because I didn't fight Saada, she added more and more responsibility onto me. After a few months, though, I asked Saada if I could finish high school. Education was so important in our family that I knew she wouldn't stand in my way, and since I was now about eighteen I was put into adult high school. My sister pointed out the bus stop and told me how to read the schedule posted there. It was so precise that most people rushed to the stop just a few minutes before the bus was due to arrive. No one screamed or played loud music to get their customer's attention. While I was impressed by the efficiency of the transportation, I also felt invisible and lonely. Desperately homesick, I even missed the catcalls of the minibus boys back in Kenya. At least they had noticed me.

My anxiety during my first bus ride was reminiscent of the day I arrived at the airport, although this time I had no sister to follow. I concentrated on each step of the journey, knowing that when I got downtown I needed to change buses. To my horror, I found out that to get to my next bus, I needed to take that man-eating escalator and, equally scary, pass through the revolving door. I was sure the escalator would make me fly off my feet when it flattened out, leaving me naked as it swallowed all my clothes. I stood at the top for a long time, watching carefully as each person stepped on to the monster. I noticed that Africans seemed to grip the handrail more desperately than white people, who got on nonchalantly and didn't even hold on! I finally gained enough courage, spurred on by the prospect of missing my bus. In my desperation, I overstepped and had to clutch the rail so I didn't fall. As the end of my ride closed in fast, I went back a step and leaped off before it could flatten out and take me with it.

I made it to my class looking like I had seen the ghost of my dead ancestors on the bus. Luckily, my English as a Second Language (ESL) teacher, a young woman named Rosalyn, and I connected right away; she was kind and patient with me and I was a quick learner, so it did not take me long to speak in full, coherent sentences. During our breaks, Rosalyn chatted with me about my life and living situation. Now that I was in school, I began making new friends and getting calls at home from students I met in my ESL class. After I hung up, Saada grilled me about the person I was talking to and the details of our conversation. I was so confused! I was the one holding the phone and I couldn't figure out how she knew exactly what we said to each other. It took a while before I learned that you could have multiple phones on the same line and that she had been listening in.

I was determined to hide the fact that I was "fresh off the boat," but buses were so perplexing that they threatened to reveal how inept I was. On some you pushed a yellow button to get off, others you pushed a red button, and on yet another you pulled a cord. Once you signaled, new problems arose. Some bus doors automatically opened, but for others you had to step down to activate the sensor. I desperately wanted to look like a competent person. Why couldn't they all be the same? I was so drained by these bus rides that I hardly had enough energy left for class!

My struggles with public transportation continued until one ride when the doors refused to open for me, even though I thought I was standing on the exact spot where the other passengers had stood. Apparently, everyone had the magic word to open this door but me. After my third attempt to exit the bus failed, I grew frustrated. But I was terrified of looking stupid, so I simply rode on, going from downtown Ottawa to the end of the line, which was at the edge of the city. At that point, I was the only person left on the bus. The driver turned to me and said, "This is the end. I am parking the bus and going home. Where did you want to go?"

Since I no longer had an audience, I told him the difficulties I was having getting off the bus. He kindly explained how every bus worked, where the button was to make it stop, and how all the doors worked. All the pushing, pulling, and stepping finally made sense to me. When he finished his lesson, he drove me back to the stop where I could get on the correct bus for home. His kindness allowed me to tackle other such problems with confidence. I laugh now to think that getting buses to let me out at the right place was once my biggest challenge.

When I lived with Saada, one of her favorite shows was *Unsolved Mysteries*, and she viewed the world through the lens of that show. "White people will kill you and put your body in a black bag and dump it in the river and no one will ever find you," she warned.

I don't know if she fully believed what she was telling me or if she was just using fear tactics to discourage me from exploring my new world. Even though her words frightened me, I had retained that same innate curiosity I had as a nomadic child, so I found a way to override her warnings. In my mind, the whole purpose of coming to North America was to have a better life with greater opportunities. How could I do that if I let fear cage me? I didn't want to just stare out that upstairs window and let life pass me by. I was happy and willing to help Saada with her children, the way I always did with Abshiro, but I was also ready to seize the reins of my own life. I imagined all that housework would be balanced with school and learning to support myself. But Saada was not happy with this arrangement, and her way of dealing with our conflict was to tighten her grip on me, giving me more chores, more responsibility, and less freedom. And my way was to fight back any time someone tried to control me. I wasn't going to cave in and let anyone break my spirit. Even when she hit me to try to get me to submit, I didn't back down.

I became disillusioned with my new world. Frankly, I started to feel that I had had a better, happier life in Kenya. In Canada,

I was turning into a sad person. And I wasn't the only one with shifting emotions: Guleed's mood swings were back in full force. One day he was acting like a fundamentalist Muslim, getting angry and looking at me like I was an infidel. The next day he would be relaxed and feel sorry for me. I did not understand him, so I avoided his hateful and judgmental gaze when he was in one of his dark moods.

One day, I walked into the house, exhausted after a long day at school, and right away I knew something was wrong. Many angry faces were fixed on me; this was serious. My sister gestured for me to join her in the living room. Saada looked furious, the dark curtains forming an ominous backdrop behind her. She held a picture in one hand, which I guessed was evidence against me. *What on earth did I do?* All I did was cook, clean, take care of children, and go to school. When did I have time to cause a scandal? I was so confused that I was glad when her lips finally moved, breaking the silence.

"Who is the man in this picture with you?"

She had dug through my few belongings and found the picture Dereje and I had taken in Kenya. *Wow, how did she find it? I hid that picture well!* Her eyes were furious, as if she had witnessed me and the boy on top of each other.

"He is my friend," I said, while at the same time thinking, *What is the big deal about taking a picture with a boy?* Her own husband was her boyfriend for a long time before they married. I never understood this hypocrisy in my people, as if they forgot that they were once young and in love. And my relationship with Dereje had been sweet and innocent, never going beyond a few kisses.

"Your breast is touching him. Did you know that?"

It had been the cold season in Kenya, so I wore a full-length skirt and a long sleeve sweater in the picture. Dereje stood next to me, his arm around my shoulder. I had no idea what "breast touching" she was talking about. I looked at her with disbelief on my face. *Is this the evidence you have on me? Is this all?*

Saada tried to intimidate me, but I didn't back down. I was not going to be beaten over an innocent picture. In the end, my utter bewilderment must have helped me out, and I only had to endure her anger, not a slap. But I was left with a dawning realization that the Somalis back home had been more open-minded than the ones in this household or perhaps even this country.

ONE DAY, I heard that my cousin Omar's wife had arrived from Kenya. She and I had been in the refugee camp together, so I was excited to welcome her to Canada. They lived a few bus stops away from us, so I knew how to get to their building without getting lost. We had a lovely visit, reminiscing about our long exodus from Somalia and all the crazy things that had happened to us along the way. I finally got up to leave, intending to take the bus back home, but Omar insisted on giving me a ride. It was so cold that we rushed to the car, but as we sat there waiting for the car to warm up, he started to talk about me. It started out harmlessly. "Here is my beautiful cousin." I listened to him and smiled back, growing uneasy as the compliments trailed on longer than

I expected. I became uncomfortable with the way he was looking at me. He blurted out more words, "It is time to give you away; we can get a lot of camels for you." Then he grabbed the back of my neck and shoved his mouth onto mine.

I pushed against him with force and demanded he let me out of the car. "I am going to take the bus, open the door."

He acted very nervous and started talking crazy. "You are my cousin. Look at how good you look. I just love you, like a cousin, I mean."

This is sickening! You are married! And where is your fear of God!? I thought. *You pray and fast for God. How could you do this?* I was so infuriated by all of the so-called God-fearing men who seemed to have one face for God and one for the women they preyed upon.

When he realized I was serious about taking the bus, he promised to leave me alone so I let him take me home. For the second time in my life, I returned to my family feeling violated, dirty, and above all, shamed. I hated feeling that way again. Once inside the house, I fumed with anger and unsettled nerves, going up and down the stairs like a lion pacing in a too-small cage. Saada, annoyed with my pacing, came down and asked me what had happened. I hesitated, but she pressed me, so I told my story, sure she would be as offended as I was by our cousin's behavior and take my side. When I was done, she immediately tried to make excuses for him. *I am alone with this*, I realized. Her refusal to stand up for me destroyed any respect I had left for her. But I had enough respect for myself and enough pride instilled in me by my ayeeyo that I was not willing to let him escape unpunished. I grew up in the shadow of that strong, proud, fearless woman, who never let any man lead her around. If no one was going to stand up for me now, I was going to stand up for myself.

The next day I called Omar's younger sister, Hibo, and told her of his disgusting behavior. She was smart, young, and had mostly lived abroad, so I thought she surely would understand and be outraged. She listened, and then said, "Abaayo, I say you are beautiful, too, that does not mean anything bad. He was just telling you how beautiful you are. You misunderstood him."

I was beyond infuriated and wanted to scream, "You weren't there, you weren't the one he forced his mouth on! You must be joking!"

She acted as if she did not hear the part about him grabbing me and forcing a kiss on me. Being told you are beautiful is no excuse for sexual violation, and it certainly wasn't cousinly behavior. We argued back and forth, and I finally hung up the phone in shock. *What is wrong with these people? They would rather make me look crazy than admit their male loved one did something wrong.* I had no choice. I had to let it go.

Saada and I were now locked in a civil war of our own. For a few weeks, I had been dealing with a toothache. I asked my brother-in-law Faysal to come home at two in the afternoon and watch his children so I could go to a dentist appointment. He agreed, but as the time got close, Faysal didn't come home. I could picture him chewing his gum with an open mouth, sitting in a Tim Hortons coffee shop with a bunch of other Somali men, ignoring the fact that he promised to relieve me.

When Faysal did not show up, I went next door and asked our nice Lebanese neighbor, Hasina, if she could help by watching the little ones for me. When I got back from the dentist my sister was seething with anger.

"Why did you leave the children with Hasina, barely clothed and without food?" she demanded.

"I fed them eggs and *malawah* before I took them!" I explained. "I didn't put on their winter jackets because they were going next door, but I did dress them well."

The whole family stood around us, staring in fear. They knew where this was going. I wanted to defuse the situation, so when Saada threw a shoe at me, a particular insult in Somalia, I ignored her. I grabbed the laundry and headed to the basement to do my chores. But Saada wasn't done. She followed me to the basement and beat me with an electrical cord. She struck me multiple times before I was able to break loose and run toward the door. Guleed, the boy who had been through hell and back with me, ran ahead of me and locked the door behind him just as I was about to exit, blocking my only escape route. He saw the look of terror on my face and left me there, knowing very well what awaited me. I was devastated by his actions. Saada dragged me back into the basement to face her anger. For the first time, I fell silent during an argument and didn't even fight back or try to defend myself. I just let her beat me. My spirit was too crushed by my brother's betrayal.

For years after this incident, Guleed denied his part, but I wasn't going to let it go; his involvement was more distressing to me than the beating itself. Years later, he came to stay with my husband and me after the birth of our first child and I confronted him once again, and this time he admitted it.

"Guleed," I said, "I saw what you did that day. I saw you lock the door on me and leave me there to be beaten."

He looked at me for a long time and then said, "I am sorry, Shugri. It was a cowardly act. I wasn't myself back then. That place was the axis of evil, Abaayo. You know I'm not like that." That was true, he was not like that anymore. During his later stay with us, we became more connected. He played with my infant daughter and made fun of me for singing Somali lullabies even when the baby was sleeping. He went on, "What I did was horrible. I am ashamed of what I did and I thought denial would make it go away." I forgave Guleed and we remain close to this day.

In Somali culture, a young woman stays with her family until she is married. But I had reached a point where I no longer cared about honoring my culture in this regard; I could not live with my sister anymore. Once I made the decision to leave, peace and clarity washed over me, and I methodically began to plan how I could obtain my freedom. I decided to confide in my English teacher, Rosalyn. I may not have known how the system worked, but I knew how to talk to people who could help me navigate it. Rosalyn offered to host me for a few days and help me find a new place to live.

Relieved to have the first step in place, I began planning my next step. Every month, after cashing my $500 welfare check, I gave the money to my sister, keeping only ten dollars for myself. I knew I needed to make my escape the same day I cashed the check so I could take all the money with me. If Saada found out I had the money, I would have to wait until the next month to run away. My biggest problem was that I had grown close to her children. The night before I left, I took them to my room and showered them with hugs and kisses as I sobbed silently. That night passed in slow motion. Both my heart and stomach felt sick, and I slept fitfully, holding my niece and nephew in my arms. When morning appeared, I got to the bank before my sister even knew my welfare check had come. I purchased my bus ticket and planned my departure for the evening, when Saada would not be home and everyone else would be occupied.

When evening finally arrived, I put all my belongings into a black plastic bag and casually stepped out the door as if I was just taking out the garbage. I trembled with fear as I made my way to the bus stop, looking around nervously while still trying to act normal. Somalis are as nosy as secret agents, always watching for any behavior they don't approve of so they will have gossip material. To protect myself, I had told Rosalyn when I was coming so she could intervene if I did not make it to her apartment. When I got on the bus, I scanned it for any Somalis. I picked a seat and angled myself so I could not be easily seen and breathed with relief. As I stared out the bus window, I was struck by the stark contrast of my circumstances. I was scared, poor, lonely, and uncertain about my future. But it was the holiday season, and as my bus drove through the cold night, colorful lights shone from every house, especially in the wealthy neighborhoods that hugged our poor one. I passed by them, feeling a world apart. But like a nomad in the midst of a terrible drought, I was now setting out with hope, a dream of green pasturelands in the distance.

After a few bus rides, I finally arrived at Rosalyn's downtown apartment. She welcomed me and made me comfortable for the night on her couch, which I shared not with little children but with a fluffy cat. The cat curled up in the crook of my neck, as if she sensed that I needed affection. I absentmindedly stroked her fur while still lost in deep thoughts.

I told Rosalyn and her boyfriend Brian that I couldn't stay in Ottawa because I was afraid my sister would find me and hurt me. After a few phone calls, they found a shelter in Toronto where I didn't know anyone and helped me buy a bus ticket. Brian felt badly that I had all of my belongings in a plastic bag, so he bought me a suitcase.

TORONTO IS A big, multicultural city. The shelter I stayed at was full of desperate people: drug addicts, the mentally ill, and anyone who was homeless due to dire circumstances. My roommate turned out to be a young but wild Somali woman. I don't think she ran away from her house; more likely they chased her out with a stick. She had a vulgar mouth and an air of unpredictability that made me uneasy. But it was also comforting to have another Somali woman nearby, and we gravitated toward each other. Unlike me, she did not care about protecting her reputation; she even ran around with rough-looking white men. I avoided all trashy-looking men, no matter what race or culture they came from. It wasn't the ominous tattoos, unkempt appearance, or vulgar language that made them scary. It was their aura, the look in their eyes that said, *You cross me and you will find your body in a black bag.* They reminded me of the characters in Saada's favorite show, *Unsolved Mysteries.* I stayed away from them.

Soon after we met, my roommate turned to me suddenly and said, "*Yaa tahay*?" ("Who are you?") Somalis ask this question to find out what clan you belong to. Your answer can provide you with a new ally or a new enemy. This mentality had fueled the civil war that killed hundreds of thousands and forced millions from their homes, and I was shocked to encounter it again so far from Somalia. I cautiously told her my clan and waited for her reaction. To my relief she said, "Oh, I know a nice woman who shares your subclan. Let me talk to her. Maybe she could help you."

I wanted to say no, but I was sick of the shelter life already. The next thing I knew, I was on the phone with her acquaintance and being invited over. My clanswoman was kind enough to let me stay with her while I figured things out. She reconnected me with my brother Aadan, who had been doing quite well in the short time he had lived in Canada. As soon as we arrived in Ottawa, Aadan had gotten a good minimum-wage job and had been living in a one-bedroom apartment downtown. He had visited us occasionally at Saada's, but he was busy building his own future. He worked two jobs, determined to bring his fiancée from Kenya to Canada, so I didn't want to bother him with my troubles at the time.

Aadan convinced me to come back to Ottawa and live with him, promising to protect me from Saada. I reluctantly agreed, although I was still on edge, convinced she would find a way to get to me. Aadan and I developed a ritual: He went to work and I went to school, helped with the chores, and got my first job, putting condiments on hamburgers at a fast-food chain called Harvey's. I was the "garnisher"! Aadan took on the role of a guardian; he even came with me when I took my English assessment test at Adult High School.

After some months, I was able to rent a room from a Somali-Kenyan woman named Amina who lived a block away from my job. As soon as I started making my own money, the first person I thought of was my ayeeyo. I had been hearing that she was in need. The war had affected everyone, even the nomads. I did not have much, but I made it a priority to send her money whenever she asked, using Hawala, Somalia's own version of Western Union. Hawala is an informal yet complex system involving, not banks, but honor, trust, and a vast network of money brokers. It is so reliable it literally delivered cash to my ayeeyo in the middle of the desert within a week. Once, my ayeeyo even asked me to send money to my formerly rich aunt Maryan, even though she had never shown us an ounce of kindness. During the Somali Civil War, everything my aunt owned had been looted or destroyed. As the war lingered, even the wealthy lost most or all of their savings. I sent money to my aunt, not because I cared for her but because I did not want my ayeeyo to be distressed. My ayeeyo blessed me for sending her money, and I took in the blessing with a full heart.

I soon settled into a routine of going to school, working, spending time with friends, then going back to my rented room. My ESL class was filled with immigrants from various countries, including Ethiopia, Sudan, Palestine, and Cambodia, which made the class entertaining. Luckily for me, my new English teacher, Lillian, had a sense of humor and a way of making me feel good even when I made mistakes. She laughed hard as I tried miserably to interpret the line of a poem, something about a dog peeing at the base of a tree. Somehow I thought the dog was a metaphor for a shy woman. I was very proud of my interpretation of this poem. The whole class laughed with me when we found out I had interpreted it wrong.

After about six months, I had made so much progress with English that I got to move from ESL classes to regular high school classes, and I began taking more challenging courses, such as calculus, computer programming, and chemistry. I also took my first history class, in which we studied the native people of Canada. I felt a profound connection with them. They had tribes and warriors just like Somalis and lived in shelters very similar to those of our nomads. For a while, I searched for these native people, sure that I would find a sense of belonging with them, but I could never find them. They seemed to be as elusive as the guduudane back in the desert. A decade or so later I finally was able to attend a native cultural event. I was mesmerized by their spirit, and their beautiful dances and transported by the sound of their drums. I felt at home with them.

Going to school with people who were refugees like myself

created the connection and sense of belonging I was searching for. Despite the horrors we had all been through, our laughter filled the hallways as we chatted between classes. We socialized after school and helped each other navigate the complexities of our new country, while sharing food and exchanging stories. For the first time in a long time, I felt truly safe. I imagined Canada to be a motherly figure watching over me, providing my basic human needs. I had the freedom to live on my own, breaking the chain of shame that surrounded women who dared to defy cultural norms.

IN THE FALL of 1994, I again fell in love, this time with a man from North Sudan. Ihab was handsome, wise, and kind. I met him while ordering chai from Tim Hortons in downtown Ottawa. He was from a middle-class family in Sudan who sent him to Canada to get an education on a student visa. We had a lot of long, late-night conversations in his car in the parking lot of my apartment building after he finished his janitorial work.

When I fall in love, I don't hold back; I give my soul to my lover. Ihab reciprocated my love. The little things we did together meant a lot to both of us. Unlike Dereje, I had more freedom to kiss him without fear of my male relatives beating me. I even told my best friend, Deeqa, that I was in love with a Sudanese man. She was happy for me. Ihab had a way of making me feel like I was the world to him, so I never thought to ask him about his past relationships. But I wish I had. I later discovered he had pursued another woman, Khadija, for three years. Though she continually refused him, he kept hoping one day she would change her mind. He finally gave up, but when he started dating me, Khadija told Ihab that she wanted him back in her life. Ihab, who was not sure who he wanted, ended up dating both of us. I had no clue. I thought Ihab and I were happy together; I never picked up on any hint of a problem until the night he dumped me.

He called me to come and meet him in the parking lot as usual. I felt something was off by the tone of his voice, but I went down to greet him. When I got inside the car he wouldn't look me in the eyes. Shame, guilt, and a whole array of other emotions I had never seen on him were plastered across his face. After a long pause, he finally overcame his fear and told me about Khadija.

"On the night of that Somali wedding, remember when you wanted me to keep you company, but I had to go?" he said. "It was because of her. I was hiding from you the whole night because of the mess I had created." It turned out that she and I had both been invited to that wedding. Ihab said he cared about me and felt for the first time that his love was reciprocated. But he also felt he had to give Khadija a chance because he had chased her for three years, even though deep down he did not trust her. Khadija knew about me and had become domineering and persistent in pursuing him. The night of the wedding, he dropped me off and then left to get her. When she saw me at the wedding, she became livid and gave him an ultimatum: "Me or her!"

I was stunned. Finally I spoke. "I won't lie to you. This hurts a lot already, and I know it will take me awhile to recover. Do me a favor, even if she dumps you tomorrow, don't contact me. She won. You broke my heart. I may even get sick, but that is my way of purging your love out of my body. No matter what, don't contact me."

He was shocked. "But I want to check on you."

"No," I said, "I want to heal from you, and if you contact me, it will just prolong my misery."

I got out of his car devastated, incredulous over what had just happened. I hated recovering from a broken heart, it felt like I was dying. In just a few days, I lost my appetite, and soon after, I was vomiting. This being exam time, within days I had to sit for my chemistry exam. I had not been able to eat since our breakup and was living off nothing but milk. One evening, it all became too much to handle and I fainted. That was when my gossip-loving roommate took it upon herself to report my misfortune to our circle of friends.

The news reached Ihab, and he called.

"I made it clear to you that this is what I go through to get over a broken heart. Please don't call me again, no matter what you hear." I hung up. I was annoyed with him, and I knew that talking to him would be a setback for me. I went to my chemistry exam, with no sleep and no food in me.

My chemistry teacher glanced at me and was concerned immediately. I broke down crying. "I am going to fail chemistry. I can't focus."

He said, "Shugri, take the exam and don't worry about your score. If you do poorly, which I think is highly unlikely, I will disregard this result."

My teacher's words were precisely what I needed. Miraculously

I did well on the test. I vowed to stay away from men and focus on school instead. *My heart is too weak to recover from another love disaster unless I am given a new one*, I thought.

TRUE TO MY vow to focus on school, I registered for an advanced summer class in one of my favorite subjects, biology. My teacher was a young, first-generation Canadian-Japanese woman, and we quickly became friends. At break time, we sat on the school steps and talked about life. Under the evening breeze she confided a secret that was troubling her. She had dated a white guy, gotten pregnant, and had had an abortion. The guilt she felt over her actions, along with that from hiding it from her parents, who would not understand, consumed her. She had grown up in Canada, but was torn between her heritage and current culture. She was independent and wanted to live her life the way she envisioned, but still wanted to please her parents. Our connection was valuable to us both, because we shared the same problem of being caught between two worlds.

I wanted to do well in her class so I studied hard for her tests. One beautiful summer afternoon the sun was shining, tempting me to go outdoors, but since I had a biology exam the next day, I headed to the Ottawa Public Library instead. When I arrived, the librarian informed me they were closing soon.

Disappointed, I said, "No worries. I will just go home and study there."

"The Ottawa University Library stays open much later than we do," she informed me. I shook my head, but that librarian did not give up. Looking me straight in the eye she insisted, "A lot of people study there. You don't have to be a student. They have an amazing library, with study rooms you can use if you don't want to be disturbed."

I thanked her and left, still thinking I would take the bus home. When my bus arrived and I started to board, however, I felt a strong urge to get off. *Strange*, I thought, as I stepped back. Conveniently, the next bus was heading to Ottawa University.

Once I got to the library, I located an empty study room and sat in the most hidden corner. I wanted to focus on my studies and not get distracted. A few minutes later, an acquaintance, Faysal, stuck his head into the room to say hello. We had a short conversation, and then he went on his way. I had just immersed myself in my books again when a young, thin, light-skinned East African man stuck his head into the room and asked me in English if I had seen Faysal.

"Yes, but I think he went downstairs," I answered in Somali, sure he was a Somali man. I smiled, not wanting to seem rude, and went right back to studying.

"I don't speak Somali," he said, smiling back. I thought he was teasing but he insisted, "No, I'm from Ethiopia." He left, but came back again to ask me something else, and when he returned a third time, it finally dawned on me, *Oh, is he interested in me?* My focus shifted from the metabolic machinery of the cell to the Ethiopian man before me.

As a scrawny person myself, I always looked for a guy with a little meat on his bones to cushion our hugs. The twenty-two-year-old man before me hadn't filled out yet, like most East Africans. But one thing attracted me to Selehdin right away: the way he smiled slyly as if he was concealing a mischievous side of himself. He was easy to talk to, and his gentleman's spirit and kind heart were clear to me from the start.

Our first conversation was bland and held no promise of two people who would one day fall in love, marry, and have three children. In fact, our first encounter was so ordinary that when friends ask me now, "How did you two meet?" I have a more exciting version ready.

"Well, he was riding a camel down the Canadian highway and I pulled over, halting traffic, to say 'Pardon me, Handsome. Do you come here often? Why don't you come down off your camel and talk to me?'" I say this with such seriousness that people who don't know me well often fall for my tale.

In reality, Selehdin told me his name and asked my name, where I lived, and how I was going to get home.

I told him home was two buses away, so when he offered me a ride, I gladly agreed.

"Are you hungry? Do you want to eat before you head home?" he asked.

And so we went to McDonald's on our first date, our conversation flowing as if we had known each other for years, not just a few hours. When I got home that night, I could barely concentrate on my biology exam. We talked every day after that, and three days later, I boldly left him a message declaring my feelings toward him.

"I just wanted to say how easy it is to talk to you and that I really, really like you." I wasn't into playing games; if I liked a man, I told him so. Years later, my husband told me that he appreciated my direct and honest nature. But two weeks into the relationship, I panicked a bit and thought, *Is this real love or just a rebound?* I called Selehdin right away and told him that I was not sure I was ready for a relationship since my last one had ended badly only three months ago.

He listened and said the words that changed my life: "Give me two weeks, and if you still feel the same, we will go our separate ways."

LIKE ME, SELEHDIN was not supposed to be in Canada. He arrived in Cairo, Egypt, after fleeing the ruthless Ethiopian dictator Mengistu Haile Mariam. Mengistu was so cruel that people said if his regime killed your son, you had to pay back the price of the bullets they used. When Selehdin was seven, he and a friend thought it would be fun to follow their house helper on some errands one night. He did not understand that Mengistu had enforced a strict curfew, trying to catch protesters who opposed his regime. As Selehdin and his friend discreetly followed the helper, they heard the sound of a streetlight shattering. Within seconds, an authoritative military voice broke through the darkness. "Who is there?" it demanded. Startled and scared, they disappeared in the darkness of the night. The soldier fired a shot at them and they cried in fear when the bullet whizzed by them. Incidents like this, coupled with food shortages, border wars, and the escalation of violence within the country, continued for years and began to take a toll on the people of Ethiopia.

As he got older and the military began drafting younger and younger men, Selehdin's parents worried he would soon be forced to serve. By that time, Ethiopia was at war with Eritrea, a small country between Ethiopia and the Red Sea, which was ironic because Selehdin is Eritrean by blood, despite having been born and raised in Ethiopia. The Soviet Union had backed Ethiopia during its war with Somalia and was now supporting Mengistu's regime against Eritrea as well. Using a Communist tactic of keeping the people so busy fulfilling their basic living needs that they had no time for uprisings, Mengistu's regime kept a chokehold on the food supply. There was always a long line for rice, sugar, and flour. Fortunately, my husband's family was able to get their four oldest children out of Ethiopia as they came of draft age.

Selehdin went to Cairo to stay with relatives while awaiting paperwork that would allow him to join his older sister Nejat in Sweden. Just as he was about to purchase his airline ticket, he developed a raging fever and pain on the lower right side of his abdomen. His relative Sofiya insisted he go to Cleopatra Hospital in Cairo, and by that time, his appendix was massively infected. The doctor told him, "If you did not come in when you did, it would have been too late."

Selehdin never did join his sister in Sweden, using the money intended for his ticket for his medical treatment instead. After his recovery, his uncle Khalil sponsored him to go to Canada. Every

time I catch sight of his scar, it is a reminder of how that rup-
tured appendix changed the trajectory of Selehdin's life and let
our destinies collide at Ottawa University Library that summer
day. His two sisters still live in Sweden, a reminder of how close he
was to ending up half a world away from me. And had I not been
switched with Hubi at the last minute, I would have missed him
at the library as well. Selehdin and I were already married by the
time Hubi finally made it to Canada.

Even though I had become fairly independent at last, I was
not yet ready to introduce an Ethiopian man to my family. Like
Dereje, Selehdin and I pretended to be apart if we came across
one of my relatives. But Ottawa was teeming with them. One
afternoon, while we were sitting in Selehdin's car at a red light, I
saw my brother Aadan standing on the corner, waiting to cross in
front of us.

"That is my brother," I blurted out. In a panic, and without
thinking, I shoved my face down onto Selehdin's lap to avoid my
brother's notice.

"That is not a good place to hide, Shugri, but don't move now.
Your brother is crossing right in front of my car."

I panicked more, realizing that nothing could be worse than
being caught by my oldest brother with my face in an Ethiopian
man's groin. Luckily he didn't see me, and we managed to laugh
about it as we drove away.

The stress of hiding our relationship, which we now knew was
serious, began to give me terrible nightmares. I often fell asleep at

Selehdin's apartment and woke screaming in terror. I once jumped on the twin bed right beside him, my arms flailing around like the rotor of a helicopter.

"Get in, get in fast! The lions are coming," I yelled.

He opened his eyes, still dazed from sleep, and saw me standing over him with an alarming look on my face. He gently told me that there were no lions here, and took his time coaxing me back to reality. The next night I took the screen off his third-floor window, ready to escape yet another horror. He simply took me by the hand and reoriented me. He physically pulled me close to him and wrapped me with his body. Feeling safe and comforted, I fell asleep.

We finally got sick of hiding and went to my brother Aadan. He talked to my father and they decided that as long as Selehdin was Muslim, we could marry. For some reason our wedding was held in Saada's basement—the very basement where I had endured the final beating that sent me fleeing into a new chapter of my life. A sheik was called, and he spoke with Aadan, Selehdin and his friends, and my cousin Omar. Dressed in a traditional Somali durah and not needed for any of this, I stood off to the side. My brother and Selehdin made a few agreements, like if my husband ever divorced me he would give me some money in lieu of goats or camels. The sheik signed the agreements and it was done. That wedding was so fast and strange that we don't celebrate our anniversary. Selehdin and I were too poor at that point for anything else, and this ritual needed to be done to uphold my family's honor. Ironically, we lost the sheik's paper and later had to get married again at a Canadian courthouse before we moved to California.

The whole time we dated, I never mentioned my circumcision. I wasn't ashamed; every Somali woman I knew was circumcised like me—it was the norm. In fact, before coming to Canada, I never looked at myself as a mutilated person. But when I told one of my nieces that I don't like it when people see me as mutilated, she disagreed. "I am mutilated," she declared. To this day, she looks down at her private parts and sees a butchered body. Each woman holds this experience differently. I have come to accept my body the way it is. For me there is no point in dwelling on the past. The scar on my private parts is a testimony to my resilience and a reminder not to perpetuate this ritual with my daughters. Compared to many, Arafo and I were lucky—at least the nomadic woman who performed our procedure had mastered the art of circumcision. For that I am grateful.

As part of the legacy of circumcision, Somali women just accept the side effects of the procedure. Most of us have painful periods and have suffered from infections. Even in Canada, I didn't know any Somali women who went to the doctor for issues relating to circumcision. It is a private matter and we all just accepted that it was our husband's duty to open up the small hole without medical help.

But after seeing the agony on my face every time we were intimate, Selehdin suggested that I see a doctor. The pain was so intense I actually banged my head against the wall to distract myself from it. Yet my initial response to his suggestion was refusal. All of my life I had been conditioned to keep this hole tight and closed, and now all of a sudden I was supposed to let this go? My young mind was full of confusion. Part of me understood that the pain was too much, but the idea of undoing this whole tradition was mind-boggling and scary. After much coaxing, though, I reluctantly agreed.

When I awoke from the surgery, the room felt crowded, as if thickened with shame, awkwardness, and failure, as my private matters had been displayed in front of all these people. It felt cold and intrusive. But there was Selehdin, holding my hand as I emerged from the fog of sedation, and he got me through weeks of convalescence, much like my ayeeyo had done when I was a little girl in that blazing desert. As I recovered, I felt like the chains that held my foremothers for centuries had been unshackled. I was starting a new era for my daughters and the generations of girls to follow in my lineage.

EPILOGUE

Two years after Selehdin and I married, my beloved ayeeyo passed away, at age ninety, and was buried in the very desert she rose from. I felt her loss deeply, but it gives me comfort that she knew I got married before she passed away, and I know her spirit is with my mother. I am glad, too, that my poetic grandmother died before she witnessed the loss of her beautiful culture. Wahhabism, with its rigid rules, has infiltrated even the nomadic way of life. I was shocked recently to see a photo of a young nomadic girl clinging to a dudumo just as I used to do, wearing a burka that covered her from head to toe. I wonder if she and her clan still sit around the fire at night telling stories. What else has been lost? The nomadic life I have been longing to see again may not be the same. Wahhabism feels like the rejection of our spirituality, our stories—the very fabric of our culture and identity. Century-old traditions were changed in a matter of years; I feel like there is nothing left for me to identify with.

As I come to the end of my story I can't help but reflect on how I survived it all. But one thing is clear to me: I was shaped by my poetic, regal, and, above all, resilient ayeeyo. Perhaps my mother saw a strength in me when she gave me as a gift to my grandmother, but I can see now that I was the one who was given a gift. The desert is one of the hardest places to live, yet I never once saw my ayeeyo in despair or waiting for a man to save her life. She commanded the desert with authority, and I watched her every move with deep admiration. My ayeeyo was my hero, who left me with the belief that I am enough. Now that she is gone, what remains is the courage and confidence that she instilled in that curious desert girl chasing the elusive guduudane.

Survival is woven into the fabric of who I am. I never ask, "Why did this happen to me?" but rather, "How can I overcome this situation?" It is easy to let past trauma or injustices rule your life forever, but I want to be free, so I needed to understand and forgive others. I know that my father was a product of his time and circumstance. When I think of my father today, I think of a man who took a stand by educating his daughters when other people thought it was not important. But above all, I keep in mind that my happiness is up to me now, not my father. I am very proud of my ancestors, my home country, and my past. I have just learned to leave out the parts that don't serve me as a woman, a mother, a human.

I am not delusional about the effect of trauma; I know the havoc it can wreak. All of my siblings and I bear lasting scars. I watched my younger brother Guleed descend into homelessness despite all of the energy and love I poured into him. He chose to numb his pain with alcohol and drugs, and this fine poet, writer, and amazing soul is today begging in the streets of Canada. My heart aches for him; I am at a loss for words to describe the pain his condition imposes on me. I often wonder, *What made our recovery so different? Why did I make it and he did not?*

HOME TODAY IS Sonoma County, California, in a town known for its occasional stench of cow manure, where my husband and I have lived for almost two decades. My husband is a software engineer, I work as a nurse, and we are blessed with three children and an amazing community. I have found my people in a group of liberal-minded, deeply grounded humans. I feel safe and content, far from my tumultuous past. I am well aware that this is a privileged life.

I have come so far from where I started that it is often comical. I am no longer that lost young woman who struggled to take the escalator, although I still have had my share of cultural confusion. Raising children in America, I had to learn about many strange customs. We roamed the neighborhood together, knocking on the doors of strangers and asking for candy on Halloween. I found out that instead of throwing a baby tooth away like we did in Somalia, I had to come back at night and pay for the tooth. I not only went along with the tradition but created crazy stories about why the tooth fairy forgot her duty some nights and came late.

My two worlds collided with hilarity one day when my kids and I encountered a hippie lady and her goats at a local farmer's market. I was immediately drawn to the goats. As my children fed them, I enthusiastically told the woman about my childhood herding goats in the desert of Somalia and added, "Isn't baby goat meat so delicious?" The look of horror on her face told me I had offended her greatly. I had completely missed her sign, which read, "Goats are pets, not dinner."

Just to make sure I wouldn't try to eat her goats, she introduced them to me one by one. "Meet Michael Jackson, Elvis, and Lady Gaga." I laughed to myself at the craziness of having a goat as a pet. That kind of thinking would get you tied to a tree and left behind in the desert.

AT ONE POINT, after moving to California, I was trying to do it all, the way I saw a lot of American women doing. I was a full-time student, a mother, and working outside the home. I neglected whatever was left of my social life. But I soon burned out; my body screamed for me to listen and slow down, but I ignored it. Soon I was having full-blown nightmares and anxiety attacks that scared me to death. It became clear that this American way of living was not sustainable for me. Things had to change. So, I asked myself, "What would your ancestors do?" The answer was clear. They would gather around the fire and talk to each other at night. During the day, they walked in nature. From that day on, I started a crusade of changing my way of life. I gathered with friends around my table to talk and to unburden our worries. I hiked in nature, both alone and with friends. When my best friend Halima and I get together, we take three-day-long hikes where we get lost in the forest. It feels good, like our bodies and souls long for it.

When we get home, we sit in a circle and share stories, poems, and riddles. Our kids listen, entranced by every word and gesture, just as I was entranced by the tales my ayeeyo told. A deep feeling of contentment and harmony fills my soul. The stories we tell now may contain some new elements from our current life, but the tradition that rooted us is being imparted to the next generation. I hope that when my children get restless, they seek answers in nature and the company of friends. This is the legacy of my ancestors that I want to leave behind for my children—and my readers.

ACKNOWLEDGMENTS

FIRST AND FOREMOST, if it was not for my dear friend Gayla Overmeer's unwavering dedication, this memoir you are holding would not have been possible. Gayla and I went through every word and sentence in this book multiple times, and I am forever grateful for her unrelenting commitment. Although I embarrassed her by demonstrating the sound of a male goat in heat in the middle of a full café, we both recovered from that scene to finish this memoir, so thank you so much, Gayla, for sticking with me to the end!

I want to thank my literary agent, Gillian Mackenzie, of Mackenzie Wolf, for her belief in me from the moment she saw my memoir. I could not have done this book without her tremendous support and friendship. Thanks to Betsy Gleick with Algonquin Books, who had a clear vision for my book from the beginning and made it easy for me to trust her judgment and guidance.

I want to thank my brother Guleed, who translated all the Somali proverbs in this memoir. Without his brilliance and deep understanding of both Somali and English, it would have been impossible to capture the essence of these unique and poetic proverbs. He is indeed a word tamer! Sadly, Guleed passed away a few months before the publication of my book. I am still heartbroken over his loss.

My sisters, Abshiro and Arafo Said, helped to excavate my childhood stories and picked up nonstop calls from different time zones whenever I had a question. Thank you, sisters!

Peter Stein is not only a fellow storyteller but an amazing human being who went to great lengths to help me find a literary agent. Thank you, Peter! Your early belief in me was instrumental in getting this book into the right hands.

Thank you to Ilana Licht, who read the early and late drafts multiple times. Her helpful critique helped to shape the book early on and her commitment was unwavering.

A whole village of women supported me throughout my writing and editing process: Linda Scholer, Jean Bean, Leah Brosio, Rebecca Pecoraro, Ellen Olah, Jenna Moore, Amiko, Amy, Maryan, Jennifer, and everyone else who read excerpts and gave feedback. Thank you all for being part of my village!

Gayla and I would like to thank our husbands and children for their patience and support throughout the hours we spent working, and for not filing missing persons reports during our prolonged absences.

And to Michael, Moose, and all our friends at Redwood Cafe in Cotati: Thank you for the Mediterranean Omelettes, tea, friendship, and free wi-fi!

QUESTIONS FOR DISCUSSION

1. The author introduces the reader to the Somali proverb, "When an elder dies, a library is burned." In *The Last Nomad*, Salh tells us that she feels a sense of urgency to archive her family's stories and keep them alive. Does your family or culture have a tradition of oral histories? Why is it important to learn from our elders and earlier generations?

2. How much did you know about Somalia, nomadic life, and/or the Somali Civil War before reading *The Last Nomad*? Did the story introduce you to events or lifestyles that you were originally unfamiliar with or to a new perspective? If so, in what ways?

3. The author was exposed to Somalia's rich oral tradition as a nomad and begins each chapter with a Somali proverb. Did any of these ring true to you or remind you of proverbs you have heard from your own culture? Which proverbs resonated with you the most?

4. As a nomad herself, Salh's mother considered it an honor for a young Shugri to help her ayeeyo with the demands of nomadic life. What was your initial reaction when the author was given as a gift of labor to her ayeeyo? Did that opinion change when you learned how Salh felt about it?

5. Salh's father fought for her to have an education instead of living as a nomad. In what ways did the nomadic lifestyle give the author an education? How does this lifestyle compare to going to school in a classroom?

6. Salh writes that her father ensured that both his sons *and* daughters got an education, which was a bold view at the time. In what ways did Salh's father raise her within traditional Somali gender roles, and in what ways did he not?

7. As a child, Salh learned a deep sense of courage and independence from her fearless ayeeyo. What are some lessons Salh learned from her ayeeyo, and how did they help her face challenges throughout childhood as well as her adult life? In what ways was Salh's grandmother different from the other Somali women in Salh's life?

8. What did you know about female genital mutilation (FGM) prior to reading *The Last Nomad*? How is FGM normalized in Somalia and how did this harmful practice become an integral procedure there, according to Salh? What is the relationship between FGM and beliefs about female virginity?

9. During Salh's FGM process, she describes herself as being brave and prideful. She even admits that she scorned "the cowardly behavior" of the other girls who were scared and tried to run. Were you surprised by the author's attitude toward the process? By

anything else about FGM? As an adult, how does Salh approach the legacy of FGM and its impact on her body and mind?

10. During the author's time at the Families for Children Orphanage (FFC), she experienced a lot of hardships, but she also had many moments of joy. Which events and people at FFC gave her the most strength, pride, and courage?

11. In *The Last Nomad*, Salh details her experience of civil unrest, instability, and violence during the start of the Somali Civil War and while fleeing from the war. How did a young Salh make sense of the everyday violence and tragedy she witnessed? How did she make sense of her new status as a refugee at the border and in Kenya?

12. When the author landed in Canada during the winter, she had never seen snow before, let alone any of the things most people in North America take for granted, like elevators and washing machines. What are some differences Salh observes, and what skills and strategies did she lean on in her new environment? Have you ever had to adjust to a different society and culture?

13. What are the ways in which Salh leans on community as she flees the Somali Civil War and finds refuge in Kenya and ultimately North America? How did Salh's expectation of North America compare to her reality?

14. What are some of the ways, positive or negative, in which Salh's childhood experiences continue to resonate in her life in California today?

15. Salh paints a beautiful portrait of her nomadic life, pre-war Somalia, and the desert and delicious foods. What were your favorite descriptions?

SHUGRI SAID SALH was born in the Somali desert. In 1992, she emigrated to North America after civil war broke out in her home country. She attended nursing school at Pacific Union College and graduated with honors. Although this is her first book, Salh has been storytelling since she could talk. From her grandmother and the nomadic community in which she was raised, she heard stories and learned of their power to entertain, teach, and transform. When she isn't writing or telling stories, she works as an infusion nurse. Salh lives in Sonoma County with her husband and three children. Her website is shugrisalh.com.